Machiavelli Redeemed

Machiavelli Redeemed

Retrieving His Humanist Perspectives on Equality, Power, and Glory

Robert A. Kocis

Lehigh
University
Press

Bethelem: Lehigh University Press
London: Associated University Presses

Associated University Presses
440 Forsgate Drive
Cranbury, NJ 08512

Associated University Presses
16 Barter Street
London WC1A 2AH, England

Associated University Presses
P.O. Box 338, Port Credit
Mississauga, Ontario
Canada L5G 4L8

The paper used in this publication meets the requirements
of the American National Standard for Permanence of Paper
for Printed Library Materials Z39.48–1984.

Library of Congress Cataloging-in-Publication Data

Kocis, Robert.
  Machiavelli redeemed : retrieving his humanist perspectives on
equality, power, and glory / Robert A. Kocis.
    p.   cm.
  Includes bibliographical references and index.
  ISBN 0-934223-42-4 (alk. paper)
  1. Machiavelli, Niccolò, 1469–1527—Contributions in political
science. I. Title.
JC143.M4K593   1998
320.1'092—dc21   97-34173
                                                            CIP

PRINTED IN THE UNITED STATES OF AMERICA

To
John and Janet Chapman,
who together taught me and my generation
how to balance justice and compassion with professional
objectivity

It cannot, however, be called virtue to kill one's fellow-citizens, betray one's friends, be without faith, without pity, and without religion; by these methods one may indeed gain *power,* but not *glory.* For if the virtues of Agathocles in braving and overcoming perils, and his greatness of soul in supporting and surmounting obstacles be considered, one sees no reason for holding him inferior to any of the most renowned captains. Nevertheless, his barbarous cruelty, and inhumanity, together with his countless atrocities, do not permit of his being named among the most famous men.

—Machiavelli, *The Prince,* Chapter 8, emphasis added.

Contents

Preface   9

Introduction   17

Part I: A Humanist Worldview
1. Humanism and Empiricism: A World Open to Human
   Effort   35

Part II: Human Nature and Potentials
2. Corruption and Nobility: Maximizing Human Potentials   59

Part III: Machiavellian Morals
3. Creating Our Moral Obligations   83
4. The End Justifies the Means—in Corruption   114
5. Obeying Laws under a Good Constitution   128

Part IV: Economics, Society, and Politics
6. Why Freedom May Require Princes   143
7. Ambition, Corruption, and Nationalism   164
8. Economics, Equality, and Justice   175
9. Machiavelli's Place in the History of Western Political
   Thought   193
Chronology of Events Shaping Machiavelli's Thought   219

Notes   228
Bibliography   251
Index   259

Preface

Was Machiavelli a Machiavellian? Given our usual meanings of that pejorative term, the answer must be an unequivocal "no." Nevertheless, my own embarrassing experience illustrates the powerful grip our negative perceptions of Machiavelli retain on our collective imagination. After receiving an invitation from Professor Manuel Paláez of Malaga, Spain, to contribute a chapter to his volume on the history of Western thought, I first conceived a project on Machiavelli. The irony is that I chose to write on Machiavelli at that time because I mistakenly thought, from the perspective of one dedicated to Lockean and Jeffersonian ideals of liberty, that he would be so easy to criticize!

The complexity of his ideas, so similar to Rousseau's and expressed like Rousseau's in oxymorons intended to provoke thought, denied me such an easy conquest. As I began to set aside my prejudices, I discovered a system of thought for which I began to feel a surprising affinity. As I recognized the validity of many of his points and discovered a perspective from which he made sense, I realized that I would need more than a chapter in Professor Paláez's book to say all that should be said. The view of his life's work that follows is a sympathetic, but not blind, defense of certain principal tenets of his views on modernization, property, and equality. He was most probably right to see that certain material conditions—equality, national unification, commerce, a new kind of property—were necessary for a flourishing democracy; and I cannot controvert his recognition of the ways that modernity meets fundamental human needs that could not be met in premodern societies, especially the need for freedom. I also fear that he may have been right to believe that coercion is sometimes necessary for maintaining freedom, so that people may sometimes need to be "forced to be free."

Yet many aspects of his thought remain "disturbing," as Sir Isaiah Berlin put it so well.[1] Most disturbing was his juxtaposing a new, modern morality with the traditional morality of Natural Law. This juxtaposition disturbs because once the two are recognized as competitors, one must choose between them, but without divine or eternal assurances that any choice is the "correct" one. Almost as disturbing was his fervent devotion to nationalism; his account of this double-edged sword was probably too optimistic, since the darker side of this kind of collectivism had not yet exhibited itself clearly. Similarly, his tactical decision to direct the attention of the Medici family away from wealth and familial interests to military affairs as a way to modernize their views may have been a brilliant error. Using Machiavelli's own criterion, I must concede that, had it worked, he would have been praised. However, having failed to win their devotion to the art of war, he is responsible for unleashing in our civilization an idea that eventually became militarism: a belief that all problems can be solved by a judicious use of force.

Finally, his moral cynicism—his conviction that believers in liberty must be prepared to do what is necessary, even what is evil, thus sinking to the depths of the enemies of liberty—may prove corrosive in its own right, while still remaining "true" in the purely pragmatic sense that believers in liberty must sometimes use force in ways that seem evil. Subsequent events, especially in our age of ideology, seem to imply that even in the name of a good ideal or purpose, doing evil does corrode our moral sensibilities; but it may be that a quattrocento Florentine should not be expected to know a lesson that history would not teach for another few centuries. Finally, his commitment to equality was not tempered by any sense of what a person deserves or what rights a person has. Without the limits of rights or desert, the pursuit of equality can cause injustices. But these criticisms and reservations remain premature at this stage.

Since I hope to keep the discussion free of jargon, I have removed many technical references to the literature of political philosophy and to professional political philosophers, placing such references in content endnotes whenever possible. It is intended that the text, which retains only those professional references necessary for the general reader, can and should be read without the endnotes.[2] Where precision requires technical elaboration and a discussion of the discipline of political philosophy, the notes are intended to provide that for the professional reader. Where the use of technical terms from political philosophy is necessary for other readers, definitions have been provided.

My intellectual debts are many, and not all can be acknowledged here. Certainly none of these sources is responsible for any of my errors or omissions. First, thanks are due to Professor Peláez for the invitation that started me on this project. Subsequently, I pre-

sented very early versions of my theses about the role of equality—
Machiavelli's belief that the gap between the rich and the poor
should be kept narrow—at the Northeast Political Science Association meeting in 1989; about voluntarism—the modern moral belief
that we create our values—at a Villanova University Philosophy
Department Colloquium; and about property—Machiavelli's belief
that excessive property excites ambition in a person, corrupting
him/her—at a Gavigan College Colloquium at the University of
Scranton. Thanks to all for providing forums for presenting and
discussing these ideas. Finally, thanks to Alan Ryan both for including me in a stimulating National Endowment for the Humanities
Summer Seminar in 1994 and for agreeing graciously to read and
comment upon the manuscript at the end of that seminar. The book
that follows is much the better for his insights.

Debts to other scholars, both experts on Machiavelli and in political philosophy generally, are not always conscious; any oversights
are unintentional exclusions. Since each person's discovery of a
theorist like Machiavelli can be compared, I believe, to a kind of
journey, I count these scholars as fellow travelers and friends. The
first stages of my own journey began with overcoming what I see as
the popular stereotype of Machiavelli: the cynical seeker of power
for its own sake, the unscrupulous "teacher of evil," who freed politics from morality by creating a new and pragmatic science of politics. For me this stage ended when a reading of Vilari's biography
showed me that Machiavelli's life was an exemplar of commitment
to one limited kind of liberty:

- he had come to adulthood while the republic of Florence was
  being formed under the influence of the friar Savonarola;
- he sought early to serve that republic;
- eventually he committed significant portions of his life and fortune to this service;
- his career was ruined by the Medicean return to autocracy;
- he was tortured after being implicated in a conspiracy to assassinate the autocratic family, to be spared only in a general
  amnesty;
- his patriotism still led him to public service, first for the Medici
  and then for the reestablished republic;
- he died, perhaps of a broken heart, when the reestablished
  republic found him suspect because he had served Florence
  under the Medici.[3]

To Vilari, then, I owe an ability to see Machiavelli's writings in
the context of his life; this gave them a new meaning and induced

my personal shift in understanding.[4] Reading Machiavelli's less well-known works, such as the poems on ambition and fortune, the dramatic comedies (*Mandragola, Clizia,* and *Belfagor*), and his proposal to the Medici to reconstitute the Florentine republic, reinforced this new perception of his commitments. But now that my misconceptions had been dismantled, chaos reigned, for I could discern little overall coherence in his views.

Bringing order to that chaos required alternative views of Machiavelli's accomplishment. Here, as in so much else, the writings of Sir Isaiah Berlin shaped my views in a number of conscious and unconscious ways. I hope that the view that follows remains true to his insight into the "disturbance" that Machiavelli ineluctably causes in his readers. While Machiavelli's disturbing moral message is most obvious in *The Prince,* it is perhaps even more disturbing in other writings (like *Mandragola*). That disturbance can be obscured if one focuses exclusively or primarily on *The Prince,* which appears to be presenting a philosophy different from, if not at odds with, the rest of the writings. Following the lead of Vilari and Berlin, then, I have sought to read *The Prince* as ground rather than figure, focusing on other writings while using *The Prince* as context for understanding the others, asking how the author of *The Prince* could also have written the *Discourses* as well as his dramas and poems.

Reassembling the different parts of Machiavelli's thought without *The Prince* as a centerpiece required a sense of what the components of a political philosophy are and a feel for how they can be combined and recombined to form various types. The influence of John Chapman, my friend and mentor, becomes most clear here. Although I doubt that he would agree with all, or even much, that I propose here, especially about equality, I know that I could never have sought to integrate Machiavelli's views on metaphysics, human nature, ethics, and politics had I not profited from Chapman's insights about analyzing political philosophies.[5] While I did not need much persuasion to see that all of these components form an integral whole, Chapman brought to my vague intuition the rigor of his own method, noting that a theory must have a kind of coherence among its various components. So, when that coherence eluded me in Machiavelli's case, I knew both that something was amiss and where to begin to discover that coherence. This method also helped me come to terms with parts of the theory that are easy to overlook (like the doctrines of *fortuna* and *gloria*) and to search until I had a clear picture that was consistent with all that Machiavelli had written relative to the philosophical approach underlying his politics. The insights, are at least partly his, but not the errors.

Finally, and certainly not least, the support and insights of Mary Emily Call contributed more to this book than she realizes. Her most obvious contribution is the title, which positions this work relative to other recent efforts. But her less obvious contributions were more important to me. Her formidable memory and insights into language stabilized my internal compass repeatedly, while her intelligence and common sense, coupled with an unfailing sense of propriety and textual coherence, enabled me to make sense of apparently self-contradictory passages in Machiavelli. Even more importantly, she urged me to change my rhetorical style to one more accessible to the reader, improving the text considerably—when I was not too stubborn to listen. Finally, as only a spouse can, she recognized the importance of this project to me, calmed me when I was frustrated, tolerated the time I spent completing this book, and still managed to take pride in the finished product.

*   *   *

I am grateful to The Putnam Publishing Group for permission to reprint parts of *The Letters of Machiavelli*, translated by Allan H. Gilbert. © 1961 by Allan H. Gilbert.

I am also grateful to Duke University Press for permission to reprint parts of *Machiavelli: The Chief Works and Others*, translated by Allan H. Gilbert (1989). Copyright Beverly B. Gilbert.

Machiavelli Redeemed

Introduction

A Modern View

REACTIONS to Machiavelli's writings have shown a remarkable variety over the centuries, but the prevailing view remains a negative one. Cast in the fires of sixteenth-century French politics, a campaign to smear his name and his accomplishments was launched, presumably by aristocratic opponents to his republicanism; to a large extent it succeeded.[1] Maintained by negative, and sometimes grossly distorted, books like the *Anti-Machiavel* of Frederick of Prussia,[2] a vision developed that equated Machiavelli, a proponent of democratic freedom and of equality, with Lucifer himself. In this tradition, Shakespeare described him as the "murderous Machiavel."[3] One of the most important books of a generation ago reported that no one would be surprised if Machiavelli's views were described as "immoral and irreligious," or if his teachings were called "diabolical and he himself a devil."[4] A decade ago he was depicted as a proponent of "predatory" republicanism.[5] More recently, a small but significant book has described Machiavelli's commitment to democracy and democratic equality.[6] Finally, a recent Pulitzer Prize-winning effort depicts Machiavelli as a "saint" occupying a corner of heaven reserved for the interesting souls of the practitioners of politics—this corner is appropriately called "Hell."[7]

Not surprisingly, given the intensity of feelings on both sides, the language attacking—and defending—Machiavelli has tended to the theological. But Machiavelli was neither devil nor saint, in any of the usual senses. No devil could have urged such political powers as the Medici to do good things (like create democratic institutions, as he proposed in his *On Remodeling the Government of Florence*, or unify the nation, as he suggested in *The Prince*); and no saint could have written as he did of his sexual escapades (Gilbert's *Letters of Machiavelli*, no. 142, pp. 151–53). Rather, like so many of us, he was a sinner, but a sinner whose soul had good in it, whose soul could be redeemed. I intend to construct a case in his defense, a perspective from which we can see that, however guilty of evil he

17

was, the redeeming grace of his commitment to modernizing his nation by freeing his people and bringing them to civilizing glory should forestall a desire to condemn or damn him.

Nevertheless, what is to follow is no whitewash; like other sinners, Machiavelli does offend, sometimes with fiendish delight. His attack on traditional morality, his deep devotion to the emerging sense of nation, his fascination with militaristic and other forms of power, and his apparent disrespect for religion were deeply antithetical to the prevailing medieval (Christian) ethos. Perhaps even more distressingly, today's ethos is no more secure against his iconclasm than was his own. Hence, to describe Machiavelli as a "disturbing" thinker, as Sir Isaiah Berlin did a generation ago, should be beyond challenge.[8] His disquieting attack on the "eternal verities" has in fact caused a large number of efforts, of tremendous diversity, ingenuity, and variety, to explain—and explain away—his hostility to our comforting certitudes, to our traditional ways of making sense of our lives. But the disturbance, rooted deeply in our human nature and the nature of the world in which we live, will not go away; nor will I attempt to explain it away, preferring to confront it and to accept its truth when necessary.

Specifying the source of the disturbance is another question, however. For instance, the dominant school of thought in American academe today, as represented by the Straussians,[9] appear to portray Machiavelli as "a teacher of evil," explaining his defiance of traditional morality as an error. To these thinkers, Machiavelli's challenge is an error akin to relativism, and so amounts to an attack on the tradition of natural right—a traditional body of objective moral truths—which they continue to defend.[10] While Straussians generally deplore Machiavelli's error as "the" error of modernity, a prominent disciple of that school also portrays Machiavelli as "liberating" politics from morality,[11] permitting the emergence of an empirical science of politics without the restraints of normative thinking. But this contribution to empirical political science does not exonerate the Florentine philosopher from the charge of having abandoned— if not destroyed—what the Straussians refer to as natural right.

But in some ways, this charge of abandoning morality and natural right is almost beside the point. First, Machiavelli was neither opposed to morality nor a relativist.[12] No consistent relativist could write in praise of law that it "makes men good" (*Discourses*, 1:3), and no opponent of morality could write that "none are so foolish" as not to know that the greatest persons are those who have founded religions or republics, or other civilizing institutions (*Discourses*, 1:10.) Second, and more importantly, his recognition of moral voluntarism (a belief, akin to the social contract tradition, that humans create their moralities in acts of will or volition) is so solidly rooted in empirical observations of moral choices and moral tragedies that the burden of proof shifts, in the light of Machiavelli's examples of moral tragedy, to those who posit the existence of a single, objective morality binding on all humans regardless of condition. For if there were a single, rational standard of right action, then moral tragedy—a choice situation where all of the options are wrong—would be logically impossible, never a part of human experience. That tragic choices confront humans is one of the most haunting moral data we can recognize, and this datum reinforces Machiavelli's view more than that of his critics.

The case of Agammenon and Iphigenia are classic illustrations. The clear moral duty of Agammenon, as leader of the Greek navy, was to win the favor of the gods at the beginning of the voyage; this duty was augmented by a rash vow he had taken. But discharging these duties required the sacrifice of his daughter, Iphigenia, in clear violation of his parental duties. The tragedy is that neither choice could be right, as a rationalist morality would have guaranteed. Though this mythic tragedy had a happy ending—the goddess Diana magically saved Iphigenia and safely placed her as a priestess in Aulis—it did not rescue Iphigenia from a similar tragic choice later. For now her religious duty was to sacrifice shipwrecked sailors to Diana, but one such sailor proved to be her brother Orestes, to whom she owed a familial duty to save his life. (Unlike her father, Iphigenia found a way around her religious duty and did save her brother's life.)

Minimally, this father/daughter pair faced conflicting moral obligations. Alternately, they confronted different moralities that placed differing and conflicting demands upon them. Either way, they had to choose among these moralities or moral duties; such choice forces itself upon us as an empirical moral datum.[13] But if there were a rationally consistent standard of natural right, one could never be confronted by the irrationality of such tragic choices. In a fully rational cosmos, irrationality of such intensity could not exist. Hence, the disturbance in Machiavelli's writings is that we are forced to choose among competing moralities, one comfortable if demanding, supported by church and tradition, and the other disquietingly new and uncertain, but promising new freedoms and new well-being.

To accommodate all the partial truths of these views, this interpretation of Machiavelli's writings will have to be eclectic; it should also be comprehensive, in order to bring all of Machiavelli's writings (the philosophical and political as well as the dramatic and poetic) together into one coherent perspective on the world, modernity, human nature and values, and political change. While this interpretation of his thoughts will remain disturbing, its strength is that it renders his philosophy plausible, coherent, and modern. Unable to intervene for him with divine forces, perhaps I can at least redeem him for modern readers.

THE CHALLENGE OF MODERNITY

I mean no paradox when I suggest that Machiavelli's *modernity* disturbs, for modernizing is a deeply disturbing and disruptive process even when it is centuries old. Whether one is dealing with the economic process whereby the industrial infrastructure of a modern society is created or one is concerned with modernizing structures of authority, the process of modernization is one of destroying old views and ways of living and replacing them with new—or renewed—alternatives. Where economic modernization would require great technical and scientific discoveries and promise to make physical life safer and more comfortable, political development is much more difficult to conceptualize, but offers equally tangible benefits. Some, like Tocqueville in the 1830s, saw the modernization process as culminating "inevitably" in the "equality" of democracy.[14] Others, like Max Weber, were to conceive of authority in terms of its becoming less arbitrary and whimsical, or in terms of its becoming more rational and routinized. In this generation, others, like Almond and Powell, have defined modernization as the progressive separation of legislative from executive and judicial functions (they call this "role differentiation").[15]

Machiavelli was most like Tocqueville of that group, except that he could not yet see the process as "inevitable."[16] He had little idea of where the modernization process was going, but he clearly felt the need to move away from the tradition, sensing that a better way of life was possible. Devoid of any incentive to protect the status quo and marginalized by the return of the Medici to power, Machiavelli did the next best thing to developing a full theory of modernization: he attacked all things traditional to make way for the modern, negatively defining modernity for all of posterity. He repeatedly attacked traditional society, in all of its manifestations: its worldview, its conception of humanity, its values, and its authority structures. He assailed traditional beliefs in the order of the cosmos in *The Tercets on Fortune;* he upended traditional understandings of humanity in *The Golden Ass;* he pilloried traditional morality and the traditional family in *Mandragola;* he mocked the follies of mixing age and infatuation in *Clizia;* and he attacked the traditional god(s), along with the Church of Rome (his church), almost everywhere.[17] All were deficient; all must be replaced with new or "renewed" alternatives. In a sense, early modernity (the Renaissance) was a recognition of the human needs mandating these changes, requiring this progress.

In another sense, after all of these traditional supports of the medieval world had been assailed, the only task remaining for *The Prince* and *Discourses,* as well as the other political writings, like those on the history and constitution of Florence, was to explore the political implications of these intellectual revolutions. Machiavelli's accomplishment in *The Prince* and *Discourses* is to propose dismembering traditional society by a modernizing authority (akin to Weber's "charismatic authority"). In like manner, his *History of Florence* was written with an eye to crediting creative authorities, even the Medici who commissioned it, whenever possible. Finally, his proposal for a new constitution for Florence, also requested by the Medici, was a proposal to reform, rather than abandon, the representative institution of the *balia,* a republican device for choosing the gonfaloniere of justice. In none of his writings does he fawn on authority;[18] indeed, it is only a slight exaggeration to assert that his approach to authority, like his approach to power, is invariably instrumental, seeing it as a device for modernizing society. More typically, his writings are critical of authority, especially moribund authority that did not or could not renew itself, whether through intellectual, moral, political, or military weakness.

Nevertheless, these attacks on authority were not intended merely to destroy it; rather, a new variant of it was to be created, a modernizing, civilizing authority on the models of Moses and Romulus. Using authority to modernize is the central theme of both *The Discourses* and *The Prince.* Machiavelli's goals in writing these pieces were to renew an authority structure that had been "corrupted" by *ambizione* (*Discourses,* 3:1), create a new replacement that could bring about national unification (last chapter of *The Prince*), resurrect commerce (*Discourses,* 2:2), and make democratic freedom possible (*Prince,* Chapter 5, and *Discourses,* 1:5). Wishing to save humanity from the "error" of not having learned from the ancients (*Discourses,* 1:1), Machiavelli sought to emulate their ancient search for republican freedom in new, more modern circumstances, in the reemerging commercial relations of the Renaissance, which could put humanity "on a new route, which has not yet been followed by any one, and may prove difficult and troublesome" (*Discourses,* introduction to the first book). Everything would have to be transformed, from our perceptions of ourselves to that of our universe, including our perceptions of morality. It is little wonder that Machiavelli should disturb us; his was a revolutionary perspective.

What was to replace these traditions when they were dismantled? Something that was different and better than what Machiavelli experienced, something that drew inspiration from antiquity but did not repeat it, something profoundly new but of ancient inspiration. Indeed, Machiavelli promised to "enter a path not yet trodden by anyone" so as to "show the way" to other investigators (introduction to *The Discourses*).[19] This new "path" or "way" was to modernize the infrastructure on which a polity is based, and then to modernize the polity, creating new room for freedom. His life positioned him as a witness to the birth of modernity, and he wanted to be a midwife to that birth. But, having been removed from the practical side of politics that he so preferred, he transformed adversity into opportunity by beginning a theory of the process of modernization. In *The Prince,* I argue, he even sought to seduce the Medici into partaking in the vision of glory promised by his view of modernity.

Unlike Tocqueville, who could see from the perspective of the nineteenth century that the modernization process culminating in "democracy" and "equality" was "irresistible,"[20] Machiavelli remained unsure of the prospects of democracy and modernization, seeing clearly only that democracy remained unstable in *pre*modern societies: the existence of a feudal aristocracy "in the kingdom of Naples, in the Roman territory, in the Romagna, and in Lombardy" is the principal reason why "it is that no republic has ever been able to exist in those countries. . . . And to attempt the establishment of a republic in a country so constituted would be impossible. The only way to establish any kind of order there is to found a monarchical government. . . ." (*Discourses,* 1:55). Despite his preference for a representative democracy in Florence, he recognized that this constitution might not be appropriate for all peoples at all levels of development. The movement from autocratic authority structures with an inherited aristocracy to the earned status of the emerging market society was, in Machiavelli's mind, genuine progress. How could he augment this progress? Might a prince be necessary along the way?

Machiavelli's achievements in political philosophy are to be found in his answers to these questions about using authority to modernize and constitutionalize a people. He was convinced that humans were not trapped by historical circumstances, whether primitive or advanced. Human choices can make a difference, he repeatedly reminds us, and the choice to advance to democratic freedom was one he urged upon his readers, even upon the Medici in *The Prince*. So he continuously urges us to take charge of our own lives and to seek the glory of modern democratic freedom under laws of our own making. This made him a humanist, a believer that we humans must take charge of the process of change and direct it to our own ends.[21] This perception of his work as humanistic has the additional advantage of placing him squarely in the mainstream of the emerging Renaissance, where he is most comfortably located.

But what if the action required to modernize a nation, making it safe for democracy, was morally objectionable? If the objection emerged from traditional morality, then, to Machiavelli, this merely illustrated again the deficiencies of an unrenewed tradition. If the older morality stands in the way of a clear good, then a newer, more modern morality must be created to permit what is necessary for that greater good. This belief that morality is a product of human creative energies (hereafter called "moral voluntarism") is arguably the greatest disturbance in the Machiavellian corpus.[22] He was, after all, the writer who said that for a prince to survive and effect real and lasting change for the better, even a good man must learn "to enter evil," need not "keep faith," and must be able to use cruelties "well" (*Prince*, chapters 18 and 8).

Like Huck Finn whose love for Jim led him to violate conventional morality and fear for his soul, Machiavelli attacks conventional morality and fears the loss of his soul, claiming in his letters to love "my country more than my soul" (Gilbert, *Chief Works and Others*, 1010). There is clearly a moral message in this, and it is profoundly disquieting—but revealingly modern: since humans create morality, if a given morality stands in the way of a clear moral good, such as the patriotic duty to civilize one's nation, then that morality can be recreated to conform to the new moral recognition. It is in this way that we make moral progress and become a more civilized or more developed people. Further, in an anticipation of the Lockean justification of revolutionary violence, sometimes this progress can only be achieved through violence. So we arrive at the centrally disturbing idea: if moralities can be improved, renewed, or recreated, then they are human creations. If they are artifacts, they cannot be eternal. The eternal verities may be neither eternal nor true; even more disturbingly, they may not even exist at times.

Let us begin, then, with a look at *The Discourses*, using them to focus on Machiavelli's thought and to place *The Prince* in context.

He described *The Prince* as a virtual subset of the larger work, and identified two subjects, republics (chapter 2) and laws (chapter 12), that he could not discuss in *The Prince*. Machiavelli's thoughts, then, on principalities and armies, the subjects of *The Prince*, must be read in this larger context, as he intended.

REPUBLICAN GLORY

We know from Machiavelli's own pen that *The Discourses* (1:1) were meant to articulate his notions of what we can learn from the study of the history of other societies. His views on history, and the historical greatness or *gloria* of Rome, frequently idealized, are the modernizing context in which his advice to the Medici in *The Prince* makes sense, even if disquieting sense. This humanist belief in historical learning rests on his conviction that the "laws" governing "the movements" of humans are as immutable as the laws governing the movements of the stars (*Discourses*, 1:2; quoted fully in chapter 3). Not only is this humanist theme a distinctive trademark during this stage of the Renaissance, but we learn that these humanist laws, in turn, require democratic freedom and are consonant with the democracies then reemerging along with "commerce."[23] The remainder of *The Discourses* is devoted to showing that these laws of human development are the causes of the powerful human need to be free—and then to exploring the political and constitutional means for satisfying that need. The central question of *The Discourses*, then, is this: how can we constitute a society so that human freedom is preserved (*Discourses*, 1:1–3)? What kind of "new order" can we create that frees the human spirit for higher and more noble aspirations (*Discourses*, 1: 4)? I take these two together to ask: How, in general, can we create the modern preconditions for liberty?

The task of *The Prince* is parallel, but narrower: How can we create the preconditions for liberty in a commercial society corrupted by personal, quasi-feudal ambition? The response is remarkable in only one sense: it is unexpected that a dedicated supporter of republican democracy should respond that monarchy is appropriate to a corrupted polity. Among people not yet civilized by obedience to law, a singular almost monarchical power is necessary to unify that people and "reduce" it to lawful habits (1:55; repeated in 1:9–11, 1:18, 3:1, and 3:8). Then, with good constitutional provisions, freedom can emerge at a later time. Machiavelli emphasized this ability to transform a people civilized by laws into a free people with his tales of the two Romans named Brutus, one of whom re-

newed the institutions given by Romulus to create the republic while
the other tried to prevent their destruction by attacking Julius Caesar. Hence, when confronted with a corrupted people, an almost
monarchical power is necessary for legislating, for creating the modern conditions of liberty. Laws and constitutions are the constant
themes of the two works, and Machiavelli advanced our understanding of both by alerting us to the conditions necessary for the emergence and preservation of freedom while recognizing that a stronger
power may be necessary to civilize a lawless people.

Indeed, constitutions emerge as the theme of *The Discourses*. If
the first book is about constitution making, the second is devoted
to the arduous task of constituting a lawful government among an
unlawful or corrupted people. Finally, in book 3, we learn how to
renew constitutions. Early in his argument in book 1, Machiavelli
rejected the six Aristotelian constitutions[24] as "pestiferous" because
the virtuous are not stable and the others are vicious (1:2). After
settling on a "mixed constitution" (one that shares the virtues of the
three lawful "pure" forms: monarchy, aristocracy, and democracy)
as a stable alternative to the vices of bad government (1:2) and
showing that the Roman provision for tribunes to represent the poor
and a senate for the rich was a glorious constitutional mix (1:3), he
comes (1: 4) to a discussion of factions within a polity, and to the
contribution they can make to constitutional stability, to freedom,
and to virtue and happiness.

Here Machiavelli gives us two of his most startling assertions.
First, faction is essential to the preservation of freedom (*Discourses*,
1:4). The key to stability in a republic is a combination of (1) a
mixed constitution and (2) the factional competition that inclines
each side (the "rich" and the "poor") to monitor the actions of the
other, preventing both from subverting the constitution and freedom
(*Discourses*, 1:3 and 37).[25] His intuitive idea is that the rich can
never steal liberty from the poor if the poor are institutionally powerful enough to prevent such deprivation; and vice versa.

Which then is the better guardian of freedom, the rich or the
poor? Here is Machiavelli's second surprise: the poor are better
friends to freedom than the rich (*Discourses*, 1:4). The preservation
of the power of the poor and the prevention of excessive wealth
appear to lie behind his assertion that "well-ordered republics ought
to keep their treasuries rich and their citizens poor" (1:37). If a
republic is to survive and preserve its freedom, it must also balance
its rich and poor factions since they are both necessary for its health.
These passages, so early in *The Discourses*, are startling revelations
about Machiavelli's theory because this advice to republics is incom-

patible with what we expect from the stereotypical teacher of evil; indeed, these ideas provide a solid base for depicting his theme as political modernization, for appreciating his modernizing emphasis. While much more must be said about the role of equality in democratic politics, we may here surmise that Machiavelli had become convinced that feudal inequalities are detrimental to democratic freedom, while the emerging (and apparently more egalitarian) wealth of commerce was more conducive to freedom.

MACHIAVELLI'S "LIBERTY"

One may well wonder how Machiavelli can be defended as a proponent of liberty when he writes so differently from, say, Locke on the question of rights. Indeed, for all of his insistence on liberty, the term rights rarely makes its way into his text and he certainly is no proponent of the classical liberal doctrine of natural rights. The quick and short response to this inquiry is to draw attention to the two distinct, but related, traditions of liberty articulated by political philosophers over the centuries. Ever since Hobhouse and Green depicted the Lockean liberty of the "classical" tradition as "too negative," proponents of the social welfare state and of equality have been wont to refer to the alternative, more modern, vision of liberty as "positive."[26] Because the classical liberties required that governments *not* do certain kind of things, the "negative" label gained currency; similarly, the rights articulated by proponents of the social welfare state required that the government take positive steps to free them. Classical, or "negative," liberty, then, came to be understood as the bundle of rights that create a political "space" where one can do or be anything one wants without fear of governmental coercion. By contrast, those bundles of liberties, like freedom from want or starvation, that require positive governmental action for their realization are called "positive liberty."[27]

So negative liberty became associated with the formal and legal guarantees that protect a citizen from the state and its actions, while positive liberty became a way of referring to the need for the state to do something for its citizens. In this way, positive liberty is typically associated with positive government, with empowering the government to "do something about" societal problems like poverty and environmental pollution. The classic Anglo-American version of this development is that the negative tradition of liberty prevailed in liberal societies from the initial stirrings of liberty in the eighteenth century until, roughly, the Great Depression, when massive human suffering appeared to justify increased governmental involvement in regulating and adjusting the economy and, more importantly, new governmental programs to aid the indigent.

Berlin describes the "notion of negative freedom" in this way: "I am normally said to be free to the degree to which no man or body of men interferes with my activity. Political liberty in this sense is simply the area within which a man can act unobstructed by others."[28] By contrast, the "'positive' sense of the word 'liberty' derives from the wish on the part of the individual to be his own master. I wish my life and decisions to depend on myself, not on external forces of whatever kind."[29] To the extent that I am unable to achieve this autonomy, however, we may infer that I require outside help to realize my freedom.

An illustration from the American Bill of Rights, typically understood as an embodiment of negative liberties, may prove useful. The Sixth Amendment's guarantee that the accused shall enjoy the right "to have the Assistance of Counsel for his defense" is notoriously ambiguous with respect to these two notions of liberty. Understood in a solely negative way, this would mean that the state may do nothing to prohibit me from acquiring counsel should I be accused. The positive rejoinder would be that this interpretation effectively guarantees this right only for those with the money to afford counsel. The indigent then are offered no protection by this amendment unless it is given a more positive interpretation—unless the state is willing to assure counsel to everyone regardless of ability to pay.[30] In this way, the positive tradition of liberty may require state help to provide for the realization of this right.

Where the negative tradition is typically associated with notions like rights, limits on governmental authority, constitutionalism, laissez-faire capitalism, and the natural laws securing one's natural rights in a state of nature, the positive tradition is more naturally associated with democracy, equality, the social welfare state, and autonomy. In this context, the quick and simple answer to our inquiry is roughly this: unlike Locke who was operating in the negative tradition of liberalism, Machiavelli's "liberty" shares many characteristics with the positive tradition. At the very least, he was an advocate of positive liberty in that he advocated democracy (understood as rule by majorities), equality, and autonomy. Implicitly, his advice to a state to keep its poor from becoming dependent upon the wealthy may recommend the programs of the social welfare state in a new and vibrant way: dependence on state programs rather than private charity prevents the degeneration of faction into sectarian violence and prevents antirepublican autocracy by minimizing the *ambizione* of the wealthy. His commitment to this liberty is an instance of his desire to "enter a new way," to modernize society. Equally importantly, Machiavelli was concerned to discover the causes of the loss of liberty in the democratic republics of Rome and Florence; knowing what corrupted these societies might serve to prevent further corruption.

CHAPTER BY CHAPTER OVERVIEW

Since Machiavelli was a humanist, he was presumably opposed to the medieval worldview of Christianity, or at least to a variant of it. What in the medieval worldview was to be rejected? As the grip of that worldview was weakening, what, in Machiavelli's mind, was to replace it? Certain truisms apply: to the worldviews of the great rationalist philosophers, Augustine and Aquinas, for instance, Machiavelli is implicitly opposed. We might well see him as standing on a threshold between the ancient and medieval world, on the one hand, and the modern world, on the other. On this, then, Strauss and the Straussians are right: since medieval and ancient worldviews incorporated a sense of natural right that is missing in modernity, and since Machiavelli stood on the modern side of the divide, he did not subscribe to their notion of a world structured by God or nature according to principles of right. Since the reemerging humanist world view is central to so much else in Machiavelli's thought, chapter one turns to an examination of his notion of the cosmic order and to his articulation of the unchanging laws governing the "movements" of things (*Discourses*, 1:1). Although Machiavelli did see rational lawfulness and regularities in the cosmos, he rejected with both hands any assumptions of a "deterministic" universe. In opposition to determinism, he depicts the cosmos as open to human exertion.

Among these laws governing things are the laws governing human change, and any political practitioner must understand these laws above all else: "it is necessary for him who lays out a state and arranges laws for it to presuppose that all men are evil . . ." (*Discourses*, 1:3). Accordingly, the second chapter is an examination of "the evil that lurks in the hearts of men."[31] Machiavelli articulates a set of laws governing human movement from corruption to glory and back to corruption in the quest for a stable polity that can resist deterioration. This examination reveals an account of human nature that is contrary not only to our stereotypes but also to first appearances in the text. For, although the passage about human evil appears to depict our nature as essentially evil, careful attention to the text reveals an explication of a radically different view of a human potential for nobility.

While his account of our evil owes much to the Augustinian view of us as transformed and twisted by Original Sin, he transcends that view by marrying to it the Roman hope for nobility, suggesting that we are capable of either nobility or corruption—or perhaps both. Given his humanist worldview, which implies that neither God nor nature will assure us of any particular outcome, Machiavelli instructs us that it is a matter of human choice which potential we realize.

How we choose is obviously a matter of morals, and Machiavelli was far from silent on this subject. Against an older tradition (the rationalist tradition of medieval Christianity and ancient Greece and Rome), Machiavelli presses the claims of a newer view of morality. Neither amoral nor immoral, he defines a new morality fit for the new way of life just beginning to emerge. Invoking the memory of the ancient Roman republic, Machiavelli contrasts the rationalist moralities of Rome and Christianity to show that neither is adequate. Then he advocates a view of morality unlike either the Roman or the Christian; this more modern view is that there are no eternal moral truths etched in stone by God, the gods, or nature. Hence, his moral reflections in *The Prince* are contrary both to the natural law tradition of medieval Christianity and to similar thinking by the Roman Stoics; even in details (like reflections on "liberality"—a willingness to spend money lavishly to satisfy the wants and needs of those less fortunate—with state funds), Seneca and Cicero are implicitly opposed as frequently as Aquinas.

In contrast to all of the ancient and medieval rationalists, for Machiavelli as for many other modern moral thinkers, our moral obligations are created by us as a rational response to the needs of living together in society. The social contract tradition of Hobbes, Locke, and Rousseau will depict this choice of morality and laws as a rational deliberation about the demands of human civilization. Machiavelli is a member of this group, which is collectively responsible for a modern belief in the possibility of moral progress. Prior to the creation of laws, for these voluntarists, actions may not be wrong. Yet, for Machiavelli, these un- or pre-civilized times are not times devoid of values; no one is "so wise or so foolish" as to fail to discern the value of civilizing an uncivilized people (*Discourses,* 1:10). These moral themes are the subjects of the third chapter.

On these modern foundations, Machiavelli erects a solidly practical and realistic political philosophy for modernizing medieval and feudal polities. Since this view of the desirability of modernization requires a moral foundation, we turn in the fourth chapter to an examination of the theory of "good" that Machiavelli posits as a sort of self-evident truth, that no one is "too wise or too foolish" to recognize. This notion of what is good for humans places its own stringent requirements upon us, although they are not the obligations of traditional morality.

Confronting the problems posed by the need to obey laws in a properly constituted modern state, examined in the fifth chapter of this book as well as in several of the works under consideration,[32] Machiavelli sounds themes dissonant with our perceptions of him as a teacher of evil. A strict advocate of a well-balanced constitution, he advises us that it must include a rich respect for the law, especially by the government (*Discourses*, 1:45); a balance of power between the rich and the poor (*Discourses*, 1:2, 4, 5, 45; 2:2); and the power of the executive to respond to real emergencies (*Discourses*, 1:34; 3:3). While it would be premature and anachronistic to detect here constitutionalism of Locke's sort, there is nothing in Machiavelli's exposition that contradicts Locke's central points, while the Lockean "prerogative" may even have intellectual origins in *The Discourses* (1:45).

Yet there are times when a republican constitution, however well formed, may not be able to survive. Anticipating Montesquieu's insights in *The Spirit of the Laws*, Machiavelli advises that a constitution must be well suited to circumstances. In conditions of abject corruption, as quattrocento Florentines knew, a republican constitution would be doomed. What is to be done then? Sometimes, as the Florentine secretary knew, a stronger form of government was needed, and cases of extreme corruption required "a power almost kingly" (*Discourses*, 1:18). The sixth chapter is devoted to resolving the apparent contradiction posed by a dedicated republican's endorsement of monarchy; in rough outline, Machiavelli comes to this endorsement of monarchical coercion as a means of modernizing a people who resist the "civilizing" effects of law.

Machiavelli's ruminations on constitutions and their renewal or corruption were not mere abstract theorizing but born of a practical need. Understanding how corruption occurs may enable us both to deal with corruption when it exists and prevent it when it has not yet corroded our institutions. Political and institutional renewal, a return to beginnings, and the power of nationalism to prevent disintegration along with the possibility of "harmony" in a state are examined in detail in chapter seven. Here we examine the differences between Machiavelli, with his faith in faction, and theorists who desire harmonious states. For example, Plato would have preferred a state in which all classes live in the harmony of justice and Rousseau desired a state in which the common good of a "general will" prevails.[33] In a powerful countercurrent to this mainstream, Machiavelli urges us to see faction as a good thing for democratic politics. The key to preventing corruption, or destroying it if present, is to comprehend the material conditions necessary for the flourishing of democratic freedom. The eighth chapter is devoted to Machiavelli's views of political economy, an anticipation of this emerging science; the characteristics that differentiate his views from alternatives are examined to emphasize his commitment to equality. It is here that Machiavelli becomes most clearly a friend of the poor (really, the *petit bourgeois* members of the lesser guilds, not of the urban masses, the unemployed, or unemployable, or the "underclasses"). Insofar as the populist movement in nineteenth-century America, along with its urban counterpart, progressivism, was also inspired by the economic interests of "small" businesses and farmers, Machiavelli, a Renaissance advocate of the small guilds, anticipates them, sharing their desire to create a government that will not "rig" the rules of the game against their interests and in favor of their wealthier competitors. Most importantly, Machiavelli fears that the *ambizione* of wealthier families like the Medici leads them to corrupt a polity as they seek familial interests at the expense of the common interest. This *ambizione*, against which Machiavelli rails in both *The Discourses* and in his *Tercets on Ambition*, leads the wealthy to protect their personal and familial interests by obtaining control of the government and writing rules beneficial to those interests, rules that confer upon them an unfair advantage in the competitive struggles of commerce. In addition, the theoretical and practical implications of Machiavelli's insights into democratic political economy are considered in this chapter, as we examine the strengths and deficiencies of his perspective. In conclusion, the populist metaphor is apt for symbolizing Machiavelli's views on class relations.

Finally, in the light of the populist and modernizing reading, we must reconsider Machiavelli's place in the Western tradition; this becomes the task of the final chapter. While it is not unusual to place him among "statists," militarists, nationalists, and other absolutists who prefigured the Fascist persuasion,[34] I argue that he has more kinship with Locke and Madison than with Bismarck, Napoleon, or Hitler. In short, his dedication to republican freedom, one variant of positive liberty, makes him deserving of a place in the democratic tradition of the West. Nevertheless, his militant nationalism, along with his moral and teleological inclinations, may be errors deserving criticism.

Let us begin, then, with the newly emergent worldview of modernity, a world where new and wonderful things would become possible, a world of uncertainty and few guarantees, but a world where democratic freedom begins to make sense. As in so many other areas, Machiavelli is here disquietingly modern—but liberating.

Part 1
A Humanist Worldview

1

Humanism and Empiricism:
A World Open to Human Effort

INTRODUCTION: RENAISSANCE REFLECTIONS
ON SOCIETY AND THE COSMOS

THE Renaissance, almost by definition, was a period of fundamental social and cultural change; it was also a time of intense perceptual change, as we came to view the world differently.[1] These changes in worldview, among other effects, reinvigorated the arts and reinforced the changes in knowledge that led to the emergence of modern empirical science. In a symbiotic reinforcement of each other, changes in the social and cultural arenas augmented parallel alterations in perception, knowledge, and science. Social scientific knowledge would also be transformed, and Machiavelli was instrumental in bringing these various strands together.

By the time of Machiavelli's birth in 1469, many societal factors had conjoined to create conditions conducive to the emergence of modernity. The resurrection of commerce had created the beginnings of a commercial class and was transforming the guilds; their feudal role would soon give rise to, and then give way to, their role as modernizing agents. The feudal margraves had begun to yield to the rising commercial class and were all but eliminated as the ruling class, with an emerging de facto aristocracy composed of the wealthiest of the soon-to-be-dominant commercial class in the greater guilds.

The confluence of many social and economic forces was transforming—and modernizing—the world. The position of gonfaloniere of justice, the chief elective executive office held by Piero Soderini during Machiavelli's tenure as secretary, had been created in response to pressures from the traders in Florence to punish aristocratic violations of the peace arising from blood feuds—because the violence interfered with trade.[2] From its original purpose of protecting townspeople and the free flow of trade, it evolved into a larger executive function. Together, emerging social and economic forces had already made the position of the feudal lords untenable; but they had not yet made democratic institutions viable.

Changing perceptions of the cosmos would challenge and change modernity even as modernity would alter perceptions of the cosmos. Central to this were religious views, and religious views remained primarily supportive of the aristocratic status quo and constituted significant barriers to democratic practice. Not surprisingly, Machiavelli came to criticize two distinct aspects of religion: its worldview and its corruption. Let us approach them in order.

A. Religion and Worldviews

Perceptions of sacred time, or of eternity, had not yet released early Renaissance minds to think in terms of secular time, or the *saeculum,* the arena in which democratic freedom could thrive.[3] Simply put, social events and even major social transformations occurred in the secular realm and were consequently, by definition, not eternal. Since eternal truths were considered more significant than transient data, social data were insignificant theologically.[4] Like the shadows on the walls of Plato's cave or the notion of *maya* (the illusions of this world that conceal the reality of deeper religious truths) in traditional Indian theology, knowledge of the events of this earth were unimportant, suspect, and perhaps even the work of Satan.

Since eternal verities, as articulated by Aquinas and Augustine, were more inclined to favor monarchy than democracy,[5] democracy was not a preferred form of government for medieval thinkers. More bluntly, in a similar and similarly modernizing situation, Mao described a parallel worldview in China as one of the "Five Pillars of Heaven" that supported traditional social arrangements and inhibited modernization.[6] So long as feudal and medieval worldviews continued to fetter human minds, humans would remain captives—and freedom would be but a dream.

Why would a Renaissance thinker believe that an entirely "new order" (introduction to *The Discourses*) is required by a new understanding of the world? Part of the answer is that this new understanding is so radically different from the old understanding, both in form and substance.[7] From the traditional perspective, if a lesson were to be drawn from an historical event, then that new knowledge is temporal; if it is temporal, then it is not eternal; if it is not eternal, then its truth is dubious and of little significance. One implication of this rationalist perspective is that one can never acquire from experience, which is "only" sensual, empirical, and historical, the type of knowledge that one would need to rule, which should be eternally true.[8] It is significant that one of the most forceful articulations of this belief that empirical knowledge is an inadequate basis for ruling was Plato's *Republic,* which proposed an ideal polity that was anything but republican or democratic.

Yet these historical sources may provide exactly what is necessary when trying to govern a real republic—a representative democracy—and when trying to stay alive in a secular world of changing fortunes. When living in the modern world that lacks an infusion of divine purpose, the knowledge needed for survival could not be theological; rather, it would have to be a secular understanding of our nature. Not surprisingly, if Machiavelli were to succeed in modernizing Italy, he would have to find a way to free humans from this mind-set; in quattrocento Italy, this would mean breaking the hold of a traditional worldview over the minds of his people.

B. The Medieval Corruption of Christianity

Since that traditional worldview was typically associated with Christianity, Machiavelli had double cause for criticizing Christianity. He was first of all opposing it from within, as a member of the Christian church, because of its corrupt practices. Further, his description of the historic figure of the Christ is friendly, even admiring. What irked him, beyond his anticlericalism, was both the Christian worldview that kept people from asserting their right to play a role in history and the role of the church in keeping Italy divided (*Discourses,* 1:12).

Consequently, even in his comedic plays like *Clizia,* characters are rarely made to show reverence to religion or the religious. When sophomoric jokes are not being made about the children of priests and popes, friars are depicted as small, venal men who would do almost anything for money. In still other scenes, even religious devotion is mocked:

Husband: Where are you going?
Wife: To mass.
Husband: And in Carnival time! Imagine what you'll be doing in Lent.
(act 2, scene 3, Gilbert, 832)

His letters are no different. Many in Florence saw a holy monk, even a saint, in Savonarola; they applauded his role in making possible the republic that Machiavelli would later serve. But the future secretary saw only an "unarmed prophet" (see *Prince*, chapter 6), unwilling or unable to secure his own welfare in an age of corruption. Although he went to hear the sermons of Savonarola, he frankly admitted that this was an exception; when a Franciscan friar came to preach in Florence, "The preaching I did not hear, because I am not given to such doings" (Gilbert's *Letters of Machiavelli*, no. 138, p. 148, also mentioned in Gilbert's introduction 70).

For those sympathetic to his cause, it is easy to make little of his animosity to religion. But his attacks on Christianity were far more than iconoclastic jokes, and although his contempt for the clergy shines through his published and private writings, he was more than anticlerical. His attacks on medieval Christianity were rooted in an opposition to what he saw as corruption and in his embracing of the "new order" that he hoped would replace it. Nevertheless, his animosity to religion may be more apparent than real, a manifestation of his modernity and a product of his desire to bring about progressive reforms. After all, he praised Numa (*Discourses*, 1:11) for the great Roman civic religion he founded, and he counted founders of religions as first among those who "deserve to be eulogized" (*Discourses*, 1:10). Since he was constantly concerned with renewing and bringing institutions back to their beginnings (*Discourses*, 3:1), I contend that he criticized the church for having failed to do so (*Discourses*, 1:13). Had that church renewed itself and become a modernizing force (*Discourses*, 1:12), there is no reason to believe that Machiavelli would have recalcitrantly continued to oppose it.

C. Moral Deterioration

A concern related to the Christian worldview is the form of life created by people who live in accord with that cosmology. So, if Machiavelli criticizes the clergy for deviating from the example of Christ, he also denounces Christian morality for making people weak. In some way, the Christian message had been contaminated, and that contamination was leaking into Italian society:

> But as there are some of the opinion that the well-being of Italian affairs depends upon the Church of Rome, I will present such arguments against that opinion as occur to me; two of which are most important, and cannot according to my judgment be controverted. The first is that the evil example of the court of Rome has destroyed all piety and religion in Italy, which brings in its train infinite improprieties and disorders; for as we may presuppose all good where religion prevails, so where it

is wanting we have the right to suppose the very opposite. We Italians then owe to the Church of Rome and to her priests our having become irreligious and bad; but we owe her a still greater debt, and one that will be the cause of our ruin, namely, that the Church has kept and still keeps our country divided. (*Discourses*, 1:12)

In other words, even worse than its internal corruption is the effect of that corruption: Christian institutions had made a mockery of morality, weakening the bonds necessary for a healthy society.

In addition, Christian morality had weakened us instead of strengthening us for the battles necessary for our freedom:

Reflecting now as to whence it came that in ancient times the people were more devoted to liberty than in the present, I believe that it resulted from this, that men were stronger in those days, which I believe to be attributable to the difference of education, founded upon the difference of their religion and ours. For, as our religion teaches us the truth and the true way of life, it causes us to attach less value to the honors and possessions of this world; whilst the Pagans, esteeming those things as the highest good, were more energetic and ferocious in their actions. . . . Besides this, the Pagan religion deified only men who had achieved great glory, such as commanders of armies and chiefs of republics, whilst ours glorifies more the humble and contemplative men than the men of action. Our religion, moreover, places the supreme happiness in humility, lowliness, and a contempt for worldly objects, whilst the other, on the contrary, places the supreme good in grandeur of soul, strength of body, and all such other qualities as render men formidable; and if our religion claims of us fortitude of soul, it is more to enable us to suffer than to achieve great deeds. (*Discourses*, 2:2)

Since it was St. Augustine who had made the case that Christian morals had *not* weakened Rome, it is clear that the republican is here directly controverting Augustine and his rationalist version of Christianity. But, to the secretary's mind, Christianity need not have become what it was in the Dark Ages:

And certainly, if the Christian religion had from the beginning been maintained according to the principles of its founder, the Christian states and republics would have been much more united and happy than what they are. . . . And whoever examines the principles upon which that religion is founded, and sees how widely different from those principles its present practice and application are, will judge that its ruin or chastisement is at hand. (*Discourses*, 1:12)

As an institution, the church had become so seriously corrupted, in Machiavelli's mind, that its very survival was in question. So there can be no doubt that, in his humanism, Machiavelli meant to criticize the Christianity of the Dark Ages and early Renaissance without criticizing Christ.

D. Rejection of the Christian Worldview

Christian cosmology seemed reactionary to Machiavelli; since it had become traditional to the point of a fault, he criticized the Christian worldview for holding back modernization, especially nation building. But Christianity had assimilated a wide variety of worldviews over the centuries and has now come to embrace an even wider range of worldviews, from strict Calvinist predestination to its Existentialist opposite. It is not clear against which version of it he was rebelling. Let us begin to identify which version he opposed by noting a distinction between two diametrically opposing worldviews within Christianity.

To illustrate the two polar opposites, let us consider the differences in worldview of two career counselors in a religious school. With relatively minor verbal differences, they might talk with their student about his/her life's calling by saying (1) "God has called you to be a priest" (or any particular vocation, say, a truck driver) as opposed to (2) "God has called you to choose a vocation." In the first version, the existence of a divine plan is assumed, and our obligation is to discover our place in that plan; but in the second version, God is said to present us with a perfectly "open" choice. To identify these polar opposites, let us call these the providential version of Christianity and the open version of Christianity.

In the open Christian view of human history, articulated clearly in Dostoevsky's *Brothers Karamazov,* for example, the all-good and benevolent God has created an open universe, in which humans are called to make almost existential choices that give meaning and purpose to their lives. The providential version, by contrast, depicts the cosmos as governed by a more rigid rational plan, presumably present in the mind of God at creation. Hence, it has two variants, according to which either (a) you have no choice but to take the role God has assigned to you, a belief we should call Christian determinism or predestination, or (b) you can make an alternative choice only by flying in the face of God's plan, refusing to accept it and the goal or meaning God had given to your life. Since the Greek word for the goal or significance of a thing is *telos,* the belief that things have a meaning and purpose internal to them has come to be known as teleology; we can call the Christian version of this belief Christian teleology. The providential version of Christianity then comes in both determinist and teleological variants.

Figure 1.1 Christian Worldviews

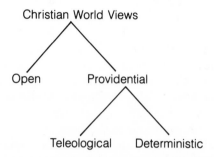

But for either variant, to act in a way contrary to the purposes that God instilled in reality is to sin. In the determinist or predestination version of providential Christianity, God requires that everything be just as it is, while the teleological version of providential Christianity, frequently associated with Augustine and Aquinas, suggests a looser texture to the reality God has created, a looseness that permits more room for human choice and sin. Most simply, then, the difference between the teleological version of Christianity (in which everything, including the human species, has a God-given purpose—or *telos*—that calls it along a certain path) and the determinist version (in which a tighter divine plan requires that everything happen exactly according to a divine script, so that human choice becomes an illusion) is the extent to which God "gives" or "imposes" meaning upon our lives. Despite the deep theological significance of the differences between these two competing Christian views, they are closer to each other than to the alternative open view, in which God has not infused the world with any particular meaning or purpose, leaving that to us.

A metaphor may make these types of worldview clearer: a cup or chalice might represent reality, being, or the cosmos, while the wine within it symbolizes the meaning and purpose of life. The teleological and determinist versions of Christianity would see the chalice and the wine as God's creations, freely given to us, though they would disagree about the extent to which the cup is filled. Presumably, the determinist would see the cup as so full of God's purposes that there is no room left for ours, while the teleological view would see room for us to put other purposes in the cup, but might see, at least on occasions, those other purposes as vinegar rather than wine. By contrast, the open version of Christianity would see the cup as God's creation but depict the wine as a human creation; God gave us the world, but life comes to have the meaning and purpose we bring to it.[9] Atheistic versions of existentialism go a bit further, asserting not only that the cup is empty of meaning but also that there is no God beyond the cup, thus denying that the cup is a divine creation. The cup "just is," and the human task is to bring however much or little significance to it as we choose.

If the teleological Christian view of reality is the archetypically medieval view, it is challenged in modernity both by the determinist views of Calvinism in the Reformation and by the denial of God as the final cause of being in secular humanism. Machiavelli belongs to this second, humanistic group that rejected the traditional teleology of the Middle Ages. Extending the metaphor to Machiavelli's views of cosmic order, we can find that the chalice is no more than half full: "In order not to annul our free will, I judge it true that Fortune may be mistress to one half our actions but that even she leaves the other half, or almost, under our control" (*Prince,* chapter 25, introductory paragraph).

THE DANGERS OF ATTACKING TELEOLOGY

Modern empirical thinkers who have challenged this teleological view—even in more recent times—often realized, implicitly or explicitly, that they were challenging an orthodoxy, and they sometimes feared the consequences of that attack. For instance, Stephen J. Gould reports that so much did "the negative effect of fear" influence Darwin that he delayed the publication of his work for twenty-one years (and then published it only because it appeared that another scientist might "scoop" him) because "he was not about to compromise a promising career by promulgating a heresy. . . ."[10] Darwin apparently felt that attacking orthodoxy could so complicate his life that it was more prudent to avoid the attack.[11]

Though the details may differ, the prejudice remains operative today: the stumbling block to our accepting Darwinian evolution "does not lie in any scientific difficulty, but rather in the radical philosophical content of Darwin's message."[12] The heresy that challenged "a set of entrenched Western attitudes that we are not yet ready to abandon" was the rejection of the teleological tradition of Aristotle and Aquinas, the claim that "Evolution is purposeless, nonprogressive, and materialistic."[13] If the evolution of species lacks a *telos,* or purpose, then the whole rationalist tradition of medieval teleology cannot have been correct; and many of humanity's hopes and aspirations are rendered disturbingly meaningless, as our sense of significance and our security and certainty are shattered.

As Galileo saw it, a similar attack on divine teleology brought modern science generally (and astronomy particularly) into conflict with religion or, more particularly, with teleological Christianity. For if the earth is a planet revolving about the sun, then it is not the center of the cosmos; and if the earth is not the center of the cosmos, then humans might not have the ultimate significance in a divine plan that we had hoped for. Modernity, then, is in many senses an attack upon the teleology of ancient and medieval world views. Entering the modern world from the Middle Ages through the portal of the Renaissance is almost like entering a completely new world. This was the voyage of Machiavelli's generation.[14]

Against the prevailing medieval view of the cosmos as structured by the will of the creating deity, Machiavelli saw it as at least partly open to human exertion. It is no accident that the Florentine secretary came to this view of the cosmos as open to human purposes; it is rather the logical outcome of his modern, almost scientific, approach to how we know the world. His attention to the data from our senses is a logically necessary step toward this nonteleological view of reality.

MACHIAVELLI'S EMPIRICISM

A. Opposition to Rationalism

In rejecting the rationalist vision of a cosmos infused with a purpose or plan, Machiavelli also found it necessary to reject the ancient and medieval theory of how we come to know the world and its significance or purpose. The theories of knowledge found in rationalist thinkers like Plato, Augustine, and Aquinas took account of the errors to which our unassisted senses were prone. Our sensual knowledge of this world lacks certainty and eternal truth; life in this world may not even be ultimately "real." Hence, according to these rationalist views, truth is available only from reason and/or revelation, usually a combination of the two.

By contrast, Machiavelli articulated a commitment to examine the real world, the material things that are available to the human senses: "I have decided that I must concern myself with the truth of the matter as facts show it rather than with any fanciful notion. Yet many have fancied for themselves republics and principalities that have not been seen or known to exist in reality. For there is such a difference between how men live and how they ought to live that he who abandons what is done for what ought to be done learns his destruction rather than his preservation. . . ." (*Prince,* chapter 15).

Plato's Socrates was one of several thinkers who had invented a "republic" that was known to have never existed in this world and that was *not* a representative democracy. It is therefore a theory of knowledge like Plato's, as it is explained in the metaphor of the cave, that is under attack here along with the elitism implicit in this theory. In the Platonic metaphor, one is to imagine oneself born into a dark cave with a slight light marking the opening onto the world outside. A fire is tended upon a shelf within the cave, and bound to the wall below the shelf are its inhabitants, who have never seen any other reality than the shadows cast by the fire upon the opposite wall.

For cave dwellers, the shadows upon the wall of the cave become the only reality. Liberation from this trap is possible only by first breaking the bonds of our senses that keep us fettered to the wall; ultimately, if we desire true liberation, we must also be prepared to leave the cave, our little illusory world, and enter the "true" reality beyond the opening. Passing through the opening into another reality constitutes a kind of death, which becomes rebirth into a new and higher being, where we no longer are aware of illusory and insubstantial shadows but of true reality. Passing through the opening, then, is a kind of death to the senses and birth to the life of reason. This is why the rationalist theory of knowledge can be attributed to the Plato of *The Republic.* This theory of knowledge also led Socrates/Plato to reject the claims of democracy, which pandered merely to the appetites at the expense of the rational truth.

In rejecting this Platonic vision of reason as the way to true, formal knowledge, Machiavelli is redirecting our attention from imagined realities to concrete realities, where freedom was constantly endangered by those elites who believed they had found, or pretended to have found, the Platonic truth. For those who have discovered the truth about how we should live are usually prepared to coerce the remainder of humanity to live according to this perception of truth. By contrast, the concrete world is always a bit "messier" than the world of ideas. Even so, Machiavelli, who though a republican was no utopian, preferred to attend to the messy, concrete, physical realities he encountered with his senses. If people are to be free to live under their own laws, this empirical attention to reality is necessary. Empirical data about concrete people and their actual desires poses fewer dangers to human freedoms (to pursue those desires) than do rationalist schemes of how we should live.

B. From Empiricism to Activism

This empirical attention to the facts was an implicit repudiation of the entire medieval outlook, a commitment to a newer, more modern outlook. This new outlook was not only conducive to modern empirical science but also to the rebirth of commerce. Hanna Fenichel Pitkin eloquently illustrates the extent to which Machiavelli's empiricist views led inexorably to a repudiation of older worldviews:

> In the medieval understanding, then, interconnectedness and dependence were taken for granted almost as the definition of the human condition. They were neither shameful nor constricting but were assumed to be natural and even sacred. . . . In such a world people felt neither an aspiration nor an obligation to be autonomous; mutual dependence was the very nature of the universe. . . . Yet no one can deny that there is a difference between the medieval and the Renaissance outlook. . . . Society had changed profoundly, and so had human self-understanding. Far from being natural and sacred, dependence had now become both contemptible and dangerous; autonomy was the goal. . . . An urban and market society gradually supplanted feudal agriculture, leaving men free (but also forced) to make their own way in life. Instead of being born into a social station, men might achieve or lose wealth, power, and status in a single generation.[15]

A lesson of commercial, capitalistic modernity, already learned in the early Renaissance, is a lesson about autonomy. Thus, a resurrection of commerce had unleashed other human needs, especially the need to be free, to live under one's own laws. This recognition of human responsibility for one's own destiny results in a kind of activism, engenders in its agents a sense that one must exert all of one's energy in making one's fortune.

Machiavelli learned this lesson well. Invariably insistent that one must seek to master one's own destiny, he is always warning princes and other political actors to rely only upon themselves and not cosmic forces like chance or fortune. There is no fatalism in his outlook:

> Not being always able to follow others exactly, nor attain to the excellence of those he imitates, a prudent man should always follow in the path trodden by great men and imitate those who are most excellent. . . . I say then that in new dominions, where there is a new prince, it is more

or less easy to hold them according to the greater or lesser ability of him who acquires them. And as the fact of a private individual becoming a prince presupposes either great ability or good fortune, it would appear that either of these things would in part mitigate many difficulties. Nevertheless those who have been less beholden to good fortune have maintained themselves best. (*Prince*, chapter 6)

Similarly, as Machiavelli is introducing (in chapter 24 of *The Prince*) his discussion of *fortuna* (the subject of chapter 25), he again insists that one must depend only upon one's own resources: "Only those defenses are good, certain and durable, which depend on yourself alone and your own ability" (chapter 24). Thus one's abilities are a stable, unvarying factor in a life swept by varying forces. Those varying factors in life are the shifting sands of a nondeterministic *fortuna:*

> I conclude then that fortune varying and men remaining fixed in their ways, they are successful so long as these ways conform to circumstances, but when they are opposed then they are unsuccessful. I certainly think that it is better to be impetuous than cautious, for fortune is a woman, and it is necessary, if you wish to master her, to conquer her by force; and it can be seen that she lets herself be overcome by the bold rather than by those who proceed coldly.[16] And therefore, like a woman, she is always a friend to the young, because they are less cautious, fiercer, and master her with greater audacity. (*Prince*, chapter 25)

Although *fortuna* is fickle and inconstant, this does not mean that one must cease trying. Rather, the inconstancy is an invitation to exert oneself and master *fortuna.*

The humanism implicit in this passage is confirmed in the following paragraph, where Machiavelli invokes the metaphor of the river to suggest that although the water seems to have a mind of its own, human exertion is capable of redirecting it, of creating dams and dikes to prevent the destruction of floods. This resurrection of the old Roman pagan belief that human exertion is possible—and even desirable—is part and parcel of the Renaissance's humanism.[17] Paying attention to such empirical realities of our lives leads us to a rejection of teleology and of the medieval worldview, driving us to an awareness of the openness of the cosmos.

MACHIAVELLI'S USE OF *FORTUNA*

A. Machiavelli's Concept of the Cosmos

Machiavelli saw one half of life under our control and the other half under the control of *fortuna;* but since *fortuna* is seen as a woman who can be overcome by an aggressive man or as a river that industrious persons could redirect with dams and levees (*Prince*, chapter 25), that other half is not beyond our control. Hence, it is reasonable to infer that Machiavelli depicted the world as completely open to human exertion. In three steps, I propose to march toward that conclusion by first demonstrating from his writings that the cosmos is at least partly open, then largely open, and finally completely so.

While it is not immediately obvious that Machiavelli saw the world as totally open, he at least begins with a basic dualism: there is a part of life over which we seem to have no control, while there is another part which does respond to human effort. The first, seemingly uncontrollable, part is governed by *fortuna;* the other is under our control:

> As I am well aware, many have believed and now believe human affairs so controlled by Fortune and by God that men with their prudence cannot manage them—yes, more, that men have no recourse against the world's variations. Such believers therefore decide that they need not sweat much over man's activities but can let Chance govern them. . . . Thinking on these variations, I myself now and then incline in some respects to their belief. Nonetheless, in order not to annul our free will, I judge it true that Fortune may be mistress of one half our actions but that even she leaves the other half, or almost, under our control. (*Prince*, chapter 25, introductory paragraph)

This belief that we control our destinies, at least in part, is a reason for believing that Machiavelli is one of the first proponents of the modern belief in activism. As a result, he must also confront directly the belief of determinists that the realm outside of our control is under the control of larger cosmic forces. What is *fortuna,* then? Is "she" merely the chance interactions of a cosmos not infused with divine purpose? Or is she a kind of goddess in her own right, a cosmic force that determines our lives? His answers to these questions are not obvious.

Since *Fortuna* was a Roman goddess, Machiavelli's invoking of her name clearly constitutes a repudiation of some dimension of Christian religiosity; it is, in an important sense, a *secular,* if not pagan, theme. Can we reconstruct a likely line of reasoning that carried Machiavelli to this conclusion? Since the Latin *saeculum* referred to an age or a time,[18] things in the *saeculum* were not things of eternity. Since the eternal is the divine, the temporal must be the nonsacred, those things of this world. *Fortuna,* we may conclude, must be part of the secular world, and that world is at least partly open to our exertions.

Given the sexism of his time, Machiaelli's description of *fortuna* in the feminine was neither an accident nor a mere following of Italian's gender conventions. Rather, in so describing *fortuna*, he was communicating a part of his perceptions of the ficklness of fortune, which is tantamount to asserting that the cosmos is *largely* open to human exertion. As stereotypically "feminine," it struck him as fickle, whimsical, not fully rational, lacking any clearly discernible purpose or *telos* that might give its trajectory any linear progression. Like a caricature of the feminine, reality was seen as moving with no linear, rational progression toward any one goal (*telos*); rather it moves with no clear sense or purpose. It "just is." Thus, Machiavelli seems to be using the notion of *fortuna* as an alternative to—or a substitute for—religious teleology.

His use of *fortuna*, then, has two possible meanings: either (1) *fortuna* refers to the vicissitudes of life in the *saeculum* and so is a reference to life's lack of purpose or structure, to its existential absurdity or lack of a divine purpose, to its openness; or (2) *fortuna* refers to the changing modes of life in the *saeculum* understood in the context of faith—which would be a rationalist reference to divine providence and similar to the providential reading of Christianity, given that changes in this world are a manifestation of divine will. Given the resistance that the secretary displayed to the providential version of Christianity, and given that *fortuna* had come to refer to the medieval sense of historical irrationality, it seems safest to guess that he preferred the more secular, almost existential, reading of *fortuna*. This existential reading of *fortuna* in turn implies that the cosmos is largely open to human purposiveness.

Finally, there are other passages in which Machiavelli describes our world as one in which human purposes only *seem* to be thwarted by recalcitrant forces; the direct implication of this is that the world is *wholly* open to human purposes. Having described reality as half under our control and half under the control of *fortuna*, he then went on (*Prince*, chapter 25) to tell us that she is like a river, which an industrious people can control with dikes and dams. If so, the movement of her current can be resisted; a people is not totally subject to the vicissitudes of fortune since she can be rechanneled. Near the end of the paragraph, Machiavelli switches to a sexual metaphor, asserting that a young, aggressive *vir*, or man, can beat *fortuna* into submission. Despite the caveman implications of this metaphor, its point remains clear: fortune can be conquered. If she can be conquered, then what *appears* to be beyond our control can *really* be dominated by humans with adequate determination.

Consequently, Machiavelli's meaning of *fortuna* is the existential meaning.

While this belief in an open cosmos might seem sacrilegious to the traditional, devout Christian, it is not an act of apostasy. That is, it is not an act of repudiating Christianity while "regressing" to the older pagan religions of Rome. While Machiavelli admired many aspects of pagan religions, his goal was not to supplant one religion with another, but to advance a more secular worldview, to modernize religion by increasing its civilizing power. Of course, the modern world will not be a world without religion; but religion would play a different role than it had played in the ancient and medieval eras.

Whatever the other changes might be, one stands out: modern states will not require religious justifications. Henceforth, the justifications of rule will be predominantly secular—and less hostile to democratic freedom. His doctrine of *fortuna* seems to present him with a formula for attempting to move his contemporaries beyond their narrow worldview and the corruption that was tainting religion at the time. The question is, does he mean to employ this secular formula in its providential or its existential sense?

Pocock presents the argument for an existential reading along these lines: since the "Greek and Roman intellects saw little reason to expect anything very new to happen in the human future," life in this world appears to have had little purpose. This "lack of expectation . . . sometimes occasioned world-weariness and *angst*."[19] The Christian belief in an afterlife was a useful corrective to this, giving life a new meaning and purpose. But it, too, depreciated events in history: "Within the *saeculum,* there remained the problem of assigning meaning to the social and historical events experienced by individuals throughout the remembered past and henceforth to the end of time."[20] Since eternal truth, meaning, and purpose were to be found in the divine, secular reality was seen as devoid of all these.

Tracing the evolution of the notions of *fortuna* and *virtus* (the Latin terms) through Boethius, who imposed Christian significance upon them, Pocock concludes that *fortuna* had come to symbolize the "darker side" of societal life in the *saeculum*. Only by leaving our physical bodies could we be freed from subjection to the vicissitudes of fortune: "Fortune thus came to symbolize the irrationality of history, the medieval sense of the absurd: history as it must seem to those who lacked faith, history as it must be if God and his providence did not exist."[21] If *fortuna* had come historically to be tied with the irrationality of history, then, when Machiavelli writes that half of life is controlled by fortune or chance, he is saying that both halves, the half under our control as well as the half beyond our control, are devoid of any superhuman meaning or purpose. Thus, both halves lack any cosmic guarantees—in the existentialist's sense of being almost "absurd"—and are open to human exertion.

B. Machiavelli's Image of *Fortuna*

While *fortuna* was surely an important idea in Machiavelli's thinking, he could not have believed literally in all the things[22] he wrote about fortune: the literary metaphors of the palace, of the wheel, and of the goddess cannot be taken as scientific, technical descriptions of reality. Similarly, his belief in *fortuna* did not conflict with naturalistic explanations in science.[23] Taken in this sense, he did not believe in fortune as a concrete reality. Fortune did not exist as an empirical force in our physical world; rather, he appears to have used the idea as an explanatory or literary device.

In this sense, his *fortuna* is akin to the notion of *chance* that Aristotle employs in his *Metaphysics*.[24] In completing his discussion of causation, the ancient thinker finds it necessary to consider the possibility that a "fifth" cause (beyond his four causes: efficient, material, formal, and final) might exist. Aristotle ultimately concludes that *chance* does not really exist; when we say that something "happened by chance," we mean only that one of the results of an action was different from the goal, or final cause, of the actor causing that consequence. Of the things that happen by chance, it is not the case that some causal agent called chance was physically operative in the world. The things that happen "by chance" seem to "just happen"; they may be the unintended consequence of some agent's seeking some other goal, but there is no causal force making them happen. Chance does not operate in pursuit of additional goals of its own, providing some kind of *telos* or purpose to reality. Chance, Aristotle concludes, does not exist as a separate causal force in the world. Something similar is true of Machiavelli's *fortuna:* events that seem to be controlled by fortune or chance are not really caused by any physical agent but are events occurring in a universe of random and chance movement.

But Machiavelli did "believe in fortune," if by "believing in fortune" one means something like responding to the world *as if* "it were mostly run by a large senior, female person, who holds men in her power to a greater or lesser extent depending on their conduct and specifically on their manliness. . . ."[25] Pitkin believes that "the textual evidence, though not conclusive, surely suggests that Machiavelli did so believe"[26] that a part of life seemed beyond the control of most men, seemed irrational and whimsical, aiming at no particular goal. However, that is not a particularly strong, and certainly not a particularly deterministic, belief. It is very doubtful that the republican believed in *fortuna* (understood as a distinct causal, physical force) any more than Aristotle "believed in" chance.

Rather, his references to *fortuna* are probably a kind of literary allusion. In particular, the ambiguous paragraph about *fortuna* in *The Prince* (at the beginning of chapter 25) offers a key to his thoughts:

> As I am well aware, many have believed and now believe human affairs so controlled by Fortune and by God that men with their prudence cannot manage them—yes, more, that men have no recourse against the world's variations. Such believers therefore decide that they need not sweat much over man's activities but can let Chance govern them. . . . Thinking on these variations, I myself now and then incline in some respects to their belief. Nonetheless, in order not to annul our free will, I judge it true that Fortune may be mistress of one half our actions but that even she leaves the other half, or almost, under our control. (*Prince*, chapter 25, introduction)

Machiavelli begins the first sentence by referring to the belief that "worldly events are so governed by Fortune and by God" but ends it by referring to the passivity that naturally results from fatalism, inducing its victims to "let things be ruled by chance." He begins, in other words, by equating fortune with providential Christianity but ends by tying it to pagan, perhaps Aristotelian, chance.

This passage is crucial in understanding Machiavelli's notion of *fortuna*. If *fortuna* consists merely of those "chance" events that "just happen" without any reason or purpose to them, then the appropriate questions are "Does *fortuna*/chance exist? Is it a concrete, observable force in this world? Can we detect it with our senses?" Here, the Renaissance man of letters within Machiavelli may be directing us to Aristotle's answer to the same question when he considered chance as a possible fifth cause. Thus, if Machiavelli's fortune is chance and not providence, then the cosmos is totally and perfectly open to human exertion. We conclude that his references to *fortuna* were a literary device rather than a rigorous philosophical effort to explicate a doctrine.

C. Machiavelli and Determinism

Before concluding that Machiavelli intended *fortuna* as a kind of existential chance, we should stop to consider the arguments for the opposite: that Machiavelli was referring to fortune as a kind of providence. Commenting on Machiavelli's assertion "that fortune is the ruler of half our actions, but that she allows the other half or thereabouts to be governed by us," at least one interpreter finds that "The implication appears to be fatalistic: It is only the forbearance of fortune that allows us partly to determine our destiny."[27]

Similarly, Mansfield has argued that since Machiavelli has suggested that men must make use of the beast within, there is no possibility for him of "detachment in the human soul."[28] Because he denied the human possibility of objectivity, Machiavelli "had to pay the price of denying that men are capable of voluntary action." A recognition of necessity, then, "replaces deliberate choice in the soul as that which begins voluntary actions. Men may choose, but the only prudent choice is anticipation of necessity." Again, the implication seems to be fatalistic.

While it is not completely certain that Mansfield is here referring to *fortuna* (he cites four passages from *The Prince* and seven from *The Discourses* by chapter number only, so he could have been referring to something else), it is highly probable that he is here subscribing to the providential reading of *fortuna*. But this reading cannot be made consistent with the entirety of the text. First, it wrongly denies Machiavelli's humanism. Second, it denies all that Machiavelli wrote about free will (see, for instance, *The Prince,* chapters 25 and 26). Finally, even if *fortuna* were to be read as providence, Machiavelli is claiming that at least one part, roughly one half, of reality is not governed by providence and so is to be understood as an empiricist's world. Even attempting this providential reading, then, we must nevertheless conclude that the Aristotelian vision of natural teleology is at least half-rejected—Machiavelli minimally stands on the threshold that separates the rationalism of the ancient world from the empiricism of modernity. In an open cosmos, even in a half-open cosmos, human *virtù* becomes possible.

MACHIAVELLI'S HUMANISM AND *VIRTÙ*

Virtù, as employed by Machiavelli, is not merely a desirable moral quality; it is a characteristic of *viri*, of men, and related to virility or aggressive assertion.[29] Hence, Pocock argues that "Civic action, carried out by *virtus*—the quality of being a man (*vir*)— seized upon the unshaped circumstance thrown up by fortune and shaped it, shaped Fortune herself, into the completed form of what human life should be: citizenship and the city it was lived in. *Virtus* might be thought of as the formative principle that shaped the end, or as the very end itself."[30]

Machiavelli's using *virtù* and *virtus* contained a wonderful ambiguity that permitted him to allude to Aristotle's moral teleology: the assertion that *virtus* could be an end of human action is an allusion to the Aristotelian principle that virtue is the natural end of humans. But since virtue also meant human exertion against chance, it becomes importantly tied up with freedom of will and so with a humanist conception of the universe in which humans can act freely—and this could only be in a universe in which there is no cosmic plan or divine purpose. In short, virtue as both moral excellence and human assertiveness is possible only in an open cosmos. In the spirit of modern empiricism, Machiavelli notes that this dualism provides room for human assertion: "God does not do everything, so as not to take from us free will and part of the glory that pertains to us" (*Prince*, the last, twenty-sixth, chapter).

CONCLUSION: HUMAN EXERTION IN AN OPEN WORLD

Thus it is that Machiavelli concentrates his, and our, energies on those parts of life over which we have control: "Those defenses alone are good, are certain, are durable, that depend on yourself and your own abilities" (*Prince*, chapter 25). Since the alternative to depending upon yourself and your skills is dependence upon fortune, whether providence or chance, the failure to exert control over those areas open to your control means certain ruin: "I say that such princes as I have described live happily today and tomorrow fall without changing their natures or any of their traits. This I believe results, first, from the causes lengthily discussed in the preceding pages, namely, that any prince who relies on Fortune falls when she varies" (*Prince*, chapter 26).

What Machiavelli infers from this recognition of a dualistic cosmos—with one part under, and the other beyond, our control—is that there are no cosmic guarantees. The cosmos guarantees neither our freedom nor our enslavement. He notes, in fact, that avoiding one evil places you in the middle of another: "And in all human affairs, he who examines them well will see this: that one difficulty cannot be removed without another's coming up" (*Discourses*, 1:6). Berlin may have been partly right in claiming that Machiavelli shared something of his devotion to the plurality of values, at least insofar as he recognized that all of the good things in life do not necessarily come wrapped in a harmonious bundle: "Let no state believe that it can always follow a safe policy, rather let it think that all are doubtful. This is found in the nature of things ... but prudence consists in being able to know the nature of the difficulties, and taking the least harmful as good."[31] Prudence—a type of intellectual, but not moral, excellence—enables us to recognize that not all of life's goods are simultaneously feasible and instructs us to accept the least bad combination of circumstances—you cannot be assured of having your cake and eating it too.

Consequently Machiavelli sees us as needing to discern what parts of life are under our control and to depend only upon ourselves: "he errs least and will be most favored by fortune who suits his proceedings to the times" (*Discourses*, 3:9). The corollary, of course, is that dependence on anything except oneself is folly: "And because transformation from private person to prince takes for granted either ability or Fortune, either of these two ... diminishes many difficulties; nevertheless, he who depends least on Fortune sustains himself longest" (*Prince*, chapter 6).

Interestingly, the very absence of cosmic purposes and guarantees is part of a Machiavellian justification of democracy: because democracies possess more potential leaders than principalities, they are more flexible in adapting to the irrational changes in fortune. They are consequently to be preferred to their more autocratic competitors on purely rational, and not merely moral, grounds:

> It is this which assures to republics greater vitality and more enduring success than monarchies have; for the diversity of the genius of her citizens enables the republic better to accommodate herself to the changes of the time than can be done by a prince. For any man accustomed to have a certain mode of proceeding will never change it, as we have said, and consequently when time and circumstances change, so that his ways are no longer in harmony with them, he must of necessity succumb. Piero Soderini, whom we have mentioned several times already, was in all his actions governed by humanity and patience. He and his country prospered so long as the times favored this mode of proceeding; but when afterwards circumstances arose that demanded a course of conduct the opposite to that of patience and humanity, he was unfit for the occasion, and his own and his country's ruin were the consequence. Pope Julius II acted throughout the whole period of his pontificate with the impetuosity and passion natural to his character; and as the times and circumstances well accorded with this, he was successful in all his undertakings. But if the times had changed so that different counsels would have been required, he would unquestionably have been ruined, for he could not have changed his character or mode of action. (*Discourses*, 3:9)

This typically Renaissance emphasis on human activity and exertion becomes the cornerstone of Machiavelli's view of the world, a humanistic emphasis that was literally liberating for people accustomed to medieval authoritarianism and elitism. The iconoclasm of this belief was directed against traditional authority; so it is not surprising that a modernizer with an eye to the future turned to the ancient past for authorities who would help challenge existing authorities. In fact, one of the key characteristics of the Renaissance is embodied in Machiavelli: the habit of using the (re-) discovery of ancients—and the authority they commanded—to challenge medieval authorities; we might almost say that Machiavelli used the past to usher in the future. As Pitkin puts it, "[T]he challenge to traditional medieval authorities and beliefs was also based partly on the recovery of a still earlier authority, the original sources—classical or biblical—to which the independent intellect reached back. Thus, the Renaissance was simultaneously a recovery of origins and a discovery of the independent self. . . . In reviving ancient authority and pitting it against the medieval, men felt liberated to exercise their own powers here and now."[32]

Machiavelli's view of the cosmos, then, is fully compatible with his deepest insights into our human capability for nobility. Although he clearly indicates that humans are by nature evil and that this evil will emerge whenever it is not restrained, he also believes that it can be neutralized by some appropriate system of laws.

To continue, we must understand how his account of human nature is consistent with his humanist emphasis upon our need to exert ourselves. Beyond the corrupt conditions in which we realize our potentials for evil, there lies the possibility of human glory—and the cosmos neither guarantees nor prohibits this. Because the world is open, we are free to go either way.

Part 2
Human Nature and Potentials

2

Corruption and Nobility:
Maximizing Human Potentials

INTRODUCTION: HISTORY AND HUMAN NATURE

In a methodological and quite original tour de force, Machiavelli begins *The Discourses* by noting that Legislators[1]—those who design constitutions—must begin with an understanding of human nature: "whoever desires to found a state and give it laws, must start with assuming that all men are bad and ever ready to display their vicious nature" (1:3).[2] This lesson about human nature, gleaned from the empirical data of history, is crucial to good governance and good laws. By contrast, he feared that political and social actors in his own time largely ignored the political lessons to be learned about human nature from history—especially from the nobility of the ancient Romans—because of intellectual barriers to the understanding of history and our nature.

In addition to religious and educational weaknesses, what kept us from imitating the Romans was "not having a true understanding of books on history, so that as we read we do not draw from them that sense or taste that flavor which they really have. . . . [G]reat numbers who read take pleasure in hearing of the various events they contain, without thinking at all about them, judging that imitation is not merely difficult but impossible, as if the sky, the sun, the elements, men, were changed in motion, arrangement, and power from what they were in antiquity" (*Discourses*, 1:1; Gilbert, 191).

Condemning the window-shoppers who read only to look from the outside, only to encounter stories or interesting places, Machiavelli urges us to taste the "goods" that books bring us. We must enter into the books to learn what they have to teach us. And what they have to teach us is of practical value: the truths about human nature.

The relative sophistication of this method enabled Machiavelli to learn more than a casual reader. Methodologically, he tacitly posited the existence of certain rules of regularity about humanity. He was convinced that understanding—or renewing—a polity requires a knowledge of the lawfulness of human change; although humans change, the lawful rules of change remain the same, and understanding them is essential to success.[3] In other words, by seeking the lawful regularities of "motion, arrangement, and power" of human behavior so as to use them to make life better, Machiavelli is moving social thought in a more empirical and scientific direction; the origins of modern, practical social science are in fact to be found here, along with the keys to modernizing and civilizing a people.

The empiricist approach of the Renaissance toward reality (outlined in the previous chapter), in turn, required a substantial reexamination of human nature. In line with this, Machiavelli surmised that the knowledge needed to survive in this secular world need not—indeed, should not—be theological; rather, the key to survival would have to be a secular understanding of our nature. Hence Machiavelli's approach to *how* we can come to know ourselves constitutes a radical break with tradition; ironically, his conclusions about human nature do not similarly deviate from tradition. Rather, there is substantial agreement between the new Machiavellian conclusions and the tradition over *what* is true about that nature. Indeed, the empirical data of social and political experience (i.e., history) suggested a view of human nature that is neither terribly different from theological doctrine nor terribly flattering. Like Augustine's notion of original sin, Machiavelli's empiricist picture of our nature is an image of humans who tend to commit evil deeds whenever it is in their interest to do so—so long as they believe they will not have to pay a penalty for their wrongdoing.[4]

Just as modern scientists were seeking to understand the laws governing physical change, like the law of gravity and other laws governing physical motion, Machiavelli sought to understand human nature—along with its moral and political implications—by seeking to understand the laws governing human change and continuity. The first such law is that humans, like physical objects attracted to other physical objects by gravity, are attracted to evil.

THE TRANSFORMATION OF HUMAN EVIL
INTO HUMAN GLORY

To make freedom secure, Machiavelli sought to convince us, we must neutralize the evil within us. Having opened *The Discourses*

(1:1) with his comment on the unchanging laws governing human motivation, "as if the sky, the sun, the elements, men, were changed in motion, arrangement, and power from what they were in antiquity," Machiavelli begins in chapter 1 with an examination of Roman greatness. Then, in chapter 2, he ties that greatness (*gloria*) to her freedom as a republic, classifying Rome as a free republic and celebrating her freedom as her greatest accomplishment. Finally, in chapter 3, he turns to the serious topic of how to constitutionalize a republic properly, and he naturally begins by offering his observations of human nature.

The pertinent eternal verity, as he saw it, about our nature is our tendency to evil:

> As is demonstrated by all those who discuss life in a well-ordered state . . . it is necessary for him who lays out a state and arranges laws for it to presuppose that all men are evil and that they are always going to act according to the wickedness of their spirits whenever they have free scope; and when any wickedness remains hidden for a time, the reason is some hidden cause which, in the lack of any experience of the contrary, is not recognized, but then its discovery is brought about by Time, which they say is the father of every Truth. (*Discourses*, 1:3)

Note first that this passage creates an appearance of maintaining that human nature is always evil while actually expressing the opposite truth. Although evil lurks within us and constitution makers must assume that we are all evil, *that evil does not always manifest itself in our actions.* Some "hidden causes," which Machiavelli reveals on the next page, are capable of preventing the emergence of the evil potentially within us. Consequently, although Machiavelli's expression of his perception of the evil within us would appear to be referring to a kind of instinctive drive, that evil instead constitutes a kind of developmental potential in his thought. Instead of a biologically determined instinct beyond alteration, this evil is rather a type of possibility that could be realized if the conditions were right— or, more accurately, wrong. So human evil will be realized unless "hidden causes" restrain it; the central point of the passage is almost the opposite of the impression Machiavelli initially creates. Hence, we must conclude that, in Machiavelli's eyes, humans are evil, but *humans can take actions to restrain or neutralize evil.*

Since we now know that evil can be concealed, we must next discover the "hidden causes" that can neutralize human evil and permit people to become "good." On the next page, after reiterating that humans will be as evil as circumstances permit, Machiavelli discloses the previously hidden cause of human nobility: "from the moment that they [humans] have the option and liberty to commit wrong with impunity, then they never fail to carry confusion and disorder everywhere. It is this that has caused it to be said that poverty and hunger make men industrious, and the law makes men good; and if fortunate circumstances cause good to be done without constraint, the law may be dispensed with. But when such happy influence is lacking, then the law immediately becomes necessary" (*Discourses*, 1: 3).

The human capacity for evil will always emerge unless *fortuna* or good laws prevent it; not one to depend on *fortuna,* Machiavelli places his hope in good laws as a way of eliciting from our human material some more noble and glorious possibility.[5]

We might graphically describe this view of Machiavelli's theory of human nature in this fashion:

Figure 2.1
Machiavelli's Account of Human Potential

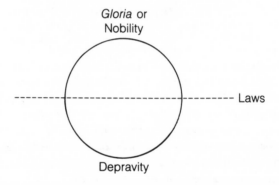

Machiavelli's vision of nobility resembled Rousseau's, which was a vision of people living freely under laws they make for themselves. He was, in this respect, quite unlike Hobbes who could imagine little more than authoritarian control of subjects by an absolute monarch. Machiavelli thought, however, that such nobility required lawful society and representative institutions, whereas Rousseau considered human nobility possible even among precivilized and presocial persons. Hence, although Machiavelli advised us that we must assume that all are evil and that the evil will come out in time, unless some hidden cause—good laws—prevents it, his was *not* the same theory of human nature that Hobbes offered: *homo lupus* (literally, wolf man), instinctively self-interested, evil, and in need of absolute authority to keep one individual from destroying another. Seeing in us a possibility of nobility that Hobbes could never see,

Machiavelli depicted us as beings with potentials for both glory and corruption—potentials that were to be elicited by appropriate social arrangements. Eliciting these potentials for nobility, and avoiding human potentials for corruption, was the virtuoso task of great Legislators. All great political leaders, manly actors or *viri* possessing *virtù* in the aggressive sense, enable their people to achieve *virtù* in the moral sense.

Because Romulus sought this *virtù* and constituted Rome to prepare its people for freedom by giving them good laws, his crimes were excused (*The Discourses*, 1:9); but even though Agathocles knew well how to wield power, he was condemned because his awful actions achieved none of the moral excellence Machiavelli associated with *virtù* (*The Prince*, chapter 8).

The contrast between the tales of two women, one from ancient Rome, the other a central character in Machiavelli's *Mandragola*, reveals the profound psychological difference between a people with *virtù* and a people lacking it. The Lucretia of antiquity was a heroic woman of virtue whose brave, but desperate, acts helped to transform Rome from a monarchy to a republic.[6] After having been raped by a son of the Roman king, she sought restoration of her honor by demanding that the king punish her rapist. Since the penalty for rape was death, the weak king was reluctant to so punish his own son. Trapped and dishonored, she made a drastic choice to escape the situation: she committed suicide. Brutus, a friend of the family who had been "playing the fool" to avoid kingly jealousy, happened to be present when her family found her corpse. Drawing the knife from her chest, he made all of her kindred swear an oath to destroy the monarchy; hence, the republic was born of unpunished rape.

In pointed reference to this heroine, Machiavelli chose Lucretia as the name for his crucial feminine figure in *Mandragola*. Yet his Lucretia is anything but a heroine who bravely makes choices to change the world irrevocably. Instead, she passively acquiesces in the schemes of the males around her, one of whom cuckolds her husband. This Lucretia, who begins as a woman of decency, puts up no resistance to her dishonor. The childless young wife of a wealthy old man, she becomes the object of the desires of a young man, Callimaco, who hears of her while studying abroad. He conceives of a scheme, aided by his "friend" Ligurio, to seduce her. Posing as a doctor, he contrives to help her husband cure her infertility. Concocting a fertility drug from the mandrake root, then widely considered an aphrodisiac, he informs the unfortunate, and gullible, husband that the drug will make her fertile; but he also cautions him that the first man to have sex with her after she takes the drug will die. Rather than face certain death, the husband agrees that they arrange to take a random man passing on the street to perform this duty; Ligurio then makes sure that the man who passed would be Callimaco in disguise. Finding a young, ardent man in her bed, Lucretia readily submits to his seduction and dallies with him in her husband's home.

Like the Lucretia of antiquity, she too loses her honor; what separates the ancient figure from the modern one is that the sexual conquest of the latter was *to no avail*. The corruption of family values that surrounded Lucretia before the events of the drama continues after her dishonor; consequently, her violation acquires no meaning or significance.

Naming this character "Lucretia" was no accident; Machiavelli almost certainly intended that we draw a comparison between the two Lucretias. Even though both women were sexually "conquered" by men not of their choice (the one by force, the other by drugs and trickery), the contrasts are stark: the ancient Lucretia kills herself, refusing to accept her dishonor, while the character in the play adapts readily to infidelity. While the deficient authority of the kings is destroyed by the suicide of the one, the deficient authority of arranged marriages is left intact in the other.

Pitkin aptly draws the contrast:

> In both tales, old and formally legitimate authorities that are substantively inadequate are displaced by new, younger, and better ones. Yet nothing could be more different than the two sexual conquests, the two overthrowings of authority, the "virtues" of the ancient and modern world. In *Mandragola* the violated wife does not kill herself but happily adapts to an adulterous life; is it for that sensible flexibility that Machiavelli (through Ligurio) calls her "wise" and "fit to rule a kingdom"?. . . . Yet the ancient rape of Lucretia led to the transformation of a social world, the birth of a republic of true *virtù*. The modern comic version leads only to the birth of a child, in a world that remains as corrupt as before.[7]

Pitkin is right to infer that in the ancient tale, the rape of a woman transforms and improves life for all; in the modern comedy life goes on much as before—in corruption. But she is wrong to depict Ligurio as Machiavelli's spokesman; more likely, he is a satiric figure. First, Machiavelli twice describes him as "a parasite" (*Dramatis Personae*, in Gilbert, 776), the second time qualifying it as "a parasite the darling of Malice" (Prolog, Gilbert, 777). Further, we must remember that Ligurio was named by a master satirist, probably with an eye to the Ligurian people, a Neolithic settlement in the area surrounding Genoa.[8] Having so named this character, Machiavelli was either hinting that Ligurio was Genoese or implying that he was less well developed than contemporary Florentines. Either way, it is unlikely that Machiavelli intended a parasite to serve as his mouthpiece: if he was describing him as Genoese, it is improbable that he intended a "foreigner" to speak for him; if he was referring to him as a Neolithic anachronism, it is even less likely that one from prehistory would speak for a theorist of modernization. In short, Machiavelli is not at "at home" in his own play, any more than he is "at home" in Florence after the return of the oligarchy; both are flawed by corruption and both are the targets of his satire.

If Ligurio is to be seen as a satiric figure, then the play as a whole is not the comedy it appears to be, but a tragedy. In a virtuous society like ancient Rome, violations of virtue resulted in changes that restored virtue; in a corrupt society like quattrocento Florence, violations of virtue went relatively unnoticed, stimulating no renewing transformation. While the suicide of the ancient Lucretia had meaning, the Renaissance Lucretia, by contrast, went from a meaningless, childless marriage to an old man to an equally meaningless dalliance with a young man capable of impregnating her. Given Machiavelli's readiness to excuse Romulus's crimes, and given his condemnation of Agathocles for similarly heinous actions because he was only seeking power, we may conclude that he found that terrible actions have meaning when corruption is destroyed, but become meaningless when corruption continues.

The tragic message of the play then becomes this: Florence and Italy had so descended into corruption that violations of virtue were no longer significant. Devoid of *virtù*, Italians were unable to renew their culture and institutions so as to enter the modern world. Machiavelli meant to contrast the two societies exactly to demonstrate that the absence of *virtù* in the latter is directly and causally responsible for preventing the social transformations necessary for modernizing.

For our immediate purposes, the important thing is that a transformation of human life is possible, and that a society properly constituted is the key to such transformation, eliciting from humans the nobility to make freedom possible. And frustrating this transformation is true tragedy.[9] Hence Machiavelli's play can be read as a comedy only at the surface, formal level; symbolically, it illustrates his frustration at his inability to reform his age, leaving parody as his only weapon against the evil he fought.

Combining his assertions from *The Discourses* about laws neutralizing human potentials for evil with the theme of *Mandragola,* we may now conclude that, for Machiavelli, social arrangements and laws are crucial variables in influencing which of our human potentials will be realized. He believed that 1) laws have a great deal to do with evoking the good and avoiding the corrupt; and 2) "the law makes men good," not simply by coercing us to be virtuous but by making possible the emergence of higher motivations, by inducing us to calculate rationally the consequences of our actions.

Human Nature and Constitutionalism

When Machiavelli writes that those constituting a state must assume that human nature is evil, he is warning that, if we want people to enjoy democratic freedom, we must not assume that people are inherently good. A constitutional assumption of human virtue fails to create the institutional framework in which freedom can thrive; but the opposite assumption enables founders to take steps to prevent the evils that destroy liberty and *gloria.* One assumes an evil human nature, then, to achieve a specific good. Machiavelli's moral theory grows naturally out of his appreciation of human potentials. Acting on the assumption that humans are capable of great evil may require terrible things of a patriot; but these terrible acts are excused if they lead to the good of neutralizing human potentials for still greater evil. To achieve good ends, one must sometimes perform terrible acts. In this, as in so much else, Machiavelli is unlike Hobbes, who sought to justify authoritarian rather than democratic government.

Therefore we should conclude that Machiavelli believed that the quest for and maintenance of power (*mantenere lo stato*), however important for being able to achieve other good things, was not the ultimate end but only a means to the end of glory.[10] From the perspective of human potentials, which is Machiavelli's perspective, a prince is not glorious for acquiring or keeping power; glory only comes from constitutionalizing a polity since this elicits from a people its greatest potential for nobility.

Machiavelli's recognition of this duality of potentials led him at times to write as though there were two different natures. Does he mean to suggest that there are two human natures or two important potentials within one nature? Let us consider the evidence for the "two natures" thesis before rejecting it. The story of Chiron in *The Prince* (chapter 18) seems to imply two distinct natures housed within one being: "You need to know, then, that there are two ways of fighting: one according to the laws, the other with force. The first is suited to man, the second to the animals; but because the first is often not sufficient, a prince must resort to the second."

Then it becomes clear that he intends that a prince should learn about our duality, so as to be able to adapt to it: "Therefore he needs to know well how to put to use the traits of animal and of man. This conduct is taught to princes in allegory by ancient authors, who write that Achilles and many other well-known ancient princes were given for upbringing to Chiron the Centaur, who was to guard and educate them. This does not mean anything else (this having as teacher one who is half animal and half man) than that a prince needs to know how to adopt the nature of either animal or man, for one without the other does not secure him permanence" (*Prince*, chapter 18).

Machiavelli appears to be referring to two natures: the human and the bestial. But his meaning is not that princes must know how to fight with beasts and with humans, but that princes must know how to fight with people behaving like beasts and with people behaving as humans. Princes need the flexibility to deal with both human possibilities. Metaphorically, but not literally, there is a "beast" within us.

A fundamental implication of our dual potentials, for humanity or bestiality, is that we must assume moral obligations if we are to achieve our humane potential. In the context of good laws, one must obey the laws;[11] in the absence of such laws, one must still recognize the values of civilization and nobility and work to establish laws that make them possible. Murder is wrong within a lawful society where human choices of rational laws have made it wrong; but murder to create a lawful civilization is morally justifiable. If we were not capable of both extremes, our moral obligations would be quite different; as it is, because people are capable of great evil, one is justified in taking steps to prevent such evil.

Machiavelli is very explicit that one must recognize whether a polity is corrupt or not and act accordingly. One cannot "seek glory" in identical ways under different circumstances; one must be attentive to circumstances (*Discourses*, 3:8). In fact, this empirical recognition of which social condition obtains is the most important knowledge that a ruler can have. The fundamental defect of rationalist political theories, like those represented in Plato's *Republic*, is the ignorance of concrete contemporary realities. Machiavelli most values people who, in contrast with such "ignorant dreamers," recognize particular realities and respond to them appropriately. Most importantly, the one crucial empirical fact upon which success depends is the factual appraisal of whether people are living in corruption or glory. Considering the success of Manlius Capitolinus, as one example, Machiavelli writes: "In this two things are to be considered: one, that in a corrupt city men have to seek glory in other ways than they do in a city still living in accord with law; the other (which is almost the same as the first), that men in their conduct, and so much the more in their great actions, ought to think of the times and adapt themselves to them" (Discourses, 3:8).

One cannot know what to do without knowing whether one's society is civilized and law-abiding. An understanding of the eternal laws of human change and an understanding of human potentials for good and evil are essential practical information only when conjoined with empirical data about the level of development of our civilization. This is especially true of great people, who must adapt themselves to empirical realities if they wish to achieve their noble goals. Without these, the seekers of glory will not only fail to achieve their objectives, but, like Socrates, they will learn their "own ruin" (Prince, chapter 15). Laws, then, are psychologically crucial in two ways: (1) without knowledge of the laws of human change, one cannot achieve glory; and (2) implementation of laws is necessary for the realization of human nobility.

VIRTUE AND LAWS

Given human nature's propensity to evil, societies must be regenerated if liberty and glory are to survive and evil is to be kept at bay:

> those are best organized and have longest life that through their institutions can often renew themselves or that by some accident . . . come to such renewal. And it is clearer than light that if these bodies are not renewed they do not last. The way to renew them, as I have said, is to carry them back to their beginnings. . . . Since in the process of time that goodness is corrupted, if something does not happen that takes it back to the right position, such corruption necessarily kills that body. . . . It is necessary, then, as I have said, that men who live together in any organization often examine themselves, either as a result of such external events or as a result of internal ones. As to the latter, the cause must be either a law, which often examines the record of the men who are in that body; or actually a good man who arises among them. . . . This good effect, then, comes about in republics either by virtue of a man or by virtue of a law. (Discourses, 3:1)

Never one to trust to chance (or *fortuna*) to provide a good "man" (person) at the right historical moment, Machiavelli again comes to the importance of good laws. Good laws do more than coerce people, then. They are a first source of societal renewal that is essential for preventing corruption. Thus, for Machiavelli, human nobility can be elicited from human material either by proper constitutional systems of law or by the example of good leaders.

There is considerable disagreement, however, as to the primacy of laws and leaders for Machiavelli. Quentin Skinner, for instance, alleges that leaders are more important to Machiavelli in avoiding corruption than are laws. Playing down the role of education in avoiding *corruzione* and making possible both *virtù* and *liberta* (playing down, in other words, the educative or developmental powers of systems of law), Skinner writes that Machiavelli instead "devoted far more of his attention to a second possibility, the possibility that a body of citizens may perhaps be capable of transcending their natural selfishness if they are inspired by the example of truly virtuoso leadership. . . . Great leaders are capable of inspiring deeds of *virtù* among their followers, Machiavelli suggests, simply by the force of their own example."[12]

As a result of his emphasis, Skinner reaches the wrong conclusion about human nature in Machiavelli's thought: he concludes that laws cannot elicit the noble rather than the corrupt potentials within us. "Taking" human nature "as it is" becomes a depressingly pessimistic judgment about human potentials: "As Machiavelli's tone throughout the above discussion suggests, he is pessimistic about the prospects of changing human nature, of transforming our natural selfishness into a willing and virtuoso concern for the common good. He prefers to take men as they are, and to recognise that in general they exhibit a strong tendency to be corrupt."[13]

While there can be no doubt that Machiavelli preferred to "take men as they are," it is doubtful that he believed that great persons were more important than laws in making possible human virtue. Rather, the great advantage of Legislators is that they legislate, that they give human communities laws. In other words, great legislators are necessary for great laws—at least in corrupt circumstances.

Four independent points support the conclusion that Skinner errs in his interpretation. First, to make his case more plausible, Skinner found it necessary to reverse Machiavelli's order in discussing the role that laws and great leaders play in avoiding corruption. Writing about the regeneration of a republic, Machiavelli said that the first cause "must be either a law, which often examines the record of the men who are in that body"; the next mentioned would be "a good man who arises among them" (*Discourses*, 3:1). To strengthen his case, Skinner reverses these, elevating great leadership over laws. Second, Machiavelli explicitly wrote that laws "make men good" (*Discourses*, 1:3), but he regarded rule by one great man as necessary to establish laws in the most adverse corrupt circumstances. Thus, the role of the historically great man (*vir*)—and all that Skinner attributes to it—is necessary *only* in conditions of corruption that require extraordinary action. Third, Machiavelli explicitly notes the limits on the role of exemplary men: "Though there were two Catos . . . they were so solitary, that with their examples they could accomplish nothing good. Especially the last Cato, finding the city for the most part corrupt, could not with his example improve the citizens" (*Discourses*, 3:1). Presumably Rome needed more than a Cato, more than a great man, to renew her.

Finally, there is Skinner's own evidence to contradict his claim that the educative power of the law is subordinate to the power of great men. In his book, Skinner recognizes that *virtù* enables us to extract from *fortuna* whatever goals we desire—so which goals should we desire? Immediately, of course, we should desire *mantenare lo stato*, to keep ourselves in power; but "there are far greater ends to be pursued" (29–30), and Skinner quotes Machiavelli's specification that these include "glory and riches." But, like the Roman moralists who preceded him, Machiavelli rejects riches as base, concentrating on glory instead: "the noblest aim for a 'prudent and *virtuoso*' prince must be to introduce a form of government 'that will bring him honour' and make him glorious."[14] Skinner has quite rightly observed this commitment to glory; Machiavelli explicitly indicates that the willingness of Agathocles to perform terrible actions "cannot be called virtue" since he performed them merely to preserve his power; "by these methods one may indeed achieve power, but not glory" (*Prince*, chapter 8).

Here it appears that Pocock—whose analysis is so similar to Skinner's in spirit and rigor—appreciates better the sophistication of Machiavelli's psychology. He contends that, for Machiavelli, the nature of humanity is altered when a society enters a state of corruption. Noting Machiavelli's play on the word *materia*, Pocock suggests that the human "matter" of the city changes as corruption progresses: "What happens as corruption develops, we are told, is that the *materia* itself undergoes change, and the reason why old laws lose their efficacy when this happens is that the same form cannot be imposed upon, or educed from, different matter."[15]

Pocock concludes by recounting Machiavelli's tale of the corruption of Rome: after Rome had conquered its enemies, its old laws became inoperative and its citizens began to elect officials on the basis of self-interest instead of qualifications; later, Rome even gave offices to the most powerful. As one commentator puts it, "These are the conditions under which reform becomes almost impossible. A republic having got so far will not reform itself; since the laws have become inoperative, reform must be carried out by violent means. . . ."[16] Under these circumstances, Machiavelli despairs of anything except a power strong enough to bring a people under laws.

When corruption, the opposite of *virtù*, has progressed so far, there is little hope except that a strong person will step in and innovate in some way, that someone will exert energies to alter this degradation. The corruption of unequal property holdings,[17] for instance, is such a great evil—given Machiavelli's understanding of human nature—that he is prepared to override his republican sentiments and call for the establishment of a principality under such circumstances. In short, though it is not the case that great men (*viri*) are more important than good laws, the absence of laws may make great Legislators necessary—precisely so that they can make good laws.

Thus it is that, at the end of *The Prince*, Machiavelli sounds the clarion call to achieve the nobility that is humanly possible under good laws, but not to set out on a moral pilgrimage to a utopian ideal:

> By no means, then, should this opportunity be neglected, in order that Italy, after so long a time, may see her redeemer come. I cannot express with what love he will be received in all the provinces which have suffered from these alien floods, with what thirst for vengeance, with what firm loyalty, with what gratitude, with what tears! What gates will be shut against him? What peoples will refuse him obedience? What envy will oppose him? What Italian will refuse him homage? For everyone this barbarian tyranny stinks. Let your glorious family, then, undertake this charge with that spirit and that hope with which men undertake just labors. . . . (*Prince,* chapter 26)

In the conditions of depravity and corruption that were prevalent in Italy at this time, the best one could hope for would be a prince who could unify the country and impose sound laws. Anyone seeking to create laws would be embarking upon a "just cause." If a prince is necessary for Italian glory, liberty, and strength, then Italy must have a principality. But let that prince, like Romulus, give Italy wise laws and democratic institutions, so that someone later could play Brutus, so that Italians will again be free. Given that these laws are necessary for human nobility, what force could resist such a Legislator?

FREEDOM AND LAWS

Finally, the human need for laws is complex; although laws *appear* coercive, they need not be coercive of a free people. Unlike Bentham, who had argued that all law is coercive, others, like H. L. A. Hart, have argued that the regulations governing the legal creation of wills, for example, do not so much restrict people as empower them to do something they could not otherwise do: create enforceable wills.[18]

Extending this argument, we might see that you are not free to live until I have an obligation not to kill you (i.e., until I am not free to kill you). In other words, freedom passes from the realm of empty abstraction into practical reality when authority prohibits the violation of freedoms. Similarly, the social contract tradition[19] supports the idea that a proper arrangement of society can evoke a range of desirable human characteristics *without coercing humans to be virtuous.*

Thus Skinner probably errs in writing that Machiavelli "puts all his trust in the coercive powers of the law" (*Machiavelli,* 8). Certainly the laws do impose upon us certain "artificial necessities" that lead us to calculate prudentially the various costs of actions—but while such prudence could prevent the worst corruptions, it would not make possible nobility. The real power of the law is not its coercive power but its power to make us cognizant of our obligations. Similarly, the occasional need for a strong, singular ruler is not simply a need for one with the strength to be cruel—"those who want only to be lions do not understand this" (*Prince,* chapter 18)—but also a need for someone with the foresight to create good institutions that will bring civility to a people.

The optimal situation is a condition of freedom for a people in a republic. Nevertheless, a civilized people could live happily under a wise and prudent ruler. Given human needs, there are times when strong leaders are needed, especially to civilize a barbaric people. Under these circumstances, nothing less than a sterner leadership can survive. Periods of princely rule are necessary occasionally to renew and regenerate a people, preparing them for democratic freedom by inculcating the discipline of law. But a principate is and remains a temporary expedient. Machiavelli's advice to princes applies to these unpleasant circumstances: "Since, then, a prince is necessitated to play the animal well, he chooses among the beasts the fox and the lion, because the lion does not protect himself from traps; the fox does not protect himself from the wolves. The prince must be a fox, therefore, to recognize the traps and a lion to frighten the wolves" (*Prince,* chapter 18).

Machiavelli introduces this provocative paragraph by indicating that "there are two methods of fighting, the one by law, the other by force" (*Prince,* chapter 18). After equating the first with humans and the second with beasts, he goes on to explain how one must defend one's interests when dealing with the latter. When a condition of corruption exists, forcing him to deal with beasts, the prince must be prepared for bestial action; when other conditions exist, human action is appropriate. In times of corruption, the human need for security calls for rule by a single person, so that laws can secure us. If a prince under these circumstances must be cruel, then cruelty is the recommended course of action.

Recognizing these needs, then, is the source of Machiavelli's preference for principalities in corruption, and otherwise for democracies, all things considered. So it is that chapter 58 of *The Discourses* is entitled "The People Are Wiser and More Constant than Princes," and chapter 59 "Leagues and Alliances with Republics Are More to be Trusted than Those With Princes." Although Titus Livy, about whose historical works *The Discourses* were written, and other authorities were of the opinion that democracies were fickle, Machiavelli reports that he trusts "arguments founded upon reason" more than authorities: "I say, then, that individual men, and especially princes, may be charged with the same defects of which writers accuse the people; for whoever is not controlled by laws will commit the same errors as an unbridled multitude" (*Discourses,* 1:58).

In a people "controlled by law," however, we shall find "good qualities," since "such a people neither obey with servility nor command with insolence." Further, such is human motivation that, "when the unrighteous ambition of some noble made it necessary for them to rise up in self-defense, they did so . . ." (*Discourses,* 1:58). The differences in the conduct of people, Machiavelli wrote, "is not due to any difference in their nature . . . but to the greater or less respect they have for the laws under which they respectively live" (ibid.).

Given what we know about human nature, then, it is not the case that one can simply say that singular rule is better than, or worse than, democracy; what is important is not how many rule but whether they rule in accord with good laws. A rich, empirical appreciation of the motivations of people is the root of Machiavelli's claim that "if we compare the faults of a people with those of princes, as well as their respective good qualities, we shall find the people vastly superior in all that is good and glorious. And if princes show themselves superior in the making of laws, and in the forming of civil institutions and new statutes and ordinances, the people are superior in maintaining those institutions, laws, and ordinances, which certainly places them on a par with those who established them" (*Discourses*, 1:58).

But while Machiavelli is committed to acquiring a voice for "the people," his commitment to democratic rule is too common-sensical and too empirical to be unconditional. If the human need for security creates a historical need for a prince in all his singularity to legislate, then monarchy is necessary, proper, and desirable. If one must commit awful acts to create a lawful monarchy in unlawful conditions, then one acquires a moral obligation to commit those awful acts. However, we should note that a monarch's proper mode of legislating, like Romulus's, results in his making the office obsolete at a later time (*Discourses*, 1:9). His very success in securing a people will unleash the human need for freedom that will, almost of necessity,[20] destroy monarchy. The success of Romulus makes the success of Brutus possible and likely; the princely founder makes feasible and necessary the democratic reformer. The glory of good princes is that they make republics possible.[21]

Princes are not enough, though, for a corrupted city or nation. They are a necessary stepping-stone on the bridge from the primitive to the modern; their success elicits the need for freedom. Once this higher need has emerged, humans cannot go back to a condition of servitude: "whoever becomes the ruler of a free city and does not destroy it, can expect to be destroyed by it, for it can always find a motive for rebellion in the name of liberty and of its ancient usages . . ." (*Prince*, chapter 5). Even when addressing the question of principalities, Machiavelli is never far from his republican commitment to freedom. Human motivation is such that people need to be free, need to live life for their own purposes, to assume obligations under laws made to meet the real human needs of a people. But people are not so moved all the time; or, at least, not all people share this motivation all the time. Sometimes, other motivations interfere, "blocking" out this need. The most dangerous motivation of this sort is ambition.

FREEDOM AT RISK

Many Americans in the 1990s consider ambition an admirable characteristic in a person, especially a young person. Those who lack it are seen as feckless and lazy, destined to accomplish little if anything; those with it can rise above backgrounds of poverty and disadvantage to whatever heights they seek. It is certainly an exceedingly powerful motivator of humans, leading them to do and accomplish much that would otherwise be beyond them.

But from another perspective, ambition can also lead people to do much that is *beneath* them. One could speak, then, of two types of ambition or distinguish between the two entities by calling one "ambition" and the other something else, like glory. Machiavelli came to use the second strategy. This, in turn, colored his opinion of ambition, which led people to seek more than their due; and the rules of the game were not seen as effective inhibitors of the ambitious. There was a difference, then, between seeking glory and being ambitious. If the pursuit of glory could end corruption, ambition would create corruption.

This contrasts with ancient Roman usage. The virtue of *ambitio* for the Romans was a striving for good things, for the common good, but Machiavelli's *ambizione* is a lawless striving for self-interest at the expense of the common interest. Rather than a strong motivator to do what is right and good, it is a corrupter of all that is good; ambition became a vice for Machiavelli. However, this vice did not infect, nor move, all people; rather, only some became ambitious.

If ambition is a preoccupation that blinds us to the common good, why are people so moved? Is it an instinctive drive that can never be resisted? Is it a drive that always moves us so that we must always be on guard? Or does it move only some of us or move us only some times? Machiavelli appears to have been convinced that ambition is a characteristic of some people. As Price notes, for Machiavelli "there are certain passions that move all men. . . . But not all passions are universal; some are characteristic of certain types or classes of men . . ."[22] Ambition is a characteristic of certain classes of men, of the *uomini grandi* or *nobili* (see the many examples cited by Price, 398–400).

Observing Machiavelli's perception of ambition in nobles leads Skinner to conclude that "the most serious danger to the balance of mixed constitutions" in Machiavelli's theory is "the danger that an ambitious citizen may attempt to form a party based on loyalty to himself instead of to the common good."[23] These dangerous ambitions of the nobles can be fostered in two crucial ways, one being that the prolongation of military commands can lead soldiers to develop a loyalty to a specific commander instead of to the state. This, Machiavelli suggests, was what eventually "made Rome a slave" (*Discourses*, 3:24). Of course, proper institutional arrangements—

including provisions that no commands are for life—can help to neutralize this ambition.

But the other source of corruptive faction "is the malign influence exercised by those with extensive personal wealth."[24] Those with massive estates and holdings of personal wealth can dispense injurious favors to those less well off that render them dependent upon the wealthy. Machiavelli lists "lending them money, marrying off their daughters, protecting them from the magistrates, and doing them similar private favors" (*Discourses*, 3:28). There can only be one result: "These make men partisans of their benefactors and give the man they follow courage to think he can corrupt the public and violate the laws" (ibid.).

So if a state keeps its citizens from becoming excessively wealthy while keeping its own coffers full, "the government will be able to outbid the rich in any 'scheme of befriending the people', since it will always be possible to offer greater rewards for public than for private services."[25] In the case of Cosimo de' Medici, who had been able to use the family patrimony to buy the loyalty of parts of Florence, one family was able to build up a party loyal to it and its interests. Instead of outbidding him, "Cosimo's rivals instead chose to drive him from Florence, thereby provoking so much resentment among his followers that they eventually" restored the Medici to power.[26]

In short, experience made Machiavelli very wary of "nobles" or "gentlemen" and their ambition:

> We may then draw the following conclusion from what has been said: that if any one should wish to establish a republic where there are many gentlemen, he will not succeed until he has destroyed them all; and whoever desires to establish a kingdom or principality where liberty and equality prevail, will equally fail, unless he withdraws from that general equality a number of the boldest and most ambitious spirits, and makes gentlemen of them, not merely in name but in fact, by giving to them castles and possessions, as well as money and subjects. . . . (*Discourses*, 1:54; Ricci–Vincent, 256)

These "gentlemen," or idle rich, are great dangers to a republic, in his eyes. Their ambition, which he defined as their seeking to advance their personal and familial interests over those of the nation, drives them to employ "private" means of achieving influence and power. Further, they do this in ways that are not obviously wicked:

> The ambitious citizens of a republic seek in the first instance (as we have said above) to make themselves sure against the attacks, not only

of individuals, but even of magistrates. To enable them to do this, they seek to gain friends, either by apparently honest ways, or by assisting men with money, or by defending them against the powerful; and as this seems virtuous, almost everybody is readily deceived by it, and therefore no one opposes it, until the ambitious individual has, without hindrance, grown so powerful that private citizens fear him and the magistrates treat him with consideration. And when he has risen to that point, no one at the beginning having interfered with his greatness, it becomes in the end most dangerous to attempt to put him down . . . so that in the end the matter is reduced to this, that you must endeavor to destroy the evil at the risk of sudden ruin, or by allowing it to go on, submit to manifest servitude. . . . (*Discourses*, 1:46; Ricci–Vincent, 232–33)

So stealthily has this evil crept up on free citizens that there is no obvious warning. Then the republic faces a "do or die" situation, and action is possible only at great peril. Now one must act against particular citizens, who, having grown strong, are a threat to the freedom of others and can only be put down by extralegal means. How much better it is, then, to prevent this evil from occurring by preventing the accumulation of wealth. Equality recommends itself to a republic on these grounds.

As we have seen, the dangerous ambitions of the nobles can be fostered in two crucial ways. First of all, with the prolongation of military commands, soldiers come to develop a loyalty to a specific commander instead of to the state; secondly the "malign influence exercised by those with extensive personal wealth" can make dependents of poor people and elevate their benefactors above the law. If a prohibition against commands "for life" is the institutional response to the one source of corruptive ambition, what is the institutional response to the "malign influence" of extensive wealth? If the poor are to be dependent (and realism suggests that, so long as people are poor, they must remain dependent upon someone), it is better that their dependence fosters loyalty to the state rather than to a sect within the state whose interests oppose those of the state.

This need to win the loyalty of the poor citizens is well understood by those who would corrupt, but not always well by those who would defend, a republic:

For in truth there is no better nor easier mode in republics, and especially in such as are corrupt, for successfully opposing the ambition of any citizen, than to occupy in advance of him those ways by which he expects to attain the rank he aims at. If this mode had been employed by the adversaries of Cosimo de' Medici, it would have been much better than to expel him from Florence; for if they had adopted his plan of favoring the people, they would have succeeded without any disturbances or violence in depriving him of the weapons which he himself employed with so much skill. (*Discourses*, 1:52; Ricci–Vincent, 244)

Of course, none of this is abstract theorizing on the former secretary's part; he drew his conclusions from concrete historical experience in Florence. The appropriate way to deal with a threat to the republic posed by a power like the Medici would be to win the loyalty of the poor for the republican government. Consequently, one appropriate institutional response to great wealth are the programs of the social welfare state: progressive taxation and transfer programs would displace the dependency of the poor from sectarians to the state. Machiavelli was, in this sense, one of the first modern proponents of the ideal of "positive liberty." Of equal significance is the fact that he rooted this defense of positive liberty in a view of human potentials.

CONCLUSION: MORAL OBLIGATIONS AND HUMAN NATURE

Thus, humans are possessed of two great possibilities: we can nurture our capacity for nobility, or we can permit corruption. The laws, along with equality of holdings, are crucial variables in determining which potential will be realized. Derivatively, great people can, through making good laws, also do much to foster the more positive developmental potentials within us. For success in our practical lives we need to determine which potential has been realized in the concrete historical circumstances of our lives. Most simply, we cannot know what is the good thing to do if we do not first make that factual determination.

Given the importance of laws in realizing human potentials for good and for evil, we might expect Machiavelli to suggest that when good laws exist, we must obey them.[27] But when there are no such laws (i.e., in the context of corruption), one's moral obligations are not those of conventional morality. Rather, when dealing with corrupt people, one must recognize the existence of objective values, especially the value of civilization, and respond to their requirements. Hence, given the value of humans living freely under their own laws, in a corrupt environment they should do whatever is necessary to establish a system of constitutional laws.

Our human needs, then, especially those for security and freedom, lead us to social intercourse, where obligations are created so that a society might satisfy human needs. There is only one reason for our having moral obligations, then: to satisfy our needs. To Machiavelli's account of our moral obligations, and of the psychological conditions in which they become real, we now direct our attention.

Part 3
Machiavellian Morals

3

Creating Our Moral Obligations

OVERVIEW

IF not literally oxymoronic, "Machiavellian morality" at least has acquired a bad reputation. When not depicted as an amoral proponent of power over morality, Machiavelli has been seen as advocating evil and immorality, whether in popularizing immorality or in "liberating" politics from morals. Everybody's "bad boy," he is damned, as Skinner observes, by "conservatives and revolutionaries alike."[1]

It cannot be denied that his thoughts on morality are decidedly challenging and disturbing, and his use of language and paradox is provocative, probably deliberately so.[2] Nevertheless, the moral theory he proposes is part of a rich, vibrant, and defensible alternative to the medieval rationalism that he opposed. The argument in support of Machiavelli's morals will be developed in three stages. In the first stage, his theory will be shown to be an instance of voluntarism and defended as such (this chapter). In the second stage (chapter 4), his account of moral values prior to the creation of laws will be explored, along with the implicit moral requirements of seeking the goal of glory, especially in corruption. Finally, in chapter Five, his account of the duty to obey the laws in a constitutional arrangement will be articulated and defended.[3]

Perhaps the most disturbing aspect of his moral theory—the assertion that our moral obligations are not carved in stone eternally by God or nature and may not even exist under certain circumstances—is not radically different from the theories of social contract theorists[4] and legal positivists whose reputations are not similarly besmirched. It is even possible, as Vilari implies, that the wealthy (who presumably control the means for forging reputations) have waged a campaign to depict him as evil because of his views on equality.[5] His caution about the corruptive potential of unequal wealth would be anathema to those with great wealth, and it would be in their interest to smear his name, exactly so that people like

Madison,[6] frequently called the father of the American Constitution and one of the coauthors of *The Federalist Papers,* would later view such proposals to equalize wealth as "evil."[7] Nevertheless, that evil image of Machiavelli should be abandoned because Machiavelli in fact advanced a view of our moral obligations that would be consistent with democratic freedom, a view of our moral obligations as human creations. This belief is generally called ethical voluntarism.

Machiavelli's was a highly developed version of voluntarism, articulated in literary metaphors rather than with philosophical precision; it is also a quite unusual variant. Like most voluntarists, he appears to believe that moral obligations are created by humans rather than forces like God or nature. Prior to human creations of value, nothing seems "really" right or wrong to him, not even Romulus's fratricide. While he is never quite so explicit as Hobbes, Machiavelli would probably agree with the other's suggestion that people's passions and actions are not sinful or wrong "till they know a law that forbids them: which till laws be made they cannot know. . . ."[8] Hence, what is disturbing about his morality is not simply his belief that our moral obligations are not always what they appear to be; what is disturbing is his implication that, before human laws, we have *no* obligations.

However, unlike other voluntarists that I am aware of, Machiavelli does not appear to believe that we are left with no moral compass in this [precivilized] condition.[9] Rather, there are certain moral values that continue to guide our actions, values so self-evident that there is no person "too wise or too foolish" (*Discourses,* 1 : 10) to fail to see them, even in corruption. Finally, although there are no duties in this condition before civilization, these moral values press their requirements upon us so that we "should" act in such a way as to maximize these values. Hence, even when living in corruption, among uncivilized, lawless people, the value of civilization requires that we should first take steps to survive and then set our eyes on bringing lawful rule into being, on developing a civilization with its glory.[10]

MACHIAVELLI'S CASE FOR VOLUNTARISM

Proving the superiority of moral voluntarism over rationalism is neither possible nor desirable here: this issue is probably one of the great philosophical quandaries of our time, irresolvable without a revolution in our ways of conceiving morality. Consequently, people of good faith will continue to espouse both views, even after weighing these arguments for voluntarism. Nonetheless, there were powerful reasons for Machiavelli's renunciation of medieval morality, and an examination of these reasons makes the case for his conception of morality more plausible.

Roughly speaking, the reasons for the emergence of this doctrine in the early Renaissance can be grouped into three categories. First, there is a question of the logical compatibility of each moral doctrine with the emerging empiricist tradition. While it is not the case that empiricism requires voluntarism, a case can be made that voluntarism is more compatible with empiricism than is rationalism. Logical compatibility, then, recommends the voluntarist alternative. Second, adhering strictly to the conventional morality of the medieval period can create (prima facie) logical difficulties; we will examine one such conundrum in detail and find therein much to support voluntarism. Finally, some apparent deficiencies of the tradition of natural law strengthen the comparative case for voluntarism.

Empiricism and Voluntarism?

Given his modern, scientific empiricism, which was based on the belief that our knowledge of this concrete world must originate in human sensation, Machiavelli might be expected to reject older, theological and teleological notions of cosmic order. Indeed, Machiavelli's commitment to empiricism does lead him to the modern belief in moral voluntarism. He begins by rejecting traditional morality and provides a series of important hints about a newer morality that should replace it as we enter a newer, more modern world. While it would be an exaggeration to assert that empiricism precludes moral rationalism or that empiricism requires voluntarism, it is nonetheless true that there is a conceptual affinity between the empiricist world view and the belief that values are a product of human reckoning. After all, most medieval versions of moral rationalism or natural law, like those of Augustine and Aquinas, required a corollary belief in a creating God, who defined standards of right and wrong (the laws of nature) at the moment of creation. But empiricist iconoclasm calls into question these notions of God and nature, and, by implication, challenges eternal standards of right and wrong.

Most simply, the problem of God for empiricists is that it is difficult to show that God exists using the usual methods of empirical verification. The God of theologians like Aquinas is a spiritual being; unlike beings with bodies, He cannot be detected by any of the senses. But moderns have come to think that things do not exist if they cannot be detected through the senses. The problem can be seen if we consider how it is that we "know" that God is, in principle, a spiritual being: spiritual beings cannot be directly detected by any of our senses (except in literally miraculous circumstances, that is, when the normal laws of nature are suspended by divine intervention); consequently we cannot know if He exists. Today, if someone were to report having seen the face of God directly, or were to report having heard directly the voice of God, empiricists would seek to replicate those sensual experiences and, failing to replicate them, would probably cynically dismiss the assertions of divine contact. In such a world, it is hard to be either saint or god.

In this brave, new, "modern" world, different formulae have to be found—or invented—to govern our actions. Machiavelli's accomplishment was seeing that a new way of life was in fact emerging. In small things and in big, he rejected antiquity and its medieval successor: not only in his celebration of heroic action; not just in his celebration of "manly," *virtuoso* conquest of the feminine[11] *fortuna;* but also and most importantly in his commitment to the emerging, modern world view and the moral challenge this posed. Included in this modern, empirical view is a recognition that no obligations exist prior to the constitution of society, prior to the creation of positive law. A further implication is an increased importance for the mortal Legislator.

Even though Pitkin did not articulate her insight in these words, she well understood the connection between Machiavelli's empiricism and his vision of modern morality:

> If one may be permitted some broad stereotypes as a way of getting started, in the medieval world people understood themselves as embedded in a hierarchical network of mutual obligation—the feudal order of fealty, which also reflected the natural and sacred order of the universe. In that understanding, the social, like the natural order, is essentially given to man, not made. Just as an individual is born into a particular social rank rather than achieving his status in a competitive market, so too the customs and rules of the social order are not subject to choice. Of course, particular individuals make decisions applying law or custom in particular situations; and people are fallible and can make bad or wrong decisions. But the law that men should be seeking to apply— that good men do seek to apply—is eternal, universal, absolute, and ultimately of divine origin. Law is not made, but found, by men.[12]

The medieval perspective that laws are an immutable part of the sacred order of things, set by God and imposed upon us, is moral rationalism; the opposing view, that moral values and principles are artificial and changeable, is the more "modern" voluntarist view.

Machiavelli was one of the first to enter that new world, and its strangeness constitutes part of an explanation of why he felt he was entering on a "new way" (introduction, *The Discourses*). A corollary of this belief that the social order is created by, and not given to, humanity is the belief that humans define standards of right and wrong.

For Machiavelli, this humanism poses a puzzle with several dimensions. Are political actors bound by traditional morality? by any morality? Is it really wrong to commit the cruelties necessary for civilized life? For Machiavelli, this requires a new conception of what is morally permissible; according to this new view, we would be morally bound only under certain social conditions. Even in the famous but, as we shall see, puzzling quotation where Machiavelli suggests that a prince need not keep faith, his point is not simply that a ruler never has moral obligations, but that we need a new approach to moral thinking: "How laudable it is for a prince to keep good faith and live with integrity ... every one knows. Still the experience of our times shows that ... a prudent ruler ought not to keep faith when by so doing it would be against his interest, and when the reasons which made him bind himself no longer exist ..." (*Prince*, chapter 18).

The fact that so many thinkers have made so many different things of this passage suggests how puzzling it is. To take one prominent scholar as an example, Harvey Mansfield has observed that the "typical view" of this passage is that Machiavelli "believed that morality can be one's guide in private affairs but not in politics,"[13] or that morality was inapplicable to political action. To bolster this view, Mansfield suggests that Machiavelli believed that "a private man should regard himself as *deprived* of office." If a person "deserves" to be a prince but is not, this deprivation of office is an "injustice." The injustice, in turn, apparently justifies using "Machiavellian" schemings to get into office.

However, this "typical view" of Machiavelli's intent becomes viable only if two dubious conditions can be validated simultaneously: first, if "private" men like the Medici are, to Machiavelli, justified in corrupting republics, and second, if Machiavelli is aiming solely at the goal of power. But, in the first case, Machiavelli explicitly condemned the rise of men to power by "private" means: when reputation and influence are "acquired by private means, then they become most dangerous and pernicious" (*Discourses*, 3:28; Ricci–Vincent, 494). After listing the various means that private persons can employ to purchase power (most of which were used effectively by Cosimo de' Medici), he concludes that permitting private persons to use their economic power this way "encourages those who are thus favored to corrupt the public and to outrage the laws. A well-regulated republic, therefore, should open the way to public honors to those who seek reputation by means that are conducive to the public good; and close it to those whose aim is the advancement of private ends" (ibid.). In the case of the first condition, Machiavelli's point seems to be the opposite of Mansfield's interpretation.

The second condition similarly cannot be supported in the texts of the Machiavellian corpus; for, as I have shown, Machiavelli's ultimate goal is the *gloria*—and the freedom it entails—beyond power. In contrast to Mansfield's assertion, Machiavelli holds even princes to this moral standard: "And truly, if a prince be anxious for glory and the good opinion of the world, he should rather wish to possess a corrupt city, not to ruin it wholly like Caesar, but to reorganize it like Romulus. For certainly the heavens cannot afford a man a greater opportunity of glory, nor could men desire a better one" (*Discourses*, 1:10).

Scheming to get mere power, as Mansfield's Machiavelli recommends, is the error recognized by the real Machiavelli as the desire to be only a lion, reducing such an ambitious prince-to-be to the condemned status of Agathocles.

To achieve real glory, one must create good laws that transform the human material of a polity from a corrupted state to a decent one. Where this most difficult of political tasks is not accomplished, evil prevails: "And truly, where this probity does not exist, no good is to be expected, as in fact it is vain to look for anything good from those countries which we see nowadays so corrupt, as is the case above all others with Italy" (*Discourses*, 1: 54; Ricci–Vincent, 253).

Hence, we must conclude that Mansfield's "typical view" of this passage is not consistent with other things Machiavelli has written and should therefore be rejected.

An obvious question is, how could one disregard what Machiavelli has so clearly written? How could rational people of good will disagree, when the passage is so plainly about everyone's knowing that it is "laudable" for a prince to keep faith? One answer is that disagreement is possible given an assumption that Machiavelli was being sarcastic in the opening sentence, sneering at weak princes limited by their compunctions to do what is right. The principal advantage of such an interpretation is that it reinforces the perception of Machiavelli as a "teacher of evil."

The first disadvantage of the sarcastic reading is that it is inconsistent with other things Machiavelli wrote. If he were being derisive in writing that it is laudable to keep faith, then all moral evaluation would become superfluous, since moral compunctions are merely barriers in the way of those who seek power. In seeking to do great things, then, one would never need to pay any attention to moral obligations or to moral values. One would be simply free of such constraints in politics. But, as has been shown, Machiavelli does not shrink from making moral judgments, noting, for an instance, that "those are doomed to infamy and universal execration who have destroyed religions, who have overturned republics and kingdoms, who are enemies of virtue, of letters, and of every art that is useful and honorable to mankind" (*Discourses*, 1:10). Hence, especially in politics, one is not free of the constraints of morality and the sarcastic interpretation seems misplaced.

The second disadvantage of a derisive interpretation is that such a reading is inconsistent with Machiavelli's expressions of his experiences and preferences. His experience in the French court of Louis XII left him thoroughly convinced of the need for modernizing— feudalism was dead, and "keeping your word" (by abiding by the oaths of feudal loyalty) was one of the pieces of dead wood standing in the way of modern glory. Such vows of loyalty bound one to a patron forever, dividing up the loyalties of a nation and leading to sectarian violence and warlordism. In *this* context, perhaps one ought not to keep faith, or in other words ought not to do what is required by conventional morality. After all, when "being moral" requires actions that create immorality, "being moral" needs to be reconceptualized.

Finally, we must note that Machiavelli begins this empirical "disproof" of traditional morality with an appeal specifically to "the experience of our times," not of all times. What he literally wrote seems to be something like this: it is usually right and good for princes to abide by the requirements of morality, although, in corrupt times like these, a prince must know how to do what would otherwise be wrong, how to behave like a lion and/or a fox, how to "enter evil." Even the conditions he attaches to his claim that the prince may sometimes break faith call attention to the fact that conventional social institutions that make the action wrong must no longer be in place, as we have seen.

But most importantly, there is, in addition to the contextual evidence, other textual evidence that Machiavelli did not here intend a sneer. For example, in *The Discourses* (1:10), as Machiavelli is preparing for his discussion of Numa and the religion he gave to Rome, he lists the Roman emperors who deserved praise; one reason they deserved praise is that they were morally incorruptible. Machiavelli urges the reader to also note how much more praise those Emperors merited who, after Rome became an empire, conformed to the laws like good princes, than those who took the opposite course; and he will see that Titus, Nerva, Trajan, Hadrian, Antoninus, and Marcus Aurelius did not require the Praetorians nor the multitudinous legions to defend them, because they were protected by their own good conduct, the good will of the people, and by the love of the Senate. He will furthermore see that neither the Eastern nor the Western armies sufficed to save Caligula, Nero, Vitellius, and so many other wicked Emperors, from the enemies which their bad conduct and evil lives had raised up against them.

A similar point is made with reference to deceit. Normally, lying is wrong, Machiavelli suggests; but in war, since morality has not been constituted (or has been destroyed), nothing is wrong: "Although deceit is detestable in all other things, yet in the conduct of war it is laudable and honorable; and a commander who vanquishes an enemy by stratagem is equally praised with one who gains victory by force" (*Discourses*, 3:40; Ricci–Vincent, 526).

In the context of these writings, we can conclude that it is legitimate to read the passage from *The Prince* without a sneer. We can therefore infer that princes should usually keep faith (and, more generally, be moral) but be prepared, in times of corruption,[14] to do whatever is necessary to battle that corruption, even if the necessary cure appears, by the standards of traditional morality, to be "bad" or "wrong" or "cruel." Machiavelli's moral truth is that, in corruption (when no viable morality exists), no action can be said to be immoral.

Consequently, however problematic his moral commitment to glory, it is a mistake to depict Machiavelli as opposing morality in the struggle for power. If Machiavelli were in fact suggesting that political action could not be judged by moral standards, he would be contradicting his own moral judgments; if he did not, however, mean to suggest that the political operative be free from moral compunction (as we have just proved), what was he attempting to say?

Recasting puzzling passages into simpler and standard logical forms sometimes helps to reveal their hidden significance. In this case, the recasting reveals that the author did not intend a blanket exoneration of all political scheming. Rather, the intent was to specify the conditions under which a prince no longer has an obligation to do what had been promised.

Let us reexamine the passage, beginning with its introduction: "How laudable it is for a prince to keep good faith and live with integrity . . . every one knows. Still the experience of our times shows those princes to have done great things who have had little regard for good faith. . . . You must know, then, that there are two methods of fighting, the one by law, the other by force: the first method is that of men, the second of beasts . . ." (*Prince*, chapter 18).

After going on to reveal the moral significance of the education of ancient princes by Chiron the centaur (he taught them how to behave as both men and animals), Machiavelli tells us that when forced to bestial action, we must aspire to be as strong as a lion and as clever as a fox (neither alone being adequate). Then he moves to the moral heart of the matter: "Therefore, a prudent ruler ought not to keep faith when by so doing it would be against his interest, and when the reasons which made him bind himself no longer exist. If men were all good, this precept would not be a good one; but as they are bad, and would not observe their faith with you, so you are not bound to keep faith with them" (*Prince*, chapter 18).

As a preliminary, let us note that this passage begins with a "therefore," which suggests that, in the mind of the secretary, this moral doctrine is a consequence of the psychological truth expressed in the prior sentence: that humans are capable of the bestial. It also ends with an additional reference to human nature: if the facts of human nature were different, a different morality would be possible. Additionally, remember that he believes that "the law can make men good" (see the previous chapter and *The Discourses*, 1:3). In context, then, the prudent ruler must make an empirical judgment as to whether people have realized their human (lawful) or bestial (corruptive) potentials. If people are basically bestial (corrupt), then we must approach morality differently than we would when dealing with civilized and lawful beings.

Logically, this passage is equivalent to a conditional (if-then) with a conjunction of two antecedents, both of which must be satisfied before the conclusion follows:

(a) *If* a prince (ruler) no longer finds it to his/her advantage to do what was promised;

(b) *and if* a ruler finds that the reasons which made him/her bind him/herself no longer exist;[15]

(c) *then* a prudent ruler no longer has any moral obligation to keep faith.

The cautious conclusion is that before absolving a ruler of a particular obligation (and of obligations generally), Machiavelli requires that two morally relevant provisos *both* be satisfied: (1) that it no longer be in the prince's interest to keep faith *and* (2) that "the reasons that made him promise are annulled" (ibid.)

The meaning of the first conditional is straightforward: sometimes rulers should consider themselves free simply to pursue their rational interest. Given that the second condition is not merely equivalent to the first, it apparently requires of us something other than a mere calculation of self-interest. What are the reasons, outside of prudence, for a prince to "bind himself"?

If traditional morality does not bind a prince, what does? More generally, how does one come to have a moral obligation? Why do obligations bind us?

The modern, positivist presumption is that social institutions provide a context in which one can bind oneself. The reasons for doing what one promises, for instance, are tied to the institution of promising (which does not exist under all circumstances), and promising is an institution that (presumably) separates civilized from uncivilized peoples. In the context of the institution of promising, a person creates the obligation to do something ("X") by uttering the words "I promise to do X." When the institution has been constituted and is effective, one's words can "perform" certain kinds of actions, creating (in this case) obligations.[16] Prior to the constitution of such institutions, obligations cannot be created in this way. Hence, an institution like promising is constituted when at least two agents reach agreement to use the institution and then begin to use it; subsequently, enforcement of obligations becomes important but enforcement is not always essential to the initial act of constituting. So the obligation to do what one has promised originates in one's own actions, not in an action of God or nature.

The fact that one promised is the reason for being bound, and, moving now to Machiavelli's concern, that reason can only be annulled in specific ways. One cannot simply, by another verbal action, un-promise. One's prima facie promissory obligation can be voided (roughly) by only two sorts of events: (1) the person to whom you are bound absolves you of any responsibility to do what you promised, or (2) the very institution in which the obligation was created is destroyed by subsequent historical events.[17] It is the latter event (corruption), tantamount to a reversion to a contract theorist's "state of nature" (Hobbes) or "state of war" (Locke), that is the object of Machiavelli's concern. So, explaining his meaning in that famous, puzzling passage about how princes ought to keep faith, Machiavelli concludes by specifying that "If all men were good, this maxim would not be good, but because they are bad and do not keep their promises to you, you likewise do not have to keep yours to them" (ibid).

To sum up, we can say, then, that (1) if all "men" were good (if people lived under good institutions that evoked their potential for being good), then we would have an obligation to keep faith (and, presumably, do all other things required by the social institutions we create to form obligations); but (2) if/when people are not good (if those institutions do not exist or are not honored), then the obligations created within those institutions also do not exist. Of course, *The Prince* was written as advice to a potential ruler in corrupt, degenerate conditions. Since the advice to princes was intended for situations when the institutions of society had been corrupted, the advice only *appears* to be that princes need never keep faith. In fact, harking back to the introductory paragraph of the chapter, we see that Machiavelli actually said the *opposite*.

We may then draw these conclusions about Machiavelli's voluntarism: the "reasons" that make you "bind" yourself are derivative from the appropriate social institution; in conditions of corruption, when such institutions do not yet exist or have been destroyed, the uttering of ritual words (like saying "I promise") performs no action, creates no obligations. We do have moral obligations, as a matter of (social) fact, but they are not eternal or divine since they exist in secular history. Machiavelli's belief that we create our institutions and our obligations defines his position as voluntarist; it also validates our classifying him as an empiricist and humanist. In context, this advice not to count yourself bound in a corrupt society sounds surprisingly like Hume's admonition that it is merely imprudent to be the only honest man in a dishonest community. This perspective also shares an important kinship with contemporary components of natural law especially the positivists.

MACHIAVELLI'S CRITICISMS OF MORAL RATIONALISM

The other side of Machiavelli's morality consists of the deficiencies he perceived in moral rationalism. His reasons for rejecting that rationalism and for becoming a modern thinker in Strauss's sense[18] of believing that the principles of moral obligation are the product of human, rather than divine, creativity, are tied to deficiencies he perceived in that tradition. Although it has other weaknesses compared to rationalism, Machiavelli detects the comparative strengths of the voluntarist belief.

In particular, voluntarism does not confront one particular conundrum faced by rationalist theories. The logical conundrum that led Machiavelli and other Renaissance thinkers to voluntarism is roughly this: if there were no moral obligations (if we continued to live in corruption), life would remain "solitary, poor, nasty, brutish, and short";[19] but if we *always* abide by what *appear* to be our moral obligations (as rationalist absolutism appears to require), we will sometimes fail to secure a legal system, thereby destroying all that is good and again reducing life to the bestial. Hence, being immoral creates human misery, but being "moral" is little better in corrupt circumstances. But given that making human life miserable is immoral, to be moral (not enforcing the laws forcefully enough) is to be immoral (to make humans miserable). It is this conundrum that leads Machiavelli, in chapter 8 of *The Prince,* to draw the distinction between cruelties "well" and "badly" used. To avoid the conundrum, we need a way of saying that that we sometimes have no moral obligations (so as to be free to perform the "immoral" or cruel actions necessary to preserve law and order) while also maintaining that we (at other times) do have obligations (so that most people would have reason to obey the laws the rest—most— of the time). In this way, we may become morally free to commit our cruelties "well."

In shaping (or responding to) the spirit of Renaissance humanism, Machiavelli sees voluntarism as a resolution of this conundrum. If we assume that we create the standards of morality, then we have an obligation to do what is right after we define it as right, but we are free to do what we must to acquire the freedom to so define things as right (i.e., to acquire the right to legislate). Believing this, when it is necessary to disregard our apparent moral obligations for the sake of achieving what is really good, we may dispense with them because they are only of human, and not divine, origin. Believing this, we can also consistently maintain that, once we have established our own laws, we must obey them. In fact, it would be self-contradictory and irrational not to do what is right after fighting for the authority to define what is right.

Machiavelli's project—to advance modernity—requires that he be critical of conventional morality/moralities. These moralities appear to depend on the truth that certain actions are always wrong, but history shows that they cannot always be wrong. The systems of moral evaluation accepted during antiquity and the medieval period become his principal moral target, especially the "absolutist" natural law tradition of the Romans and, later, of the Christians. The central point here is that Machiavelli was not simply opposed to the "weak" virtues of Christianity; he also opposed some moral theories of the ancient Romans.

It was logically necessary that he oppose Roman morals (in addition to Christian morals) because that morality also assumed that our obligations are natural and thus independent of our creative decisions. In viewing Christian and Roman morals as similar, he agreed with Augustine, who argued in the first ten books of *The City of God* that Christian morals were merely a logical extension and completion of Roman morals, rather than a repudiation of the older tradition. Machiavelli repudiated both moralities when he praised Romulus (who killed his brother to found Rome), Cleomenes (who purged Sparta of its bad blood before restoring the laws of Lycurgus),[20] and Brutus (who, after creating the Roman republic, oversaw the execution of his own traitorous sons). We are reminded by McIntosh, a Machiavelli scholar, that these three men would have evoked far different moral reasoning from the ancients than from Machiavelli, or even from Christianity: "the three stories have quite a different ethical meaning for the pagan mind than for Machiavelli. From the Stoic point of view all three exemplify civic virtue, not as using a bad means if necessary to a good end, but as doing one's duty regardless of the consequences."[21] Where Machiavelli might see these actions as justified by their consequences in conditions of corruption, they would be seen, from the traditional Stoic perspective, as cases of performing one's duties (under the laws of nature) regardless of the (undesirable) consequences; from the Christian perspective, they would presumably be seen as violations of duty.

To focus on but one of the examples: from the Stoic perspective, Brutus's responsibility as consul was to preside over the trial of his counterrevolutionary, traitorous sons—even though the consequences were quite unpleasant for him. Presumably, this would be a case of "cruelties well used" for Machiavelli. But if "Brutus treacherously had spilled the innocent blood of his children in order to save Rome, the act would have been a case in point for Machiavelli, but anathema to the pagan ethical and political sensibility."[22]

If McIntosh is right, the problem (for Machiavelli) with ancient Roman (traditional) morality is that it is at once both too arrogantly certain (relying on natural reason for certainty), too rationalistic, and too legalistic (looking more to one's duties under laws rather than to the consequences of political action). Nevertheless, Machiavelli was right to note that the actions of these three men were judged approvingly by the Stoics, but not by medieval natural law; if natural law were a single, coherent tradition, such inconsistencies would be impossible.

A more apt example for the voluntarist (Machiavellian) perspective might be Catherine Sforza, reputed (by Machiavelli in *The Discourses*, 3:6) to have left her children as hostages with conspirators (who had already murdered her husband, the count) to guarantee her good behavior while she prepared to turn over control of her domain to them. Once out of personal danger, though, she determined to abandon her children to the butchers, opting to punish the conspirators and defend her rule at the expense of the lives of her innocent children. Here Roman and Christian morality would presumably converge to condemn her actions, citing both her familial duty to her offspring and also their innocence. At most, they might admit a conflict of duties, with patriotic duty opposing familial duty.[23]

But Machiavelli admires her courage as she taunts her torturers, the murderers of her husband and kidnappers of her children, by pointing to her reproductive organs and telling them that more children can come from whence the others had come, while it is not within her power to beget the domain (*Discourses*, 3:6). For Machiavelli, not even the sacrifice of innocent children is wrong in warfare. In conditions this corrupt, no principles can stand in the way of the pursuit of the goal of glory. The actions of Catherine Sforza may have been tragic, bringing great sorrow and remorse to her; but they could not be wrong.

To conclude this example, we might note that Machiavelli's admiration of the countess might not be misplaced. However bestial it may seem to abandon her children to butchers, she may have chosen wisely. First, there was no real assurance that transferring control of the domain would have spared the lives of the children, since a powerless countess and her children would have been defenseless and at the mercy of the butchers. Finally, it is not certain that the countess was actually guilty of any wrong under the circumstances. If there is any "natural" wrong associated with the death of such innocent children,[24] it should attach only to the souls of the murderers and not to that of the tortured parent. To affix guilt in any other fashion would be to blame the victim of cruel and inhumane torture. Machiavelli's admiration of the Sforza countess might not be misplaced after all.

In many respects, then, the Florentine republican was as opposed to Roman morality as to Christian morality, because both pretended to have moral certitude. Even the famous quotation about a prince's need to fight like a man and like a beast takes new meaning in this light: one meaning, reinforced by the preceding paragraph that sets the context, of this passage is that, in conditions of corruption, one must be prepared to fight as a beast, being both clever and strong since neither alone can save you. As we have seen, after beginning by noting that "everyone knows" that princes should keep faith, the secretary reports his experience of corruption before advising: "You must know, then, that there are two methods of fighting, the one by law, the other by force: the first method is that of men, the second of beasts; but as the first method is often insufficient, one must have recourse to the second. It is therefore necessary for a prince to know well how to use both the beast and the man" (*Prince*, chapter 18).

The point is hammered home by the ancient tales about the education of princes by Chiron, the half-man/half-beast.

But while it seems that this meaning contradicts the rationalism of Christian morality, the secretary is giving us less obvious messages, indicating that the target is larger than Christianity. His invoking of metaphors—used universally to make the opposite moral point from the originals—implies that the target is the larger moral category that includes the Romans. This less obvious meaning becomes clear when it is compared to Cicero's use of the same metaphor (the fox and the lion) in arguing that our obligations are natural.[25]

Similarly, the Florentine secretary's discussion of liberality and niggardliness opposes Cicero's, as does his claim that a prince should prefer to be feared over being loved. Finally, his discussion of mercy directly confronts Seneca's writings on the same subject.[26] Thus, Machiavelli did not believe that medieval Christianity monopolized moral error since the Romans also failed to appreciate the complexity of moral choice. The intellectual deficiencies of conventional morality evoke his contempt, but not because Machiavelli scorned all duty and values; rather, whenever necessity permits, even conventional morality is highly recommended. Instead, he saw the inconsistencies of all older moralities as evidence of a need for a newer morality, a more modern valuing of things—the need to "enter a new way."

MACHIAVELLI'S NEW MORALITY

Machiavelli seems to have been convinced (*Discourses*, 1:2) that legislating, the glorious act of creating social institutions that evoke higher human potentials, is also the act of creating our moral obligations. It is for this reason, presumably, that founders of republics and principalities are to be valued almost as much as founders of religions (*Discourses*, 1:10). This perspective is the opposite of the natural law tradition, in which certain actions are wrong or right because a cosmic force greater than humanity, whether nature or God, has so decreed. From Machiavelli's moral perspective, nothing is wrong or right until some human choice—or volitional act—has made it so.

Like Hobbes and Locke (but not Rousseau), Machiavelli believed that human life without obligations was inconvenient at best and intolerable at worst—"poor, nasty, brutish, solitary, and short," as Hobbes put it.[27] Because corruption was a condition that was without obligations and unquestionably evil, Machiavelli was not a moral relativist but a moral reformer, one who sought to improve upon existing moralities by creating a newer one. From this more modern perspective, the obligation to remain faithful to one's spouse (to take one example) is not an obligation imposed by a god or nature (whether whimsical or rational) but an obligation one creates for oneself in making a pledge of fidelity. In other words, this modern voluntarist perspective would require no divine plan preordaining that any individual be faithful to a spouse in order to recognize an obligation to do so. The obligation would not be seen as originating in an act of God but in a person's decision, at a point of time, that life could be made fuller and more rewarding by making and keeping such a pledge.

For Machiavelli, moral truth does not exist as a metaphysical chimera; it is instead an intensely social reality, contingent upon certain empirical conditions in which people find themselves. In this respect, his morality is distinct from the prevailing morality that he sought to reform. In contrast to that prevailing morality (Christian and absolutist), he had a dual vision of our moral obligations: in lawful societies, he recognized our duty to obey the laws; but, in conditions of corruption where no such duties have yet been created, he believed that one should seek the highest good of lawful, civilized life (*gloria,* understood as noble freedom under laws of our own making in a republic). If his belief about the duty to obey law in a properly constituted republic seems similar to the deontology of Kant or Locke, the other dimension of his moral philosophy contains distinct similarities to Mill's utilitarianism. ("Deontology" is a moral belief that an action is required if morally right and prohibited if morally wrong, regardless of consequences; consequentialism is its opposite, a belief that the good consequences of an action make it obligatory while bad consequences require its prohibition.) If humans have legislatively defined right/wrong, then we must abide by this reckoning; if they have not yet done so, then we must "seek glory" by pursuing the goals of freedom and civilization. But even before civilization, even before we have created laws defining right from wrong, the importance of freedom and civilization to humans place moral requirements upon us. This implies that Machiavelli's

theory was a complex of at least two accounts of our moral obligations: on the one hand, a democratic people has a moral obligation
to obey the laws it freely makes for itself (a fusion of deontology
and voluntarism) while, on the other hand, the values of civilization
and freedom place moral requirements upon us even in the absence
of laws (teleology) so that actions taken in the absence of laws will
be judged by their consequences. Moral evaluation, then, is always
of a conditional sort: if one set of conditions obtains, one's obligations
are to do X but if another set obtains, then one's obligations are to
do not-X.

Machiavelli is indeed explicit that our moral obligations depend
upon whether we live in corruption or glory, the empirical conditions
of our social existence. First, in the context of discussing the successes of Manlius Capitolinus, Machiavelli wrote that those who
seek glory must attend to the complexity of empirical circumstances:
"in a corrupt city men have to seek glory in other ways than they
do in a city still living in accord with law . . .; [and] men in their
conduct, and so much the more in their great actions, ought to think
of the times and adapt themselves to them" (*Discourses* 3:8).

Manlius Capitolinus, like Romulus, judged empirical circumstances correctly and won eternal praise. Agathocles failed to do so
(having mastered the acts of the lion and the fox, as necessary, he
never moved to the higher mode, seeking glory when possible), and
he won condemnation. Making appropriate empirical judgments is
essential, then, to acting correctly from a moral point of view since
moral obligations are not eternal and immutable, but are conditioned by empirical reality.

Second, Machiavelli supported this voluntarist view with empirical observations of political and historical events. What would at
first seem to be good for all times and circumstances turns out to be
not so good at a later, different, time. There can thus be no eternal
standard of what is good. For example, "Cesare Borgia was considered cruel, but his cruelty had brought order to the Romagna,
united it, and reduced it to peace and fealty" (*Prince*, chapter 17).
In fact, when all is considered, his sort of cruelty is to be preferred
to the false sense in which the Florentines were "merciful" to the
Pistoians, who suffered incredibly under such "kind" mercy.

Hence, a prince "must not mind incurring the charge of cruelty
for the purpose of keeping his subjects united and faithful; for, with
a very few examples, he will be more merciful than those who, from
excess of tenderness, allow disorders to arise, from whence spring
bloodshed and rapine . . ." (ibid.). If cruelty is necessary to preserve
law and order, one must not flinch from being cruel, since it is more

cruel to be tender and thereby destroy the lawful foundations of civilized life.

So it is that in good conditions—i.e., of human lawfulness—"the best fortress is to be found in the love of the people" (ibid., chapter 20), but when conditions are such that one cannot be loved and feared simultaneously (i.e., when humans are corrupt), "it is much safer to be feared than loved . . ." (ibid., chapter 17). A single, rationalist principle in the form "always do X" ("always be loved by the people" or "always be feared by the people") simply is not adequate to the complexity of choices in our empirical reality. The complexity of real life imposes upon us the necessity for a multitude of principles, all of them in conditional ("if X, then Y") form.

Hence, what is most necessary is recognizing the differences in historical situations and responding appropriately: "This brings us to two important considerations: the first, that the means of attaining glory are different in a republic that is corrupt from what they are in a republic that still preserves its institutions pure; and the second, (which is in a measure comprised in the first), that men in their conduct, and especially in their most prominent actions, should well consider and conform to the times in which they live" (*Discourses* 3:8).

Politics can be turned to glorious ends, if political actors attend carefully to the circumstances in which they are called upon to act. Failing to notice differences brings ruin.

This passage also enables us to resolve an apparent—but not real—ambivalence noted by Pitkin in Machiavelli's writings about the need of a military leader to be either harsh or kind. Sometimes, Pitkin notes in *Fortune Is a Woman,* he praises leaders for their cruelty; at other times, he praises leaders who can win loyalty of their troops by kindness. "He attempts to resolve the apparent contradiction by distinguishing: the crucial variable, he suggests, is the commander's status vis-à-vis his troops. If the soldiers are his comrades and equals, temporarily under his command, he must be kind; but if he is dealing with 'subjects,' with 'the multitude,' then harshness is called for" (74). But Pitkin is aware that this simple formulation of Machiavelli's meaning does not describe adequately the complexity of his views. Turning to the passage in which Machiavelli praised Hannibal's harshness and cruelty, Pitkin comes to a second formulation: "Again, he appears to resolve the dilemma, asserting that method does not matter compared with *virtù.* . . ." As satisfying as this formulation is, it is inconsistent with the fact that Machiavelli was a political scientist very attentive to method. Attacking the subject a third time, Pitkin tries a last formula (actually the opposite of the first): "harshness like that of Manlius Torquatus is best in a republic, for it imposes discipline, can be used to renew public spirit, and cannot even be suspected of currying favor with some faction for private gain. Kindness, by contrast, is profitable to a prince because it will win him the loyalty of the army; such personal loyalty to a commander would be suspect in a republic but is beneficial to a prince. And there the matter is left, except, of course, that this conclusion contradicts both the doctrine of *The Prince*, that it is safer for a prince to be feared than loved, and the doctrine in both works that armies must be harshly governed" (ibid., 74).

But there is no ambivalence in Machiavelli's text: sometimes harshness is necessary in both republics and principalities, and it is certainly tied to the possession of *virtù*. The key variable, it seems, is corruption; corruption is the context in which *virtù* is most necessary and it can require harshness. Paying attention to one's empirical situation allows one to determine whether conditions are corrupt; in a civilized society, the man of virtù can obey the laws most of the time. It is only when conditions are corrupt that a prince need not keep faith and is otherwise free to perform terrible actions. Similarly, military commanders must be considerably harsher when dealing with corrupted troops than when dealing with honorable warriors.

Similarly, Machiavelli's advice to a prince about the use/abuse of cruelties must be construed as a conditional imperative; if and only if a state is in a condition of depravity, a leader must be cruel. Machiavelli is explicit that this advice applies only to leaders acting to end corruption; discussing the differences in the fates of cruel leaders, he writes that "I believe this comes from cruelties badly used or well used. *Well used* we call those (if of what is bad we can use the word well) that a conqueror carries out at a single stroke, as a result of his need to secure himself, and then does not persist in, but transmutes into the greatest possible benefits to his subjects. *Badly used* are those which, though few in the beginning, rather increase with time than disappear" (*Prince*, chapter 10).

Cruelties that serve efficiently to establish modern states and civilize their populations are well committed; bad cruelties are those that do not so serve. When there is a cancer upon the body politic, swift and decisive surgical action is required, and there will be only moral praise for it.

This is why a conqueror, in taking a state, must determine exactly which actions are required to secure his regime and

> does them all at once, so that he need not repeat them every day, because, not repeating them, he makes men feel secure, and gains their

support by treating them well. He who acts otherwise, through either timidity or bad advice, is obliged always to hold his sword in his hand; he can never rely on his subjects, and they, because of fresh and continual injuries, cannot feel secure. Injuries are to be done all together, so that, being savored less, they will anger less; benefits are to be conferred little by little, so they will be savored more. (ibid., chapter 8)

The abuse of cruelties, as well as the inability to employ them as a kind of precise surgical removal of a growth upon the body politic, is a mark of a ruler unwilling to exercise *virtù,* unwilling to bend fortuna to his/her ends, or a prince with the wrong ends (like Agathocles whose ends were other than glory)—ultimately, a mark of a prince ruined.[28]

Finally, as we have seen, even the "sin" of fratricide, of which Romulus was ostensibly guilty, is not wrong under certain circumstances. Not only does the end of founding a free republic exonerate him, but the conditions under which he acted made it clear that society had not yet been constituted, right and wrong had not yet been legislated, and therefore nothing could be considered wrong. Rather, like their lupine surrogate mother, the brothers were existing in a presocial condition where nothing need be right or wrong. If humans had not yet made laws prohibiting murder, by what standard is it wrong? If humanism is a belief that humans are the standard of all that is good, Machiavelli's humanism committed him to the belief that there could be no divine standards making actions wrong.

In other words, Romulus and Remus were living in a kind of Hobbesian state of nature or a Lockean state of war, where society had not yet been constituted and people failed to live up to the obligations that would be incumbent upon them in other circumstances. Can anyone be guilty of wrong under these circumstances? Is there any wrong before laws defining right and wrong are made?

This should not, however, lead us to conclude that Machiavelli was a moral nihilist. He displayed contempt for conventional moralities—he was not one to hide his contempt—but this must not blind us to the very real respect he had for morality and even religion. His introduction to chapter 18 of *The Prince,* in which he considers the ways in which a prince must keep faith, is a classic illustration of this healthy respect for moral compunctions: "How praiseworthy a prince is who keeps good faith and lives with sincerity and not with trickery, everybody realizes." Since we have already examined this passage in some detail, we need only note here that it is only in corrupt times that one has no obligation to keep faith; otherwise, one should abide by the dictates of morality. This rule obviously admits of exceptions, and Machiavelli is realist enough to attend to the exceptions: "Still the experience of our times shows those princes to have done great things who have had little regard for good faith. . . ." So, we must conclude that not keeping faith is the exception to the rule, not the rule.

VOLUNTARISM AND LEGAL POSITIVISM

Defending Machiavelli's voluntarism, unlike attacking it, apologizing for it, or explaining it away, requires making a plausible case for that voluntarism. But proving beyond any rational doubt that moral voluntarism is superior to rationalism would be far beyond any rational expectation; if two thousand years of philosophical reflection have not removed doubts about this, this short book is not likely to do so either. Fortunately, the positivist tradition in jurisprudence or legal philosophy does, however, provide a guide in the search for a plausible defense of Machiavelli's voluntarism.

Like Machiavelli, theorists of this jurisprudential tradition deny the existence of any law of nature, recognizing as laws only "positive" systems of law, only concretely existing statutes. Positivism is for law what voluntarism is for morals: the modern, empiricist alternative to the rationalist doctrines of yore. And it confronts a similar difficulty: if there are no "higher" laws of nature or god, we seem to be unable to judge the validity of existing systems of law. In morals, the parallel concern is: if there is no single, highest morality, given by god or nature, we seem unable to judge the validity of existing moral systems.

For example, if we abandon the belief in eternal laws, it seems difficult to criticize a law (or a system of laws) for not being what it should be, and it becomes hard to condemn "injustices" that might not be "really" unjust. Attending to the empirical "is" seems to blind us to the rational "ought." Without the eternal laws of nature or god, can we say that Nazi (or any other) laws were defective? Without eternal moral truths, can we claim that laws permitting slavery, although they existed, were wrong?

H. L. A. Hart is one of this century's most articulate, rigorous, and famous proponents of positivism. Like Machiavelli, he is forced by the logic of his position to confront this question: does voluntarism require that there are no higher standards by which we can judge a legal system invalid? Is a system valid if no one abides by its rules?

Although in his text Hart does not use the word "corruption" to describe the phenomenon, his questions from the "positive law" perspective about the possibility of judging a legal system "valid" are similar to Machiavelli's.

> From the inefficacy of a particular rule, which may or may not count against its validity, we must distinguish a general disregard of the rules of the system. This may be so complete in character and so protracted that we should say, in the case of a new system, that it had never established itself as the legal system of a given group, or, in the case of a once-established system, that it had ceased to be the legal system of the group. . . . In such cases it would be generally pointless either to assess the rights and duties of particular persons by reference to the primary rules of a system or to assess the validity of any of its rules by reference to its rules of recognition. To insist on applying a system of rules which had either never actually been effective or had been discarded would, except in special circumstances . . . be as futile as to assess the progress of a game by reference to a scoring rule which had never been accepted or had been discarded.[29]

Construing all laws upon the model of rules of a game, Hart argues that their validity is not to be found in some abstract, rationalist model but in concrete observations of applicability.

Like Machiavelli, Hart believes that the obligations (say) of the president of the United States alter when legal systems supplant one another. In this (political) sense, the duties and obligations of the chief executive of the country were different under the Articles of Confederation from those under the Constitution of 1789. But one need not posit the existence of a natural law or a perspective of eternity to judge the Constitution preferable to the Articles of Confederation. It is enough to examine the various reasons put forward by the drafters of the newer constitution, as in the *Federalist Papers,* to understand why the newer document was preferred. This preference, a kind of moral valuing, is rooted solely in concrete historical circumstances and theoretical perspectives on politics, not in any transcendental beings or entities. Moral valuation, for Machiavelli, becomes conditional rather than eternally and immutably set by a nonhuman standard. So, *if* you accept Madison's assumptions about human nature and *if* you desire a stronger union, *then* you should favor the 1789 document over its predecessor.[30]

Or, in another example, deciding which team in professional football has a "right" to a particular round's draft pick is not arbitrary. Yet it is also not defined by divine rules. Rather, particular legislative enactments of the NFL define this right. Indeed, these enactments are the rules constitutive of the "draft." But if all the teams refuse to establish such rules, or refuse to recognize their validity, no appeal to the Laws of Nature can rectify the situation. In this situation, the rule, simply, has become invalid, or, according to the Machiavellian vocabulary, "corrupt."

Applying this to the perspective of quattrocento Italy, we might note that, since there are no laws in a corrupt state, there are no standards for evaluating actions, and consequently neither right nor wrong exists (i.e., there are "no reasons" for a person to be bound). Whatever one does is neither right nor wrong; it is only conducive, or not conducive, to glory. (Of course, by implication, there are also no natural rights.) Simply, there are no natural, eternal standards nor natural rights to guide our way. In the absence of eternal assurances that our way is the "right way," we must rely upon ourselves and define what is an appropriate way to live. Nothing that one does can be judged right or wrong in such conditions; the only obligation one has is to seek glory in the appropriate (if necessary, even bestial) way.

Hence, it is not the case that Machiavelli creates an additional (political) standard for judging the actions of princes. Rather, he has recognized that, in some conditions, there are *no* moral standards and we must create them to make civilized and social life possible. In such corrupt circumstances, the only question is whether the agent has sought glory effectively. In this respect, his position on morals is akin to the positivist perspective on law.

Of course, the problem with Hart's metaphor (and for Machiavelli's position) is exactly that politics may not be like a game; at least, it may be the case that we have no choice but to play. We may be impelled, as Aristotle suggested, with a kind of "natural" necessity, to live together.[31] There is much that is attractive about a view of politics as "natural" to the human species. It affords us, at least, with a sense of significance and with a degree of moral certainty.

But, unfortunately, one must make a series of premodern, Aristotelian, assumptions of a natural order to reality to reject the game metaphor: if politics is not an artificial game, then it must be "natural" to humans.[32] If we are by nature political, then obligations may apply even prior to our choosing to "play the game." When Aristotle wrote that "man is, by nature, a political animal,"[33] he meant that people, like all natural objects, have a principle of motion within them.[34] As natural beings, we have a "final cause" or *telos* that impels us toward our natural resting place. Since the distinctive human *telos* is virtue, we are naturally pulled to virtue.[35] Finally, since the *polis* is the place in which human virtue can be made to exist, we are naturally drawn from the household (*oeconomia;* where production occurs) to the market (*agora*) and then up to the *polis.* Since the very nature of our being draws us to this activity, it is inhuman to exist apart from it. Hence, we have no choice but to play the political game, and there is no escaping the obligations that come from playing.

This argument is undoubtedly one reason why Strauss finds fault with the modern rejection of the ancient ideas of natural right. But to make the rationalist objection against Machiavelli (and other voluntarists, like positivists) stand, one would have to establish beyond any reasonable doubt many metaphysical claims—like natural teleology (the belief that everything in nature has a purpose or *telos*)— whose truth is open to doubt for most moderns and whose spirit is alien, even hostile, to the ethos of modernity and of empirical science.

In line with Renaissance humanism in general, and Machiavelli in particular, instead of seeking an abstract rationalist morality, we should assess the strengths and weaknesses of existing, positive moralities. Those conducive to human *gloria* should be judged good moralities, while those tending to corruption and dishonor earn "universal execration" (*Discourses,* 1:10; Ricci–Vincent, 141). Not all moral systems are equally good from his perspective; some deserve condemnation. Only those moralities that can be renewed will survive for any time, but none is eternal and above human volition. All moralities are human creations or conventions.

A RESPONSE TO MACHIAVELLI'S CRITICS

To complete this defense of Machiavelli's views, several barriers to a proper understanding of his accomplishment must be removed. These barriers are considerable, for weighty reasons along with powerful images support his opponents. First, in offering certainty, rationalist doctrines possess a strong emotional appeal. Second, a strong image continues to support the idea that Machiavelli deserves to be called a "teacher of evil." Third, the "disturbance" caused by Machiavelli's morals will be seen by others as a "horror," and that horror must be defused. Fourth, his morality might prove not to be modern after all, but to constitute a type of anachronistic throwback to Homerian conceptions of virtue. Finally, the appearance that the modern belief in voluntarism might culminate in nihilism and relativism must be dispelled. When these and other concerns are laid to rest, it becomes easier to accept the Machiavellian insights.

Moral Appeal of Rationalism

Perhaps the moral disturbance that Machiavelli evokes is a natural reaction against the rejection of rationalism implicit in the secular humanism emerging in Renaissance thought. As we (Westerners) began to think of the world in less theocentric terms, the role of human choice expanded in the realms of action and knowledge, logically moving to human choices about morality (about what is of value, about what is right or wrong). But for the religious consciousness of the medieval period, this perspective is profoundly disquieting. If God views a thing as wrong, how can mere humans declare it right? Yet modern voluntarism professes exactly the opposite of such consciousness, positing instead that values and principles are of human, not divine, origin.

Nor is the "older" consciousness merely a thing of the past; the challenge of Machiavellianism rankles among at least some of us modern Westerners even today. The tradition of natural law offers at least one major psychic payoff of tremendous magnitude: moral certainty. If God has decreed that murder (or anything) is wrong, then it clearly and eternally is wrong.[36] An easy way to end moral debate and confusion about abortion or health care, for instance, would be to "discover" a law of nature that prohibits or requires either policy. Hence, moral rationalism appears to offer moral certainty, and we seem to need it.

The resistance of so many religious Westerners to the modern (voluntarist) view is natural since, given socialization patterns in Western civilization, we tend to fear that if there is no God (or if there are no divine, eternal commandments), then nothing is "really" bad/wrong. In short, many of us have been taught that, since God makes natural and eternal laws, rejecting a belief in the divine origin of obligations necessarily leads to an end to moral certainty.

Nevertheless, our desire for moral certainty may tempt us to error. As Isaiah Berlin has argued, "Indeed, the very desire for guarantees that our values are eternal and secure in some objective heaven is perhaps only a craving for the certainties of childhood or the absolute values of our primitive past. . . . To demand more than this is perhaps a deep and incurable metaphysical need; but to allow it to determine one's practice is a symptom of an equally deep, and more dangerous, moral and political immaturity."[37] The reaction to

Machiavelli's moral theory is evidence that Berlin was right about our cravings.

Despite his attempts to save us from such "moral and political immaturity," Machiavelli continues to suffer a bad reputation. Since the image of Machiavelli as "a teacher of evil" continues to evoke associations with Strauss's book (which probably remains the single most influential and famous work on Machiavelli in English), this negative image remains associated (though not exclusively) with his tradition. In Strauss's depiction of him, Machiavelli was a rabidly anti-Christian thinker who corrupted modern thought by teaching that the traditional values of the medieval and ancient traditions— especially natural law, as in Cicero and Aquinas—are not the eternal verities they appear to be.

Other Straussians see Machiavelli as an inspiration for the "empirical" political scientists who look to him as a symbol of the "liberation" of politics as an autonomous activity from the constraints of religious morals.[38] This, in turn, leads others to depict Straussians like Mansfield as finding Machiavelli "right where Straussians have always found him, in the text, goading modern man into a conspiracy against Christian and classical virtue."[39] Further, Straussians tend to sense (and deplore) the absence of a sense of "soul" in this theory, claiming that this absence entails that "there could be no universal principle *beyond* one's country,"[40] implying that Machiavelli recognized no higher moral requirements and so was committed to moral relativism, a belief we have already refuted.

The "Horror" of Machiavelli's Standards

Even Machiavelli's defenders find his moral doctrine repugnant. For example, Vilari, in his nineteenth-century classic, *The Life and Times of Niccolo Machiavelli,* accurately depicts him as a patriot and nationalist committed to freedom in a democratic republic, and he is glad that Machiavelli's time for "justice to be done"[41] had at last arrived. But he too rejects Machiavelli's moral theory as fundamentally flawed:

> He never puts himself the question: whether the excessive immorality of the means employed, may not, even while momentarily grasping the desired end, sap the very foundations of society, and render in the long run all good and strong government an impossibility. He forgets to inquire whether, just as there is a private morality, there may not be also a social and political morality, imposing certain inviolable limits, and furnishing rules for the statesman's conduct, which, although varying with the times and different social conditions, are yet equally subject to righteous principles. This is the weak and fallacious side of his doctrine;

that which disgusts us with its author, arouses our horror, and has been a perennial source of accusation and calumny.[42]

While Vilari raises some interesting moral points concerning the corruptive potential of evil means to good ends and the limits of creative power, to which we shall return later,[43] still his "disgust" blinds him to a portion of reality: in our moral commitment to the ideals of democracy, we run the danger of ignoring the threats to democracy coming from arenas where such moral compunctions will not limit actions. In practice, Vilari's "morality" may cripple a democratic regime in dealing with its less moral adversaries.

So Vilari depicts Machiavelli as guilty of proposing a standard of evaluating action so different from, and so much more lenient than, that of conventional morality that it permits a prince to do almost anything. In this sense, his Machiavelli is like that of the Straussians' in "separating" politics and morals, or creating two distinct standards for judging human exertions. The conventional moral standard is meant for common folk in their private lives while the other, the extraordinary political standard, is applicable to the actions of statesmen in the public arena. The latter would excuse much that the earlier would condemn.

Thus, despite all of his approval of Machiavelli's political insights, Vilari ultimately agrees with the Straussians about his morals: Machiavelli's theory is "horrid" because he recognizes no eternal standards to regulate political behavior, because he opposes the rationalist natural law doctrines of an earlier time.[44] It must be kept in mind, though, that while a) Machiavelli did divide moral judgment into two realms and b) there is much force to the criticisms of his morality, it is questionable that he ever meant for the public and private to be those realms. From the perspective of Machiavelli's theory, whether one is dealing with the private or the public realm, one's moral obligations are radically different when dealing with a corrupt as opposed to a civilized people. Hence, the central duality in Machiavelli's theory is the corrupt/noble divide rather than the public/private divide, and Vilari was wrong to deplore a mistake that was not present in the theory.

Machiavelli as an Anachronism

Even when an analyst like Terence Ball begins to approach Machiavelli's moral theory by noting that it "used to be fashionable to say that Machiavelli was immoral, or at any rate amoral; but now it is more fashionable—and arguably more accurate—to suggest that he did in fact subscribe to a system of morality,"[45] Machiavelli's morality is still a target for unfair criticism. While there is much that is disturbing and wrong in Machiavelli's moral philosophy, Ball also criticizes him for errors that are not his, ignoring Machiavelli's modernism and voluntarism and depicting him as an anachronistic throwback to a discredited moral theory, a believer in an older morality not at home in the modern world: "My claim is that Machiavellian *virtù* shares some crucial affinities with the older Homeric conception of virtue. In attempting to reinstate something like this archaic conception of virtue, Machiavelli's model prince rather resembles Don Quixote. For both are alike in failing to recognize the mutability of our moral concepts. From this perspective Machiavelli emerges as a misguided moralist from whose mistakes we might yet learn something about morality, and about moral change in particular."[46]

For all the justifiable parallels between Homeric and Machiavellian moralities, the comparison with Don Quixote remains strangely off-key. Since Machiavelli did recognize the mutability of our moral concepts (his plays are all about the changing of human values, and his claim that no one value system is eternal is exactly what offends the Straussians), he could be no such tilter at windmills. Rather than a feudal soul lost in a bourgeois and nationalist era, he was perfectly at home in the new era and devoted his life to opposing the corruptive ambition of the throwbacks to feudal aristocracy. He is also one of the first to become aware of the emergence of the new commercial era and of the need to adapt our actions to this new world. Thus, he is not regressing to an earlier ethic that no longer has any place in the modern world, but searching to articulate an ethical theory for the modern world. However, this commitment to modernity (i.e., to empiricism and moral voluntarism) did not make of him a nihilist nor a relativist.

The Machiavellian Alternative to Nihilism and Relativism

Finally, defending Machiavelli as a proponent of a newer, more modern morality also requires anticipating certain other objections to moral voluntarism. There are indeed dangers in this modern approach to morality, some stereotypical and some real. Stereotypically, a voluntarist can avoid neither nihilism nor relativism, and both are errors. While neither is quite the evil it first appears to be, a refutation of them is outside the scope of my argument. The important point here is that Machiavelli is guilty of neither.

Let us first examine the assertion that Machiavelli is a "relativist."

Stereotypically associated with anthropological and sociological research aimed at understanding cultural variety, relativism is a belief that any existing morality is as "good" or as "valid" as any other. It is futile, if this view is correct, to try to ascertain whether British or Japanese morals are "really right." Each is thought to perform some socially desirable function for its respective society, and there is no need to view either from the perspective of eternity or any particular God. One should simply live in accordance with the norms of one's own society: while in Rome, do as the Romans do.

The nihilist simply goes a bit further, casting doubt upon the validity even of existing norms and moralities. According to the caricature foisted upon Nietzsche, no morality has any hold upon us. We are simply free to do as we choose, to forge any goals for our lives as we choose. If God is dead, then all is permitted.

Whatever the merits of these two views when not so caricaturized, we pause now only to establish that Machiavelli was not committed to either belief. When considered as an integral whole, Machiavelli's writings simply preclude both interpretations. Of course, given his historical circumstances, Machiavelli did not expressly address these moral alternatives; but one can show that it would have been contradictory for him to subscribe to these doctrines.

Let us begin by noting certain Machiavellian preferences: he believed too much in the importance of morality and in certain civilizing values to subscribe to strict relativism; because life is better after the creation of obligations, we have strong incentives to create them. No one is "too wise or too foolish" to miss this basic moral truth (*Discourses*, 1:10).

Machiavelli's own observations and assumptions about human nature can be used as premises:

1. we rarely know all that is necessary for fully rational decisions (*Prince*, chapter 21; *Discourses*, 1:6);
2. unless restrained by good laws, we typically seek our own self-interest without regard for the rights and interests of others, even with cunning and duplicity (*Discourses*, 1:3);
3. we typically prefer to enjoy the fruits of our labor in security (*Discourses*, 2:2);
4. if security is "purchased" by assuming obligations, we usually prefer to assume our own obligations over having obligations imposed upon us—i. e., we humans prefer freedom over slavery, but law and order over insecurity (*Prince*, chapters 5, 8, and 17).

Machiavelli would have had to repudiate some of these convictions to have been a consistent relativist. Strict relativism, the belief that all moralities are equally valid, would require that we not condemn, say, the disciples of Marquis de Sade, because they hold their beliefs sincerely, and small societies could exist where these values might become the norm. Strict relativism is consistent with, but not required by, Machiavelli's first assumption about our limited rationality. It could also coexist, albeit unhappily, with the third assumption (about our preference for security). But strict relativism is inconsistent with Machiavelli's second and fourth assumptions. If, as Machiavelli posits, humans pursue their interests with cunning and without regard to the interests of others, and if humans prefer security, then humans will need protections from one another. This is because unrestrained and cunning pursuit of self-interest by one agent renders others insecure. The resulting need for protections implies that a morality must secure persons by imposing obligations to protect us from one another or it would not be a valid morality. A sadistic morality, or one permitting slavery, would be acceptable to a consistent relativist, but not to Machiavelli. Similarly, the fourth assumption (preference for the freedom to choose obligations) precludes some moralities that a consistent relativist would have to accept. If this assumption about human nature is accurate, then only moralities with adequate provisions for glory would count as legitimate moral systems to Machiavelli. Consequently, he cannot be a relativist.

If nihilism is the belief that there are no valid moral obligations, it is consistent enough with the first two Machiavellian assumptions; but it clearly violates the last two conditions. A nihilist might well agree with Machiavelli that humans rarely know what is good, and that human actions rarely are good. But a nihilist of the caricature would have to oppose the Machiavellian assumptions of the need for security and liberty. The need for security seems to require a moral system of one sort or another; in particular, the need to enjoy the fruits of one's own labor seems to require a morality with property rights (or some moral equivalent). Similarly, the human need for liberty seems to imply that any form of life that deprives humans of this need is not adequate to humanity's needs. In short, Machiavelli is advocating a challenging moral doctrine, but it does not fit of the caricatures of relativism and nihilism.[47]

CONCLUSION

We should also note in conclusion that these same assumptions about human nature, born of an empiricist appreciation of human frailty, are likely the cause of Machiavelli's rejection of natural law doctrines. First, to be valid, natural law doctrines require that humans know something (the eternal standards of right and wrong) that corrupt humans do not, as a matter of fact, seem to know. Similarly, unless natural law doctrines become natural rights doctrines (like Locke's), they do not accord enough recognition to the human need to be free, failing to appreciate the significance of Machiavelli's fourth assumption. The psychological reality of our humanity precludes certain kinds of morality for Machiavelli; the rationalist moralities of the Romans and of contemporary Christians were not adequate either to our perversity or to our nobility. But while Machiavelli was opposed to these moralities, he was not opposed to the idea of morality.

Understanding Machiavelli's moral theory as an instance of voluntarism precludes a number of erroneous interpretations. Seen in this light, his theory is also a plausible alternative to the rationalism of the natural law tradition that Machiavelli opposed. Distinct from both relativism and nihilism, voluntarism provides a way of discerning that a necessary action may be morally permissible prior to civilized living but morally reprehensible under other circumstances.

Now we need to examine the possibility that, prior to the civilizing act of legislating, certain moral values demand certain courses of action from us. Even in the absence of moral obligations, a moral person may still find that certain values are sufficiently pressing as to require that we act in a virtuous way. To this logical possibility we now direct our attention.

4

The End Justifies the Means—in Corruption

GENERAL PERSPECTIVE

Gɪᴠᴇɴ that Machiavelli believed that we have no obligations prior to the act of legislating, it would have been easy for him to infer that "everything goes." This temptation to relativism, to the belief that there are no true moral obligations, is blocked, however, by other insights he articulated in his writings. While he may have maintained that our duties under law are human creations, he also posited the existence of objective moral values, and he offered original insights into the two types of moral systems generally recognized by moral philosophers.

These systems can be categorized as consequentialist and deontological. *Deontological* systems are based on our "duty" or "obligation" to perform an action, given a moral axiom or principle. By contrast, *consequential* systems evaluate our actions by reference to their consequences or the goals at which they aim. In the last chapter, we examined Machiavelli's beliefs that deontological systems are created by human decisions and legislating; as we will now see, a consequential system is viable even in the absence of deontological systems.

Indeed, Machiavelli clearly proposes a theory of the "good" that applies even in corrupt conditions, where there are no principles nor duties. This vision of what is morally good is rooted in human nature, it is "good for humans," and it is tied to the values of civilization. Oversimplified, it is an assertion that all persons are objectively better off when living within a civilized community and that none are too blind to see this objective value (*Discourses*, 1:10). Since our actions are not all neutral in relation to this value, with some advancing civilization and others inhibiting it, we find a different kind of call to moral virtue under corrupt circumstances than under nobler ones. If, in nobility, we seek the goal of glory by obeying laws and "being moral" or "fighting" by the methods "of the law"

(*Prince,* chapter 18), then, in corruption, other methods recommend themselves. The moral value of civilization, then, may beckon to us to act in different ways; if we respond to that invitation in corruption and are successful in reaching the goal of civilizing people, all will praise us. As Machiavelli commented on Piero Soderini, chief executive of the republic who refused to move against the Medici when they threatened freedom, "he should have borne in mind, that as his acts and motives would have to be judged by the result, in case he had been fortunate enough to succeed and live, everybody would have attested that what he had done was for the good of his country, and not for the advancement of any ambitious purposes of his own" (*Discourses,* 3:3).

Most importantly, Machiavelli is passing moral judgment in this passage, not denying the applicability of moral criteria. Some great moral goal, which was tied to the "good of his country," called Soderini to act to preserve freedom and law; but that goal required actions deemed "immoral" by the prevailing morality of the day.

Indeed, true morality dictates to a prudent ruler certain actions, based on civilizing values; when no socially established morality limits people, when other people are not moral, a good leader will "reduce" his/her subjects to "peace and fealty," as Cesare Borgia did for Romagna (*Prince,* chapter 17). Hence, even when others are immoral, one is not free morally to pursue any course of action. Even in the depravity of corruption, moral beacons call to us, drawing us to noble actions; it was this that Agathocles could not see. The fact that we must approach these goals in ways different from those that we would otherwise use should not blind us to the fact that moral evaluation retains an important role in depravity.

One may thus face moral requirements in corrupt circumstances (like seeking the consequential goal of glory), but these are neither the obligations of conventional morality nor of an eternal law. In fact, in citing the case of Romulus, another half-bestial man, Machiavelli was describing his notion of these moral requirements: when in depraved and corrupt circumstances where others recognize no moral obligations, one's most important moral duty is to survive so as to create moral duties, to unify the polity and constitute it lawfully in accordance with the needs of civilizing modernity. Even fratricide can be excused under these circumstances, since it has not yet "become" wrong by human decree.

But there is no reason to suppose that Machiavelli would render a similar judgment of fratricide *after* Numa "reduced" the Romans to lawful civility. Similarly, conventional morality and its familial obligations cannot prevent a Brutus from performing his duty to reconstitute Rome as a republic, because the accomplishment of Numa was reversed by the corruption of succeeding kings. The rape of Lucretia and her inability to get justice are but evidence of this corruption. But to kill one's sons simply to gain power, without the republican vision of *gloria,* is a kind of sport that would make of you an Agathocles, not a Brutus.

Given this voluntarist picture of his moral theory, it is too simplistic and even wrong to claim that Machiavelli is suggesting that we "liberate" politics from morality or that it is guided by different standards of evaluation, as Mansfield contends. Rather, it is corruption, and not the messenger who chronicles it, that "liberates" one from moral obligations. Sometimes one has no obligations; at others, even conventional morality is binding. We must then conclude that Machiavelli is suggesting that no single moral standard is adequate to the empirical complexity of moral choice.

Thus, it is not the case that Brutus is acting under different moral rules because he is a politician. Rather, it is because the Tarquin monarchs had failed to maintain the laws and because Rome had become corrupted that the social foundations of conventional morality had been destroyed. Since universally applicable eternal principles are not to be found and conventional moral rules no longer apply, one is left to calculate the consequences of one's actions and to calculate how best to civilize a people. Machiavelli puts this most bluntly in *The Prince:* "in the actions of men, and especially of princes, from which there is no appeal, the end justifies the means" (chapter 18). In the context of corruption, in the absence of a viable morality or prior to civilization, this precept that the end justifies the means to it is valid; in other circumstances, one must seek *gloria* in other ways.

In the absence, then, of the social institutions that define our obligations, our first duty is to survive—by whatever means necessary—and then to constitute social order by legislating wisely, by achieving glory. Under corrupt circumstances, *gloria* is to be found in this, and this alone: creating the material and social conditions for civilizing modernity and democratic freedom. As we have seen, there is a need to move beyond the mere search for power to the quest for glory. In other words, while one has no obligations in corrupt circumstances, the existence of these values still requires that we then seek glory in an appropriate way. More precisely, one's obligations in corruption are defined by the consequences of one's actions rather than by principles of law, whether human or divine. Should one achieve *gloria* and survive, everyone will remember the achievement and forget the means employed to get there.

Overlooking the difference between Romulus, praised for his quest for glory, and Agathocles, condemned for his ambition, leads to a common but erroneous depiction of Machiavelli urging the maintenance or acquisition of power at whatever cost. In considering bestiality, liberality, mercy, and fear in government, even Quentin Skinner, who comes so close to getting Machiavelli's economics right, concludes that a prince will see that being criticized from the perspective of conventional morality is "merely an unavoidable cost he has to bear in the course of discharging his fundamental obligation, which is of course to maintain his state."[1]

But Machiavelli's advice to princes is more complex than this; from his voluntarist perspective, a commitment to true values, like civilization, requires that a prince must legislate in conditions of corruption, creating our moral obligations. Such a prince has no obligation to abide by conventional morality and, from the humanist perspective, there is no higher morality. But he is not simply free to do whatever strikes his fancy, arbitrarily. Given that humans are capable of corruption and of glory, human needs (including, in particular, the human need for the security of civilized life) begin to define our obligations in the absence of laws. Since humans need the discipline of law, one must legislate; since humans need to be free, one must seek the glory of republican nobility; since humans need a more civilized way of life, one must begin to build it.

Indeed, Machiavelli has clearly set priorities for moral evaluations, and they are strongly conditioned by his dedication to the goal of civilized glory:

> Of all men who have been eulogized, those deserve it most who have been the authors and founders of religions; next come such as have established republics or kingdoms. . . . On the contrary, those are doomed to infamy and universal execration who have destroyed religions, who have overturned republics and kingdoms, who are enemies of virtue, of letters, and of every art that is useful and honorable to mankind. Such are the impious and violent, the ignorant, the idle, the vile and degraded. And there are none so foolish or so wise, none so wicked or so good, that, in choosing between these two qualities, they do not praise what is praiseworthy and blame that which deserves blame. (*Discourses*, 1:10; Ricci–Vincent, 141–42)

Glory, itself, is justified by reference to the consequences: "In free countries we also see wealth increase more rapidly, both that which results from the culture of the soil and that which is produced by industry and art; for everybody gladly multiplies those things, and seeks to acquire those goods the possession of which he can tranquilly enjoy. Thence men vie with each other to increase both private and public wealth, which consequently increase in an extraordinary manner" (*Discourses*, 2:2).

In corrupt circumstances, then, morality requires actions that effectively achieve glory, actions that create the material conditions for democratic freedom under laws. Machiavelli effectively draws moral implications from his observations of human potentials. His advice to leaders is always to begin by recognizing whether one is situated in corruption or in glory; if conditions are corrupt, then the lure of the values of decency and civilization beckon to us, and our obligations are to do what has to be done to achieve these values; if, by contrast, a people has been civilized and freed, then duty becomes our operative moral category and consequentialism is replaced by deontology. The operative variable becomes the existence of a functional system of laws, as illustrated in Figure 4.1.

Figure 4.1: Drawing Moral Implications from Human Potentials

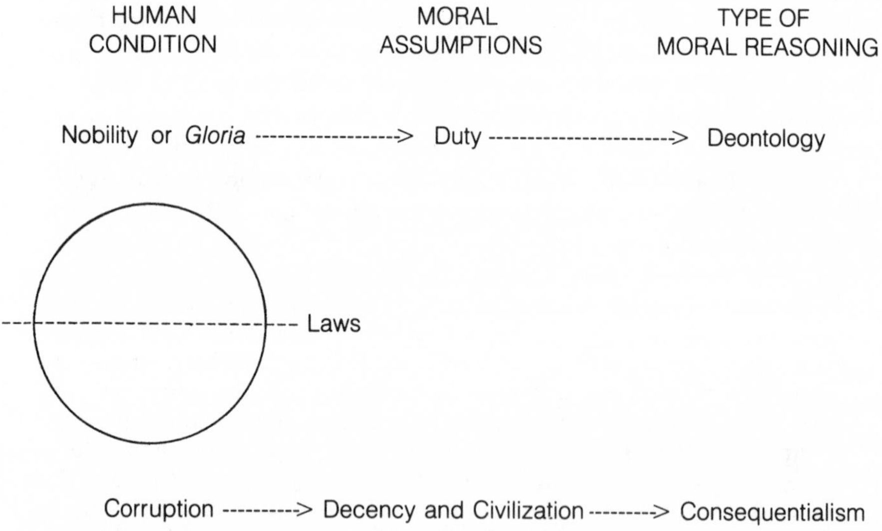

HUMAN CONDITION	MORAL ASSUMPTIONS	TYPE OF MORAL REASONING

Nobility or *Gloria* ------------------> Duty ----------------------> Deontology

---|-----------------------|--- Laws

Corruption ---------> Decency and Civilization --------> Consequentialism

In corruption, one is dealing with beasts and must be prepared to act in a beastly way, unrestrained by the laws of nature; but one cannot be content to be an Agathocles. This is the point of the story about the ancient education of princes by Chiron the centaur (*Prince*, chapter 18):

> You must know, then, that there are two methods of fighting, the one by law, the other by force: the first method is that of men, the second

of beasts; but as the first method is often insufficient, one must have recourse to the second. It is therefore necessary for a prince to know well how to use both the beast and the man. This was covertly taught to rulers by ancient writers, who relate how Achilles and many others of those ancient princes were given to Chiron the centaur to be brought up and educated under his discipline. The parable of this semi-animal, semi-human teacher is meant to indicate that a prince must know how to use both natures, and that the one without the other is not durable.

A prince being thus obliged to know well how to act as a beast must imitate the fox and the lion, for the lion cannot protect himself from traps, and the fox cannot defend himself from wolves. One must therefore be a fox to recognize traps, and a lion to frighten wolves. Those that wish to be only lions do not understand this. . . .

While this chapter of *The Prince* is widely interpreted as advising the ambitious[2] to do anything they must to gain power, it is saying exactly the opposite: "those who wish to be only lions do not understand" that being strong—acquiring power—is not enough. Nor is it "enough" to be strong like a lion and cunning like a fox—one must also know how to rise above the bestial and become human by freeing a people and bringing civilizing laws to them. It was for this reason that Agathocles was condemned: that he did not understand how to rise from bestial to humane behavior.[3]

DEMOCRACY AND THE MORAL VALUE OF GLORY

Now that we have seen the foundation in moral philosophy for Machiavelli's commitment to the civilizing value of glory, we need now only to show that this commitment is equivalent to freedom in a democratic republic. The equivalence of glory with freedom under laws that we make for ourselves is in fact the key to understanding his celebration, and even romanticization, of Rome and to understanding *The Prince*. Since the value of glory was the moral beacon to guide actions of leaders and potential leaders in corrupt conditions, we now ask: What is glory? What does glory entail?

A. *Gloria* in *The Prince*

Machiavelli clearly draws the distinction between *power* and *glory* in *The Prince*. It would not be surprising to find this distinction in *The Discourses,* where Machiavelli clearly enunciated his respect for the Roman republic and wrote of the *gloria* that Moses, Theseus, and Romulus brought to their peoples. But that he drew this distinction in *The Prince* should be surprising; reputed to be a work in which Machiavelli was pandering to the Medici to reestablish his career, *The Prince* is the work most responsible for his reputation as a teacher of evil. If *The Prince* were only a handbook for the seekers of power, then he would not need to distinguish it from glory. Yet, it is in this work that Machiavelli felt compelled to draw the distinction. Why would a republican like Machiavelli dare to distinguish between power and glory in a book dedicated to the Medici? Why would he end the book with a call to seek glory when the ambition of the Medici, though seemingly so similar to glory seeking, had been anything but beneficial to his government and his career? Why arouse more ambition in a family already too ambitious? What was he doing?

A related surprise is to be found in his celebration of faction. How could he celebrate faction when he had seen how the Guelph-Ghibelline conflict had torn Tuscany apart, and how the Soderini-Medici split had destroyed Florentine freedom? Was there a difference between faction and violence? How can we provide a good theoretical account of this distinction in the context of his notion of *gloria?*

B. Glory versus Ambition

To all appearances, Machiavelli's appeal to glory in *The Prince* is all the more strange given his condemnation of ambition in other places. Defining ambition as an elevation of personal and familial interests over those of the community, he satiricized this evil human motivation in both his *Tercets on Ambition* and in *The Golden Ass.* In addition, political experience had given him good cause to fear the ambitious, especially ambitious autocrats like the Medici.[4] So it is quite unlikely that he sought to stir their ambition. Might he actually have been trying to reduce their ambition? Or replace it with something else?

Whatever his personal feelings about the Medici, there was no doubt that events had placed them in a position of power, and he had to appeal to them both to help save his career and to help save his country. But given his nature and their nature, the most obvious course of action was blocked; an appeal on moral grounds (like the one in his *Exhortation to Penitence*, Gilbert, volume 1, 170) would probably be ineffective. Recognizing that "all men are evil" (*Discourses,* 1:3), Machiavelli's project must be to find a way to turn their vice to good purposes. One possibility, then, is that *The Prince* was an effort to divert the ambition of the Medici, to lure them to seek something similar and similarly ego gratifying while more conducive to the common good. In short, in this imperfect but real world, the vice of ambition must be turned into an unspecified virtue.[5]

We know that Machiavelli maintains that the vice of ambition must be recognized as a fact of the real world. Because Luigi Guicciardini (to whom the *Tercets on Ambition* are dedicated; lines 1–3) does not recognize the prevalence of the evil of ambition, "it does not seem to me that you take the world as it is." The empirical fact is that ambition and avarice are "two Furies [sent] to dwell on the earth" to "deprive us of peace and to set us at war, to take away from us all quiet and all good" (lines 28–31). But these facts do not mean that we are doomed; Machiavelli still sees the possibility of neutralizing ambition: "she will burn their [Tuscan] towns and their farmsteads if grace or better government does not bring her to nought" (concluding line). Grace or divine intervention might halt ambition, but no humanist could wait for that. Our hopes become tied to an improved government or a "new order," an idea that came to be called *civilizing* in the nineteenth century and *modernizing* in the twentieth. Our preliminary conclusion is that an appropriate constitution can neutralize ambition, making possible a better life by introducing a new order, by modernizing. To aim at this modernizing goal is synonymous with seeking *gloria*.

But how can we expect better government of the Medici, whose ambitions were well known to Machiavelli? It would be naive and unrealistic to assume that their ambition could be curtailed by moralizing, but is there another way to direct it to better goals? Just as in his later proposal to the Medici for a new republican Florentine constitution, Machiavelli here appeals to their self-interest, implying gently—perhaps even surreptitiously—that the Medici are *not ambitious enough,* are not seeking enough in their political lives. Seeking to create an autocracy in Florence is aiming too low; creating an Italian nation that will later make possible peace and freedom is the only appropriately "ambitious" goal.

Counting ambition as an evil desire to "dominate" others (*Discourses,* 1:5), Machiavelli believes that seeking glory is rather different—and good. The last chapter of *The Prince* begins with a discussion of the conditions making glory possible: Italy had to "be reduced to her present condition" in order that "the might of an Italian genius might be recognized." This is an appeal for "glorious" liberation of the nation, not for "ambitious" domination of a people. Then a list of divine signs or omens is recited, concluding with this appeal to seek a glory higher than ambition: "[E]verything has contributed to your greatness, the remainder must be done by you. God will not do everything, in order not to deprive us of free will and the portion of the glory that falls to our lot" (*Prince*, the 26th and last chapter).

Aspiring to *this* goal of glory is good; but reaching it will require much skill and ruthlessness. Nevertheless, skillful cruelty could win for a man (*vir*) and his family the *gloria* to ensure an illustrious reputation for the ages. Although traditional morality would condemn the necessary cruelty, a newer morality, just emerging, would count it good. In this brave new world, things that were once bad would now be deemed good. But even this newer, looser morality imposes its limitations upon our actions. Not just *any* exercise of cruelty, even if it be technically well executed and effective in securing power, is justified. For cruelty to be good, it must be moved by a desire for true glory rather than by mere ambition.

C. Power and Glory

How are we to distinguish power from glory? Consider the contradiction between the notorious and widely quoted passages in *The Prince* about not "keeping faith" and Romulus's fratricide on the one hand, and a more obscure passage about Agathocles, on the other. While the obscure passage reveals a powerful sense of this newer moral decency and propriety, the first two seem to suggest that no one (or no political leader, at least) ever has any real moral obligations to refrain from bad—and even terrible—things. Nevertheless, these passages also suggest an answer to our question about higher virtue that can substitute for ambition.

Despite the appearances created by his defense of Romulus and his acceptance of princely deceit, Machiavelli's true goal is larger and more noble. We must put the passage on princely deceit in the context of the discussion of Agathocles, as Machiavelli did, first distinguishing power from glory. He discusses some who came to power "by means of villainy" as he prepares to draw the distinction between "cruelties used badly" and "cruelties used well," on his way to excusing deceit and breaking promises. Agathocles, tyrant of Syracuse, was one prince who knew well how be cruel; but Machiavelli is not urging the Medici to imitate him:

> It cannot be called virtue to kill one's fellow-citizens, betray one's friends, be without faith, without pity, and without religion; by these methods one may indeed gain power, but not glory. For if the virtues of Agathocles in braving and overcoming perils, and his greatness of soul

in supporting and surmounting obstacles be considered, one sees no reason for holding him inferior to any of the most renowned captains. Nevertheless, his barbarous cruelty, and inhumanity, together with his countless atrocities, do not permit of his being named among the most famous men. (*Prince*, chapter 8, "Of Those Who Have Attained the Position of Prince by Villainy")

Governing is not simply a technical concern, then; morality—though not traditional morality—does have something to do with good government. Employing the most efficient, effective, and brutal methods is not enough to win Machiavelli's approval and respect—so the Medici should be aiming higher than Agathocles. By this newer morality, cruelties can sometimes be employed *constructively*, while at other times their use is *destructive*; traditional morality does not make that distinction clearly enough. Using cruelties constructively is good, both morally and technically, while using them destructively is not. Apparently, Romulus and Agathocles knew equally well how to act terribly, how to be cruel. Yet one had a vision of glory while the other did not, and the one with a glorious vision was praised while the one lacking it was condemned. For the one with such a vision, terrible acts are praised if they are considered necessary to reach that end; for the one without such vision, terrible acts earn condemnation. However important terrible acts may be as means to power, power is not enough: Romulus is praised and even fratricide is excused; but Agathocles is condemned exactly because he sought nothing beyond power. In this passage, Machiavelli contends that by doing terrible things without a vision of glory, one can achieve *only* power—but not any higher good. Clearly, glory is something greater than power; power may even be only a means to glory. I conclude that Machiavelli is inviting the Medici, or even trying to trick or to seduce them, to aim higher than they and Agathocles had; he is inviting them to seek the glory that their power makes possible, securing eternal praise for themselves.

What is the relevant difference between glory and power? Here we can gather an answer from the more famous passage from *The Discourses*. Those who commit terrible deeds with an eye to moving a people from corruption to glory earn what Agathocles missed; Romulus is a classic example:

For he is to be reprehended who commits violence for the purpose of destroying, and not he who employs it for beneficent purposes. . . . That Romulus deserves to be excused for the death of his brother and that of his associate, and that what he had done was for the general good, and not for the gratification of his own ambition, is proved by the fact that he immediately instituted a Senate with which to consult, and according to the opinions of which he might form his resolutions. And on carefully considering the authority which Romulus reserved for himself, we see that all he kept was the command of the army in case of war, and the power of convoking the Senate. This was seen when Rome became free, after the expulsion of the Tarquins, when there was no other innovation made upon the existing order of things than the institution of two Consuls, appointed annually, in place of a hereditary king; which proves clearly that all the original institutions of that city were more in conformity with the requirements of a free and civil society than with an absolute and tyrannical government. (*Discourses*, 1:9)

The text explains that Romulus possessed what Agathocles lacked—a vision of glory. One key to understanding the difference between power and glory is ambition: because Romulus acted to achieve this glory, while Agathocles acted only out of personal ambition, Romulus was to be excused while Agathocles was condemned. And how do we recognize this glory that excuses even fratricide? One simple fact excuses Romulus: the fact that he sought to create institutions that would enable people to be free. The proof that his actions were infused with a goal of glory—and consequently devoid of ambition—is found in the fact that he immediately created the institutional foundations of electoral representation. His preparing for a republic, calling into being a legislature, and reserving for himself only the command of the army are all evidence that he aimed at the common, rather than personal, good.[6] Although he did not grant freedom to the Romans immediately, he did everything necessary to make the heroism of Brutus possible later. The fact that freeing the Romans, after the Tarquins were deposed, required only minimal institutional restructuring is even taken by Machiavelli as final proof of this hypothesis (*Discourses*, 1:9).

We must conclude, then, that Machiavellian glory is intimately tied to laying the institutional and material foundations of republican government, or in other words to modernizing or civilizing a polity. Brutus's heroic role in the overthrow of the Tarquin monarchy would never have been possible without the institutional arrangements put in place by Romulus. The freedom made possible by this constitutional design is the glory that was Romulus's. Machiavelli's notion of "glory," then, can be seen in two ways: glory is either a condition in which a people is free to live under its own laws or glory is a characteristic of actions creating that condition. In different circumstances, one achieves glory in different ways. Achieving glory requires a careful, empirical attention to one's time and circumstances—what is conducive to glory today might be inimical to glory under different conditions tomorrow. But achieving glory ensures an illustrious reputation; corruption is its proper opposite, and ambition is its impostor.

Now we have a context in which to make sense of his passage on a prince's need—or lack of need—to keep faith: "a prudent ruler ought not to keep faith when by so doing it would be against his interest, and when the reasons which made him bind himself no longer exist. If men were all good, this precept would not be a good one; but as they are bad, and would not observe their faith with you, so you are not bound to keep faith with them" (*Prince*, chapter 18).

We have already seen that this passage is intimately tied to his moral voluntarism. But we can now see that it is also tied to securing glory. When social conditions are different, one must seek glory differently (*Discourses*, 3:8); but when a people is corrupt, then a "power almost princely" (ibid., 1:18) is needed to bring them to a lawful status. When advising a legislator in conditions of corruption, devoid of laws and obedience, Machiavelli suggests that a prince need not keep faith. Under such conditions, when the reasons that would make acts wrong do not exist, one's only obligation is to seek glory or freedom for one's people by achieving the power to legislate.

The Prince and The Discourses

Drawing together this distinction between power and glory with a few other things we know about *The Prince* and *The Discourses*, we can begin to see his perception of the logical connection between these two works. First, as Machiavelli says (chapter 5), *The Prince* is a more limited discussion of politics than is the larger *Discourses*. Second, Machiavelli himself notes that *The Prince* avoids the questions of republics and laws (ibid.). Is *The Prince* then a subset of the larger work and consistent with it, or is *The Prince* inconsistent with the larger work? Since our immediate concern is to discern Machiavelli's perception of the connection, it is worth noting that he mentions the larger work in *The Prince;* if he saw the two as inconsistent, he would not have mentioned the larger work, lest its democratic message indict him in the eyes of the Medici. At least as he saw it, the messages of the two works were not radically different, with *The Prince* containing advice appropriate to the particular circumstances of Florence at that time.

Our examination of the moral voluntarism of the two works reinforces such a relationship in two ways. First, the voluntarism is one of many consistencies that permeate the two works. Second, we learn in both that actions that seem "terrible" may not be terrible under corrupt circumstances. Now we can make one empirical observation—that Florence was judged corrupt by Machiavelli because of the destruction of republican glory by the *ambizione* of the Medici—before concluding that the advice Machiavelli gives in *The Prince* is advice he would give to any powerful man (*vir*) during corrupt times.

Looking at *The Discourses,* we find the celebration of Roman glory centered on the achievements of three great men: Romulus, Numa, and Brutus. The first gave Rome its institutions and laws, using brutal force to begin to civilize his people. The second gave them a religion to reinforce the emerging civilization. The third "renewed" the institutions given by Romulus, transforming their potential for human freedom into a realization of that potential. The phenomena of birth, growth, and renewal of constitutions are all dealt with in a complete theoretical perspective on politics, corresponding roughly with the three books of *The Discourses.*

The Prince, by contrast, is admittedly and deliberately an incomplete picture. Given Italian corruption, the glory of Rome could not be achieved immediately. The regaining of the lost glory would have to occur in stages. Of the three Roman heroes, Numa's role was least helpful to Machiavelli; he apparently concluded that imitating Numa, achieving religious renewal, was outside of his arena of competence. That left Romulus and Brutus. The role of Brutus would be the one Machiavelli would most love to play; it could even be said that he had been trying to play the role of Brutus all his adult life, but to little avail. Before he or anyone else could play Brutus, someone else would have to play Romulus a second time. But this descendent of Romulus would have to found a nation-state rather than a city-state. At one point, he hoped that Cesare Borgia could do so, but he died prematurely. Now the Medici, his enemies in Florentine politics, could become his allies in Italian politics—if he could move them from the mere *ambizione* that had characterized their dabblings in politics and trick them into seeking the real article: *gloria. The Prince* was the means to this trickery.

CONCLUSION

The distinction that Machiavelli draws between "power" and "glory" is central to any understanding of his thought. Knowing that he makes this distinction early in *The Prince* precludes reading it as a "cookbook" of recipes for getting and maintaining power. It is rather what it purports to be: a call to the Medici to seek the glory of nation builders. Of course, it is possible as Strauss argued that there is an "esoteric" or hidden meaning of the text.[7] But, given the consistencies of this work with all of the remainder of his writings, it is more elegant methodologically to posit a continuity in his work—unless there were some overriding reason for seeking other meanings.

We may summarize this portion of Machiavelli's moral theory by noting that in corrupt conditions we have no duties or obligations under laws or principles; but morality still demands appropriate action of us. Moral action here is defined by reference to the goal of democratic glory. But conditions are not always bestial; in civilized conditions, obedience to the laws becomes the foundation of our deliberations about what to do, so that Machiavelli shifts our attention to our duties under law.[8] For a fuller understanding of his position, we must shift our attention to the duties we have under good laws in that noble condition of democratic freedom called *gloria* by Machiavelli. We also need to know what constitutional arrangement is best suited to achieving that condition of human glory. These topics are best considered under the rubric of "constitutionalism," the subject of the next chapter.

5

Obeying Laws under a Good Constitution

ORIGINS OF THE DUTY TO OBEY THE LAW

A. Defining Constitutionalism

CONSTITUTIONALISM is a natural bridge between morality on the one hand and politics and law on the other. Broadly understood, constitutionalism is the belief that the authority of government can be curtailed by law—legitimately. While it is conceptually tied to "negative government"—a belief that the powers of government best serve the needs of a people when those powers are minimized—it is associated, historically but not necessarily, with religious and other metaphysical notions. For instance, in the European battles between emperors and popes, the religious conviction that there is a higher law, the laws of nature or of God, developed into an effective restraint upon government. A belief in the sanctity of person can and has also performed this function, though one can equally believe in the sanctity of human life without any particular religious conviction, and, without subscribing to any religion, one might still believe that governments should not violate that sanctity of person. For example, atheists can often see the desirability of restrictions on government like the first ten amendments of the American Constitution of 1789; they may even value freedom of religion more highly than religious people, given a religious culture and fears of social tyranny.

But without a god to fall back on, a ruler might legitimately ask, "Why should I obey these, or any, restrictions on governmental authority? If I have effectively fought for and won the power to rule this nation, why shouldn't I do as I please?" Why, in fact, should any ruler abide by constitutional restrictions? If not a ruler, why should anyone obey any government? Given his commitment to republican government, this becomes a broader question for Machiavelli: why is anyone bound to a democratic government? Is a citizen

128

bound to obey a republican law? And why should a government abide by its constitution and its restrictions?

B. Advantages of Obeying Good Laws

While there are many reasons why a government should, all other things being equal, abide by its own laws, Machiavelli prefers to "take men as they are" (self-seeking) rather than as they should be (amenable to reason). Characteristically for him, one of the best reasons for abiding by laws is a simple calculation of one's own self-interest, a calculation that carries one back to one's own human need for security: "And finally to sum up this matter, I say that both governments of princes and of the people have lasted a long time, but both required to be regulated by laws. For a prince who knows no other control but his own will is like a madman, and a people that can do as it pleases will hardly be wise" (*Discourses*, 1:58).

Machiavelli here invites rulers to calculate their own self-interest and realize that establishing and using laws is the best way to retain power—and he then recommends a similar restraint upon popular government.

Nonetheless, Machiavelli's moral commitment to government by laws is more complex than this; and although his commitment is sincere, it seems rather different from Locke's. For Locke, any government guilty of "cruelties well-committed" would be a government guilty of warring against its citizens and thus a government deserving a revolution. Further, this is not just because Locke is more optimistic about human nature, recognizing less clearly the human potential for depravity and corruption. The difference centers exactly upon their theories of duties with respect to law.[1]

For Locke, constitutionalism became a political expression of a natural law—actually, a natural rights—theory, a commitment to obey the laws of nature that are the foundations of our liberties. A government could be prohibited from violating certain of its citizens' rights because there were natural laws, derived from a higher authority that conferred these natural rights upon all citizens. Since there was a law of nature prohibiting wanton killing of people, for instance, the innocent citizens of a state had a right under that higher law not to be killed, even by their government—even though their government clearly had the power to take human life in punishment of crime. Given these natural rights, Locke believed that constitutional restrictions can be violated only at the expense of liberty, so that such violations are always wrong.[2]

But this was not the case for Machiavelli, for whom laws of nature did not exist; according to him, therefore, duties under law were genuine but conditional. If a lawful state is constituted, a Machiavellian could explain, then the citizens have certain rightful claims against the government, and it is in the self-interest of that government to respect these claims. But if that first condition is not satisfied, then all duties under all laws evaporate. We are then existing once again in corruption (Machiavelli's term), a state of nature (Hobbes's), or a state of war (Locke's).

When living under the opposite condition (*gloria* to Machiavelli), one's duty is generally to obey the laws; the principal exception is when the laws are "bad." But since legal systems are "bad" primarily when they do not enable a government to preserve rule by law, this exception can be set aside for now. Generally, since freedom requires good laws, disobeying them threatens freedom. Hence, for Machiavelli it is "inconsistent with a proper regard for liberty to violate the law. . . . For I think that there can be no worse example in a republic than to make a law and not to observe it; the more so when it is disregarded by the very parties who made it" (*Discourses*, 1:45).

So, when humans are free to live under laws they make for themselves in a democratic republic, their first obligation is to obey the law. In other words, central to Machiavellian morality is this conditional imperative: "If humans are living under good laws, then you must obey the law." Indeed, disobeying laws under these conditions is "inconsistent with a proper regard for liberty," and there can be "no worse example" for a government to set for its people. If Machiavelli was a consequentialist in conditions of corruption, he becomes a deontologist in glory.

Finally, a government should have so much respect for the laws that it cannot even disregard the laws in order to reward someone to whom it owes a debt of gratitude: "[N]o well-ordered republic should ever cancel the crimes of its citizens by their merits; but having established rewards for good actions and penalties for evil ones, and having rewarded a citizen for good conduct who afterwards commits a wrong, he should be chastised for that without regard to his previous merits. And a state that properly observes this principle will long enjoy its liberty. . . ." (*Discourses*, 1:24).

Liberty requires of its citizens and of its governments that there be a strict adherence to laws, an adherence that not even emotional commitments should diminish. The last thing a free republic should permit is an injustice under the law, even for its most popular heroes, since that injustice will tend to destroy the system of law and, with it, the free republic.

CONSTITUTIONAL WEAKNESSES

A. Constitutionalism under Pressure

One's belief in constitutionalism is most truly and sorely tried under direct pressure from contemporary emergencies. The greatest exigency of Machiavelli's professional life was the collapse of the republic headed by Soderini, who had employed Machiavelli as secretary. What would he find acceptable as means to prevent that collapse?

At first glance, Machiavelli's comments on this issue sound like those of a coldly calculating schemer, unrestrained by the niceties of constitutional law. Let us first recall that the secretary has advised us, and probably advised Soderini also, that, if one wants to establish a free republic, one must eliminate all "gentlemen" and establish equality (*Discourses*, 1:56 and 3:3). In *quinquocento* Florence, the greatest threat to democratic equality and freedom came from the wealth of the Medici. Yet Soderini felt restrained by the constitution from doing what he knew had to be done: removing the corruption by destroying the power base of the Medici.

Commenting on Soderini's refusal to eliminate his Medicean enemies, Machiavelli sounds as though Soderini was a fool or a coward to yield to restrictions on his power to deal with the Medicean threat to his rule:

> And although his natural sagacity recognized the necessity of destroying them ... yet he had not the courage to do it. For he thought, and, several times acknowledged it to his friends, that boldly to strike down his adversaries and all opposition would oblige him to assume extraordinary authority, and even legally to destroy civil equality. ... This respect for the laws was most praiseworthy and wise on the part of Soderini. Still, one should never allow an evil to run on out of respect for the law, especially when the law itself might easily be destroyed by the evil; and he should have borne in mind, that as his acts and motives would have to be judged by the result, in case he had been fortunate enough to succeed and live, everybody would have attested that what he had done was for the good of his country. ... (*Discourses*, 3:3)

It is almost as if Soderini was a nice and noble man for not violating the law, even in the name of the law, but a coward and a fool nevertheless. Perhaps one should never recognize such a constitutional restriction on one's power? If Machiavelli is here saying that we should violate the laws any time we deem that an evil may undermine the rule of law, then we may want to say that he lacked the subtleties and sophistications of Lockean constitutionalism.

B. Weak Constitutions Destroy Freedom and Glory

But Machiavelli was not so foolish as to believe that constitutions can be set aside so easily. Rather, consistent with his commitment to constitutionalism, Machiavelli is here concerned with the proper arrangement of a society—the laws Soderini was seeking to protect and defend were defective because they did not permit such a defense. Hence, Machiavelli's position is more complex than it first appears: the strictures of a good constitution should never be violated; but a good constitution must have the strength to defend the law: "Yet it is not good that in a republic anything should ever happen that has to be dealt with extralegally. The extralegal action may turn out well at the moment, yet the example has a bad effect, because it establishes a custom of breaking laws for good purposes; later, with this example, they are broken for bad purposes. Therefore a republic will never be perfect if with her laws she has not provided for everything, and furnished a means for dealing with every unexpected event, and laid down a method for using it" (*Discourses*, 1:34).

Soderini then was not ruined just by a personal weakness, although personal strength could have helped to offset the other deficiencies; but his own shortcoming was coupled with an institutional defect that failed to help him move effectively against those who would destroy the freedom of the Florentines. Thus, we may conclude that a proper constitution would never have positioned Soderini where he would have to choose between obeying the law and preserving the laws, where he would have to choose between abiding by the improper restrictions on his power and doing what was necessary to preserve any semblance of legal rule. In a properly constructed constitution, it would be legal to do what is necessary to preserve the rule of law.

Further, as Machiavelli saw it, Florence was not the only republic to flounder because of constitutional defects. Rome, too, finally lost her freedom and was ruined as a republic because of two such defects: "If we study carefully the conduct of the Roman republic, we discover two causes of her decadence; the one was the dissensions consequent upon the agrarian laws, and the other the prolongation of her military commands. If these matters had been better understood in the beginning, and proper remedies applied, the liberties of Rome would have endured longer, and she would probably have enjoyed greater tranquillity" (*Discourses*, 3:24).

Like Florence, Rome need not have lost her freedom; there are no causal laws so deterministic that there is no escaping them. Rather, human exertion, especially at the time of foundation building, is the key to remaining gloriously free, to becoming all that we can be as humans. If we forge good constitutional laws, we can preserve freedom by periodic regenerations or renewals. Then it becomes our duty to obey these good laws that we have made for ourselves.

CONSTITUTIONAL TYPES AND LIBERTY

If a constitution is to preserve liberty, it must prudently permit unusual action that is needed to combat corruption. In short, it must effectively provide for its own renewal by assuring that the *ambizione* of the rich never destroys the people's freedom: "As to those who have prudently set up a republic, one of the most necessary things they have arranged has been to set up a guardian for liberty, and according as they have placed him well, that free government is more or less lasting" (*Discourses*, 1:5).

The way a polity is constituted, then, is central to the possibility of human nobility and freedom, and a crucial question is therefore, which way of constituting a polity is best?

The first part of our answer is to be found in Machiavelli's praise for the advantages of free polities: "It is easy to learn why this love for free government springs up in people, for experience shows that cities never have increased in dominion or in riches except while they have been at liberty. . . . Riches multiply in a free country to a greater extent, both those that come from agriculture and those that come from industry, for each man gladly increases such things and seeks to gain such goods as he believes, when gained, he can enjoy" (*Discourses*, 2:2).

To anticipate a later argument, freedom and economic development seem to be related for Machiavelli. That is, the economic consequences of freedom are so desirable in themselves as to justify free institutions. But the story is larger than this. A good constitution must first of all provide for institutional means of balancing power between social classes, so that no class can unjustly harm another. In short, if we value freedom—and our considerations of Machiavelli's theories of human nature, of knowledge, and of reality all imply that we should—then we should seek a constitution that is "mixed" (i.e., contains elements of all the "pure" types) and provides for "checks and balances."

A. Toward a Typology

Despite the fact that Machiavelli was obviously aware of the six types of constitutions conceived by Aristotle—the three lawful ones being monarchy, aristocracy, and democracy, and the three lawless variants being tyranny, oligarchy, and mob rule (see the next section for quotations illustrating this awareness)—he sometimes reduced his conceptual categories to a bare minimum: "All states and dominions which hold or have held sway over mankind are either republics or monarchies. Monarchies are either hereditary in which the rulers have been for many years of the same family, or else they are of recent foundation. . . . I will not here speak of republics, having already treated of them fully in another place. I will deal only with monarchies, and will discuss how the various kinds described above can be governed and maintained" (*Prince,* chapters 1 and 2).

But his simplifications in this case appear to have been deliberate. First, given that the Medici family responsible for destroying the republic was the audience to whom he directed *The Prince,* it would not have been wise for him to employ any system that might imply that their regime was illegitimate. Second, the "democracies" of his time may have been, in practice, little more than aristocratic rule by those with varying degrees of property, while the "oligarchy" he opposed was some combination of monarchy and aristocracy. Finally, we know from Machiavelli's own pen (chapters 2, 5, and 12) that *The Prince* is not the place where we will learn what he believes about lawful government. So his task here is not one of exhorting the prince to be lawful, but of demonstrating to the prince that it is in his self-interest to abide by the law. Hence, we must turn to *The Discourses* if we seek to know which constitutions, strictly speaking, are to be preferred.

B. The Defects of Pure Types of Government

Constitutions are in fact the central theme of *The Discourses.* The first book discusses the features that consitutions must possess if liberty is to survive. The second is devoted to the steps that must be taken, often with great difficulty, to bring a corrupt people back to the constitutional straight and narrow. Finally, the third book is devoted to a discussion of renewing constitutions that are not yet corrupt, but merely straying from their origins. Not surprisingly it is in the first book that we should expect to find the answers to our questions about the best constitution, all things considered.

Nor should we be surprised to find Machiavelli, the empiricist, turning to actual experience to find a reason to recommend a "mixed constitution," which borrows good elements from all of the various types. The notion of a mixed constitution is at least as old as Aristotle, who was favorably disposed to the idea under many circumstances. But traditional justifications of this sort of constitution are typically of the "second best" sort. That is, given that, for one reason or another, we cannot have the "best" constitution that we would otherwise prefer, a mixed constitution becomes desirable as the second best alternative.

Machiavelli, too, seeks to justify a mixed constitution, but his defense is not of the "second best" type. Rather, the various "pure" forms are, for him, not very desirable, considering the human penchant for ambition and corruption. This more important part of his justification of a mixed constitution is to be found in his complex story of the "degeneration" of the different pure types of government. This imaginary history of the political evolution of the human race, which undoubtedly owes much to Polybius, contains the seeds of social contract theories. Machiavelli begins by noting that "These varieties of government sprang up by chance among men because in the beginning of the world, since the inhabitants were few, they lived for a while scattered in the fashion of the beasts. Then, as their number increased, they gathered together, and so that they could better defend themselves, deferred to him among them who was strongest and bravest, and made him chief and obeyed him. From this came understanding of things honorable and good, as different from what is pernicious and evil. . . ." (*Discourses,* 1:2).[3]

Politics and society are not "natural" to humans, who initially live in isolation. But social progress resulted in urbanization, and people had to forge appropriate governments. This process of social creation began with our defining what was good and bad, right and wrong. But, since we are not angels, we wronged one another, and these wrongs rendered us insecure. Sensing the human need for security and recognizing that people did wrong one another, the residents of the primitive world then undertook "to make laws and to establish punishments for those who broke them. Thence came the understanding of justice. As a result, when afterward they had to choose a prince, they did not prefer the strongest, but him who was most prudent and most just" (*Discourses,* 1:2).

The first significant progress in human affairs arose from this thirst for a just ruler, which emerged from the human need for security and protection. But monarchy is not an appropriate institution for humans; it cannot long meet their needs, since their imperfections make some rulers lazy and others ambitious. Nevertheless, having chosen a prince to lead them, the people wanted to avoid the need to make choices again, so they made sovereignty hereditary. "[But] the heirs quickly degenerated from their ancestors and, leaving off actions requiring ability, thought that princes needed to do nothing else than to surpass the others in lavishness and in lust and in every other sort of licentiousness. From this came, next, causes for destruction and for conspiracies and plots against princes. . . ." (*Discourses*, 1:2).

One of the shortcomings of a principality is exactly the wealth and the corruptive ambition of the prince and the nobles surrounding him or her stirring up ambitious desires for extravagant living that ultimately lead to excessive taxation and oppressive rule.

The oppression, in turn, excites resentment in the ruler's subjects; distress over his licentiousness, coupled with a desire to be free of what amounts to a political vampire, leads the people to plot his overthrow. Of course, as we have already seen, a good—i.e., lawful—prince need fear little from such conspiracies. The undoing of tyrants is a predictable reaction of the people against the outrages and excesses inherent in tyranny and all lawlessness.[4] Thus there have been times when the masses had to arm themselves against the tyranny by finding leaders among them strong enough to rise successfully against the tyrant; "and, when he was destroyed, [the people] obeyed them [the few leaders] as its liberators. The latter, hating the name of a single ruler, formed a government of themselves and at first . . . conducted themselves according to the laws they had laid down. . . ." (ibid.). Aristocratic government, under reasonably good laws, could meet human needs better than the old principate, at least for a time.

But again the leadership became hereditary, Machiavelli reasons, and the aristocratic children (ignorant of the changes of fortune, having never experienced its reverses), "turning to avarice, to ambition, to violence against women, caused a government by the best men to become a government by the few, without having regard to any civil rights, so that in a short time it happened to them as to the tyrant . . ." (ibid.). Again, ambition undid the leadership. The aristocratic few, as prone to domination as a single ruler, degenerated into tyranny without an appropriate constitutional restriction. The people, disgusted with their oligarchical government and the violations of their freedom, submitted to anyone willing to attack the new tyrants "and so quickly one rose who, with the aid of the multitude, destroyed them" (ibid.).

Having no desire to restore the principality or the aristocracy because of bitter memories, the people next opted for a popular government "and organized the state in such manner that neither the few powerful men nor one prince could have any authority. And because all governments get some respect at the beginning, this popular government was kept up for a while, but not long . . . because it rapidly went on to abuse of liberty, in which there was no fear either of private or of public men, so that since each one lived as he pleased, every day a thousand wrongs were done . . ." (*Discourses*, 1:2).

Even popular governments, unrestrained by good laws, are incapable of ruling for long. After "fortuitous circumstances" evaporate, only good laws can keep a people good.

Now, in order to escape this anarchy, people have "returned once more to the princedom" (ibid.). As the cycle begins again, one becomes more cynical about the prospects of liberty and stability, and Machiavelli himself concludes that all of the pure forms of government are inherently defective and unstable: "I say then that all the said types are pestiferous, by reason of the short life of the three good and the viciousness of the three bad" (ibid).

C. Freedom, Mixed Constitutions, and Checks on Power

Most importantly, this imaginary history leads Machiavelli to the notions of a mixed constitution and of checks and balances as a means of protecting freedom: "Hence, sagacious legislators, knowing the vices of each of these systems of government by themselves, have chosen one that should partake of all of them, judging that to be the most stable and solid. In fact, when there is combined under the same constitution a prince, a nobility, and the power of the people, then these three powers will watch and keep each other reciprocally in check" (*Discourses*, 1:2; Ricci–Vincent, 115).[5]

One means of turning factional distrust into an institutional protection of liberty is to position different branches of government, representing different factions, as rivals of one another for power. A representative democracy (or "republic," to Renaissance analysts) was best able to achieve this "mixture." Here the "power of the people" is maintained by having choices of governmental leaders depend upon the electoral decisions of the people. But one also has an aristocracy among democratically elected legislators and judges, as well as in an elective monarch, whether it be called a president, prime minister, or gonfalonier.

Thus the notion of a mixed constitution, born in antiquity, is here given a modern twist—people have a potential for evil, but are also capable of glorious freedom, and mixing the constitutional modes thus becomes a way of protecting liberty and avoiding corruption by keeping each power in check. Later in *The Discourses*, Machiavelli abandons the three-fold analysis and settles on a dichotomy between classes. The balance of the two "estates" or factions in a society is the key to Machiavelli's constitutionalism:

> [A] republic that has no distinguished citizens cannot be well governed; but, on the other hand, it is often the great influence of such distinguished citizens that is the cause of states being reduced to servitude. And to prevent this the institutions of the state should be so regulated that the influence of citizens shall be founded only upon such acts as are of benefit to the state, and not upon such as are injurious to the public interests of liberty. And therefore attention must be given to the means employed by citizens for acquiring such influence; and these are twofold, either public or private. The former are when a citizen gains reputation and influence by serving the state well with his counsels or his actions. The way to such honors should be open to every citizen, and suitable rewards should be established, that will be satisfactory and honorable to those who merit them. Reputation and influence gained by such pure and simple means will never prove dangerous to any state. But when they are acquired by private means, then they become most dangerous and pernicious. (*Discourses*, 3:28)

"Private means" of achieving reputation are, not surprisingly, associated with personal wealth. The incident that gave rise to this lecture about corruption concerned a famine in ancient Rome, during which one Spurius Melius resolved to feed the starving masses at his own expense, an act of magnificent and grand philanthropy. But the people's dependence upon him, a private person, was not good for liberty; so the senate, cognizant of the threat to its legitimacy arising from the fact that "this liberality attracted crowds of people, and so won him the popular favor," and "fearing the consequences that might arise from it," created a dictator "expressly against Spurius . . . who had him put to death" (*Discourses*, 3:28).

Rich men tend to want to use their wealth to purchase favor with the masses, which confers upon them new power. Then they naturally desire to turn that power to private uses; once they seek to advance their private interests at the expense of the public interest, the masses are oppressed. Only a good constitution can prevent this, and that peculiar mixture of constitutions, a democratic republic, has an inherent advantage over principalities from this perspective of oppression: "For the aim of the people is more honest than that of the nobility, the latter desiring to oppress, and the former merely to avoid oppression" (*Prince*, chapter 9; Ricci–Vincent, 36).

As a class, *il popoli* (the people) were less likely to be corrupted by the ambitious desire to oppress; as a result, Machiavelli reasoned, their need to be free remains alive. But *il nobili* (the nobles) have lost that characteristic of humanity. Hence, the capacity for this goodness can be had and lost. Is there any institutional mechanism for preventing the loss?

CONSTITUTIONAL REGENERATION

Regimes can be "reborn" to the vitality of their youths under appropriate circumstances. Constitutions can foster such rebirths by recognizing the differences of origins of renewals: "And those are the best-constituted bodies, and have the longest existence, which possess the intrinsic means of frequently renewing themselves, or such as obtain this renovation in consequence of some extrinsic accidents" (*Discourses*, 3:1; Ricci–Vincent, 397).

External forces are outside the control of constitutions and constitution makers, while the internal sources of renewal are of two types:

> It is necessary then (as has been said) for men who live associated together under some kind of regulations often to be brought back to themselves, so to speak, either by external or internal occurrences. As to the latter, they are either the result of a law, that obliges the citizens of the association often to render an account of their conduct; or some man of superior character arises amongst them, whose noble example and virtuous actions will produce the same effect as such a law. This good then in a republic is due either to the excellence of some one man, or to some law. . . . (*Discourses*, 3:1; Ricci–Vincent, 399)

Since one must often rely upon *fortuna* for people "of superior character," any activist humanist will want to resort to reliance upon laws rather than upon good people for renewing the virtue of a people. Hence Machiavelli's constitutionalism carries him, as it carried Jefferson, to a belief that the tree of liberty is watered with blood. But where the "blood" in Jefferson's version is that of patriots, it is for Machiavelli the blood of miscreants and criminals: "It would be desirable therefore that not more than ten years should elapse between such executions, for in the long course of time men begin to change their customs, and to transgress the laws; and unless some case occurs that recalls the fear in their hearts, the delinquents will soon become so numerous that they cannot be punished without danger" (*Discourses*, 3:1; Ricci–Vincent, 400).

Machiavelli valued public punishments for their deterrent effect. His analysis implies that it is good for a republic to have public executions and scandals, which serve to remind the people of the sanctity and fragility of their freedoms in the face of unfettered ambition and to reinforce in their minds the importance of observing the laws. It is also consistent with Machiavelli's notions of development that, as a people becomes more civilized, less radical punishments may serve the same purpose. In this respect, the press may also serve a constitutional role, becoming a kind of "fourth" branch of government whose task becomes the policing of the branches; it can help to redress imbalances of power by bringing miscreants to public punishment.

But most simply, a constitution must set up opposing factions whose rational calculation of self-interest becomes an institutional barrier to constitutional collapse. Rome's use of the rich and the poor, up until the triumph of the rich, serves as a model for this constitutional arrangement: "I believe it therefore necessary rather to take the constitution of Rome as a model than that of any other republic, and to tolerate the differences that will arise between the Senate and the people as an unavoidable inconvenience in achieving greatness like that of Rome" (*Discourses*, 1:6; Ricci–Vincent, 130).

CONCLUSION: MACHIAVELLI AS A REPUBLICAN

This is, of course, not to say that all of Montesquieu's insights about checks and balances were anticipated by this passage in Machiavelli. But it does enable us to recognize how similar to the ideals of the American founders[6] were the ideals of Machiavelli. Such an arrangement, a mixed constitution with checks and balances, was most likely capable of resisting that most deadly of evils, corruption. Consequently, it was also most likely to preserve freedom. Machiavelli's clear constitutional preference, then, is for a strong republican constitution with internal branches that represent different classes and watch each other jealously.

Given this republicanism, we must inevitably ask how Machiavelli could then have written *The Prince*, a book in which he gives advice to princes on how to break "faith," be "cruel," and use the power of the military to press a people into subjection.

Part 4
Economics, Society, and Politics

6

Why Freedom May Require Princes

POWER AND FREEDOM

A. *The Prince* and *The Discourses*

GIVEN this commitment to republican constitutionalism, how could Machiavelli have offered advice to princes? And how, when offering this advice, could he have advised them to be faithless and cruel? Worse, how could he offer this advice to the Medici, whose ambition and wealth repeatedly destroyed Florentine freedom? Did Machiavelli betray all that he believed in writing *The Prince?* Did he stop believing in republican freedom? Did he "convert" and become a monarchist?

Such questions are natural, and because of them there is a temptation to read *The Prince* and *The Discourses* as radically different works, with the crass *Prince* a pandering to the Medici for a job and the other revealing something more secret, his hidden commitment to the freedom of a democratic republic. While a correct understanding of the relationship between these two works is essential to any coherent reading of the Machiavellian corpus, this particular view, of two radically discordant works, leads to blind alleys and dead ends, suggesting that Machiavelli was either incoherent or hypocritical. Methodologically, it is more elegant to begin with an assumption of coherence, leaving open the possibility of rebuttal. Meanwhile, even more extreme than those charging incoherence are those who believe that reading *The Prince* alone is the key to understanding Machiavelli, so that we need not even consider *The Discourses*.[1]

While *The Discourses* are more openly and obviously democratic, the two works are nevertheless a seamless web. Machiavelli is seeking to accomplish the same goal in both books, and this goal remains exactly the one he articulates in *The Discourses:* to find a "new" way of preventing ambition and corruption from destroying freedom and, as a corollary, to find a "new" way of reversing corruption so that people can be free again. Hence, *The Prince* concerns a subset of those larger issues: what to do when ambition has corrupted a city, what to do to move from feudal aristocratic privilege to more modern democratic freedom.

By what reasoning can we infer that Machiavelli was attempting to seduce the Medici into the modernizer's trap? The first premise, that Machiavelli desired to transform ambition into glory seeking, is the conclusion of this argument: (a) if Medicean wealth and corruptive ambition are a barrier to freedom, and (b) if we are to take men *(viri)* as we find them, then (c) the ambition of this family must be aimed higher toward *gloria*, and (d) the power deriving from their wealth should be aimed at the common good. If this account of his reasoning is correct, then the "evil" of the Medici could be transformed into a higher good, and *The Discourses* can be seen as a tract on corruptive ambition and the danger it poses to democratic freedom, while *The Prince* suggests a way to transform ambition into a search for glory by seducing the Medici into a militaristic quest for unifying Italy. The repeated references to glory in the final paragraphs of *The Prince* constitute good evidence that such conclusions about Machiavelli's aims are valid.

B. The Glory of Republics and Laws

To examine in closer detail the question, how could the democratic author of *The Discourses* also pen *The Prince,* it is wise to begin with what Machiavelli himself wrote: that he intended *The Prince* to be a more limited discussion of politics than were *The Discourses.* Of necessity, then, the goal of *The Prince* cannot be comparatively very grand—or obvious. If he was attempting to lure the Medici into modernizing and unifying Italy, he could not simply announce that to them nor inform them of the entirety of his analysis. Rather, he would have to find a way of convincing them that it was in their interest to do what was morally necessary and desirable. Hence, *The Prince* covered only part of what Machiavelli found to be important about politics: "I shall omit discussing republics because elsewhere I have discussed them at length" (*Prince,* chapter 2). Similarly, Machiavelli believed that the "principal foundations of all states, the new as well as the old and the mixed, are good laws and good armies. And because there cannot be good laws where armies are not good, and where there are good armies, there must be good laws, I shall omit talking of laws and shall speak of armies" (ibid.). So what is missing in *The Prince* that Machiavelli thought important were discussions of *republics* and of *laws;* a discussion of armies replaces these topics, with the aim of tempting the Medici to see military conquest as a means to become glorious and so as a means to redirect their ambition.

Second, Machiavelli's assessment of the comparative desirability of principalities and republics cannot be prominently displayed in *The Prince.* While Machiavelli thought that a principality could play an important historical role *under certain circumstances,*[2] still he clearly preferred government to operate under laws suitable to a republic. Hence, in *The Discourses,* he notes the glory of the Roman republic: "Those who read in what way the city of Rome began, and by what lawgivers and how she was organized, will not marvel that so much vigor was kept up in that city for so many centuries, and that finally it made possible the dominant position to which that republic rose" (*Discourses,* 1:1). He is unstinting in his praises of its freedom as a republic: "Either way it will be seen that Rome was from the first free and independent . . ." (*Discourses,* 1:1; Ricci–Vincent, 109). Even in *The Prince* (chapter 5), he cautions the Medici that "whoever becomes the ruler of a free city and does not destroy it, can expect to be destroyed by it, for it can always find a motive for rebellion in the name of liberty." In fact, it is little exaggeration to suggest that he was so committed to the idea of republican freedom that he had idealized and romanticized the freedom of the Roman republic.

His admiration of Rome is largely a function of the wisdom he saw—or imagined—in her institutions. So wise were these institutions that with a bit of luck or skill, Roman glory could have continued for centuries. For the Romans had accomplished one crucial institutional feat: they had found an appropriate institutional guardian of liberty.

All the legislators that have given wise constitutions to republics have deemed it an essential precaution to establish a guard and protection to liberty; and according as this was more or less wisely placed, liberty endured a greater or less length of time. As every republic was composed of nobles and people, the question arose as to whose hands it was best to confide the protection of liberty. . . . the Romans entrusted it to the people. . . . I will say, that one should always confide any deposit to those who have least desire of violating it; and doubtless, if we consider the objects of the nobles and of the people, we must see that the first have a great desire to dominate, whilst the latter have only the wish not to be dominated, and consequently a greater desire to live in the enjoyment of liberty. (*Discourses,* 1:5)

Roman institutions, Machiavelli was convinced, were wisely designed to preserve human freedom. Central to that wisdom was the foresight to place the responsibility for preserving freedom in the hands of the people, since they had the least desire to destroy freedom.

Finally, Machiavelli seems to equate the freedom of a republic with the greatness and glory he has been advocating: "certainly it is wonderful to think of the greatness which Athens attained within the space of a hundred years after having freed herself from the tyranny of Pisistratus; and still more wonderful is it to reflect upon the greatness which Rome achieved after she was rid of her kings. The cause of this is manifest, for it is not individual prosperity, but the general good, that makes cities great . . ." (*Discourses*, 2:2).

In short, Rome could not have remained a monarchy and become great: "I think it was necessary for royalty to be extinguished in Rome, else she would in a very short time have become feeble and devoid of energy" (*Prince*, chapter 17).

Thus even in *The Prince*, monarchy is held to be inferior to republican freedom; even for princes true *gloria* is to be found in constituting new republics.

OTHER PERSPECTIVES ON MACHIAVELLI'S ADVOCATING A PRINCIPALITY

A. The "Actual and Potential Princes" Thesis

An example of the misreadings that can occur when the two works are seen as radically different is Strauss's failure to understand Machiavelli's nationalism and misconstrual of the central connection between the two works. Opting to define the relation in terms of "potential" versus "actual" princes, Strauss overemphasizes the fact that *The Prince* was written for the Medici, who were the actual princes of Florence, and misses the significance of the fact that *The Discourses* were dedicated to Buondelmonti and Rucellai, who "deserve to be" princes (dedication, *Discourses;* Gilbert, 189). In his first articulation of this perspective, Strauss gives this preliminary formulation: "Machiavelli says explicitly that in the *Prince* he will deal solely with principalities and will not discuss republics there since he has done so elsewhere at length. The reference to a work on republics fits the *Discourses*, and fits no other work by Machiavelli which is extant. . . . It therefore seems reasonable to describe the relation of the two books as follows: The *Prince* is devoted to principalities, the *Discourses* to republics."[3]

However, Strauss was aware that the relation between the two is not so simple as he had at first suggested; if it were, he asks, "why did Machiavelli not call his treatise on republics simply *De Republica?* It might be suggested that when Machiavelli wrote, republics were not timely in Florence, in Italy, or anywhere else on earth; principalities were in the ascendancy; republics were rather a matter of the past."[4] While it appears that Strauss is not prepared to take ownership of the "suggestion" that "republics were not timely," his mere mention of such an implausible idea suggests the need created by his (mis)interpretation; he seeks explanations for that which needs no explanation in a more elegant reading. Besides, his interpretation is inconsistent with three things we know about Machiavelli's writings: his modern empiricism, his nationalism, and his visions of class conflict.

First, *The Discourses* is an empiricist tract about how to make freedom possible and stable by studying history and historical experiences. One need not explain, as Strauss tries to do, why Machiavelli named *The Discourses* as he did: Machiavelli tells us in the introduction that his goal is to learn from historical, i.e., Roman, experience the republican lesson on how to preserve freedom; the book deals with its subject, republics, by focusing on historical events. In other words, since Machiavelli's purpose is to provide a historical discourse, the title is appropriate; *De Republica* would in fact disguise the actual focus. What was needed, in the eyes of Machiavelli, was not another theoretical rumination on republics but an experience-based discussion of what was necessary for people to be free.

Further, there is little cause to believe that Machiavelli would have hesitated to put "republic" in the title if there had been reason to. While it may not have been as evident to all practitioners as it was to Machiavelli, democracy was about to become "inevitable," as Alexis de Tocqueville described it in *Democracy in America*. This was the beginning of the era of republics. In some of the commercial city-states of Italy at the time, there were the first modern stirrings of the desire for democratic freedom and, as Strauss himself was to write, "Florence herself had been a republic until a short time ago. . . ."[5] It was not the case, then, that modernization had rendered republics anachronisms and that Machiavelli feared dooming his book by giving it an unpopular title; on the contrary, modernization was moving polities toward democracy—but sometimes this process needed help from a "prince" whose *virtuoso* task would be to lay the foundations. Moreover, titling the work as a series of discourses on Titus Livy's history of Rome was a manifestation of Renaissance humanism, perhaps even empiricism, rather than a product of a desire to avoid the topic of democracy.

Second, and more importantly, *The Discourses* cannot be interpreted without reference to Machiavelli's nationalism. Strauss errs in focusing too narrowly on Florence, ignoring the wider Italian context: while the Medici may have been actual princes of Florence, they were potential princes of Italy. Hence, Strauss was wrong in suggesting both that *The Prince* was about principalities and that it was only written for actual princes. *The Prince* both articulated a preference for democracy and was intended for potential princes— and in fact contains advice for those who would be prince, reminding them that either luck or skill can make a prince of a private person and urging reliance on skill rather than chance.

Finally, the relation between the two works cannot be understood without attention to Machiavelli's equivocal notions of class. Machiavelli thought constantly, if fuzzily, about the conflicts between the greater and lesser guilds, and the insights and errors of his class perspectives infused almost everything he wrote. It is an insensitivity to Machiavelli's attention to "factions," a discussion of which opens *The Discourses* and constitutes the principal disagreement between Machiavelli and Titus Livy, that leads Strauss to misunderstand Machiavelli's view of the relation of these works. Knowing that Machiavelli sees the existence of a class of gentlemen or aristocratic nobility as necessary for a principality and inimical to a republic (*Discourses*, 1:17–18, 1:55, and 3:28), we cannot accept as a Machiavellian idea Strauss's suggestion that "princes can be presumed to know certain harsh truths which gentlemen must not be presumed to know."[6] This interpretation is unacceptable because it is exactly "the rich" and "gentlemen" like the Medici who, corruptive with their "ambition," must be presumed to know those "harsh truths." Hence, Strauss is wrong when he reaches his conclusion: "To summarize, Machiavelli presents in each of his two books substantially the same teaching from two different points of view, which may be described provisionally as the points of view of the actual prince and of potential princes."[7] While he is right that the teaching is the same, the difference between the two books cannot be a matter of *these* different points of view, no matter how well they are qualified after this provisional first stab.

More accurately, corruption is the key to understanding the relation of the two works. Under conditions of the most abject corruption, like those prevalent in early *quinquocento* Italy, a strong, unifying prince may be necessary to lay the material foundation for the creation of a new modern state, and *The Prince* is written to someone who can end that corruption. By contrast, *The Discourses* are a more complete description of the evils of corruption and the good of its opposite, *gloria*. The larger book deals not only with what to do in corrupt circumstances but also with the possibility of autonomy in a democratic republic; it is not merely about corruption but also about the constitution and reconstitution of republics upon legal foundations that make nobility possible. The relation between the two works, then, is not so "simple." This is at least partly because, in the passage of *The Prince* that Strauss refers to, Machiavelli had conjoined "laws" with "republics" as subjects not fit for *The Prince*, confining himself instead to arms and princes. But arms are to a prince what laws are to a republic—part of a coercive apparatus that is needed for the creation of a new state and for the maintenance of it in the face of corruption. *The Discourses*, then, are about the constitution, corruption, and reconstitution of republics; princes are, of necessity, included because they have a role to play in ending corruption, in reconstituting republics by creating the material conditions (national unification, laws, and social equality) necessary for democratic autonomy.

B. The "Deceit and Conspiracy" Thesis

Many other interpretations of the message of *The Prince* have been offered, some of them superior to Strauss's. Rousseau's is only one of the more audacious when he reasons that *The Prince* was written for subjects, i.e., those who deserve to be princes, so as to forewarn them of the devious stratagems princes will employ to strip them of their liberty. Of similar audacity and power is Mary Dietz's claim that Machiavelli systematically sought to undermine principalities by giving them bad advice.[8] Hers is a most fascinating and well-reasoned thesis about the relation between *The Prince* and *The Discourses* and serves as a necessary corrective to the Straussian view—although her thesis is not fully correct. If *The Discourses* reveal an advocate of democratic freedom, Dietz reasons, then *The Prince* must do the same, although not obviously. Nor *could* the meaning be obvious, according to her interpretation; Machiavelli was, after all, attempting to destroy the Medici and he could not risk assuming their stupidity. For Dietz, then, *The Prince* "was a masterful act of political deception"[9] aimed at trapping the Medici in a republican assassination conspiracy.

Dietz notes several instances in which the advice Machiavelli offered the Medici in *The Prince* would have destroyed them, given the circumstances of *quinquocento* Florence:

1. relying on the good will of the people of Florence rather than on that of the *ottimati* or nobles would have undermined the strongest support available for the restoration of noble rule;
2. avoiding *liberalità*, the generous spending of government funds to keep the people happy, would have stripped the younger Medici of the most successful tactic of their elder, Cosimo, namely the use of wealth to purchase favor among the people;
3. arming the citizens of republican Florence while forgoing fortresses would have delivered the Medici over to the republican forces, which (as Machiavelli warned in *The Prince*, chapter 5) would use the excuse of the ancient usages of liberty to "destroy" any prince who hoped to subjugate them.

So Dietz concludes that "The mystery or oddity of Machiavelli's treatment of arms and fortresses can be explained in only one way. He offers Lorenzo advice on security, with the intention of delivering him into republican hands"[10] so that a new assassination conspiracy might succeed. Dietz is right to conclude this article by claiming that "*The Prince* has for five centuries accused this Florentine patriot. His vindication is long overdue."[11] But she is not right to depict Machiavelli as involved in an assassination conspiracy.

This thesis—so provocative on first sight and so seductive on examination of the actual advice Machiavelli offered the Medici—does, however, suffer from two defects. One, its range is too narrow since Machiavelli was concerned with the nation of Italy as well as the city of Florence, and two, it fails to recognize the extent to which Machiavelli was a modern and modernizing thinker.

First, although Dietz is right that Machiavelli was a Florentine republican and should have harbored some hostility to the oligarchs, especially after his torture, he was nevertheless modern enough to realize that the nation of Italy and the Italian cities were open to foreign domination so long as there were other united nations like France in existence. The vision in the last paragraph of *The Prince* then may not be a false vision of glory (ambition being such a false vision, as we have already seen) aimed to seduce the Medici into reckless abandon in dealing with Florence; it may well have been Machiavelli's true vision of glory. What would it profit the Florentines, after all, to lure the Medici into a republican trap and resurrect a republic if it remained an isolated and surrounded city-state?

The republic would remain in perpetual danger, which its secretary was not fool enough to ignore—his trips to the French court had convinced him of the need to end the warlordism of Italian politics and to unify the nation.

Second, to read Machiavelli as wanting to revert to the divisions of feudal sectarian violence and corruption would be to mistake the modern sense of republican virtue that infused his thought for a feudal dedication to the city-state. Sectarian violence is, after all, a degenerated version of faction, an evil for Machiavelli. Perhaps before the destruction of Soderini's republic, he considered such violence (see his comments about advice given to Soderini, presumably by him, in *The Discourses*, 3:3), but *fortuna* had closed that avenue, and larger forces, like the emerging nationalism, were rendering city-states obsolete.

Reexamining the advice he gave the Medici in this light reveals a different, and more noble, project. When he advises the Medici to seek the loyalty of the people and turn their backs on the *ottimati*, he is urging them to embrace the emerging and powerful feelings of nationalism. When he advises them to abandon *liberalità*, he seeks to transcend the loyalty to factions and transfer loyalty to the nation-state. Abandoning their fortresses is a way of turning their attention from *ambizione* and efforts to imitate the disappearing royalty, substituting instead the commercial ways of the city. (He might even have glimpsed darkly the connection between urbanization and modernization, but any assertion of that would be mere speculation.) And finally, in recommending the arming of the citizens so as to create citizen soldiers, he is recommending modernizing the military in a more democratic way. In its own way, each of these recommendations is a recommendation to modernize Italy into a strong, free nation-state.

We must conclude, from this examination of context, that Machiavelli's goals in *The Prince* were larger, more modern, more noble, and more consistent with the remainder of his philosophy than would be a vengeful conspiracy against the Medici. If the problem was the corruption of the Italian nation, the solution could not be merely Florentine; but it could originate in Florence and the power of the Medici—if they could be persuaded to use their power to seek glory and avoid the errors of Agathocles. In short, the goal of *The Prince* is nothing less than to lure the Medici into the trap of becoming lawful, modern princes, princes who could lay the foundations for a modern republic by modernizing and unifying the nation. In short, Machiavelli sought to transform corruptive ambition in "men as they are" into the quest for glory.

MACHIAVELLIAN USES OF PRINCELY POWER

A. Why the Medici?

In corrupt conditions like those of *quinquocento* Italy, a strong leader like Romulus would be needed to create conditions preparing for a later Italian freedom, which might entail forcing the Italian people to submit to good laws. Machiavelli saw, or at least tried to see, in the Medici what he had earlier seen in Cesare Borgia: the strength and ruthlessness needed to unite a people and bring it to lawful civility. As we shall see, textual evidence supports the thesis that Machiavelli planned a modernizing trap rather than an assassination trap.

That he sought to rouse a devotion to glory in the hearts of the Medici when he wrote *The Prince* is made evident in this passage from the more inclusive *Discourses:*

> And truly, if a prince be anxious for glory and the good opinion of the world, he should rather wish to possess a corrupt city, not to ruin it wholly like Caesar, but to reorganize it like Romulus. For certainly the heavens cannot afford a man a greater opportunity of glory, nor could men desire a better one. . . . And, in fine, let him to whom Heaven has vouchsafed such an opportunity reflect that there are two ways open to him; one that will enable him to live securely and insure him glory after death, and the other that will make his life one of constant anxiety, and after death consign him to eternal infamy. (*Discourses*, 1:10)

It is not always possible, after all, to seek glory in the way that the "good" Roman emperors had: by obeying good laws. In the absence of good laws, one must position oneself to make such laws, by amassing power—if necessary, in cruel ways.

But why the Medici? How could one count on their doing right by the Italian nation when they had already corrupted Florence? Although it would be easy to assume that he carried an undying hatred for the oligarchs in his heart, Machiavelli was too much of a patriot to let his feelings cloud his head. Almost immediately after the restoration of the oligarchy in 1512, he placed the Medici under a microscope, examining their mettle to determine if they were like Cesare Borgia. It is almost as though, having lost Florence and his place in it, he resolved to work on the larger project of Italy. So in 1513, we find Machiavelli writing of his ever present fear of renewed incursions by the French and the Spanish. While he lacked the respect for the French armies that he had for the "Swiss" (since the nation of Switzerland did not yet exist, these people were not quite identical to today's Swiss; the reference is apparently to a rather loose confederation of Germanic peoples from the North and Northeast of Milan), still he feared the impact of their power in Italy: "I do not believe [the French] will produce an empire like the Romans, but I do believe they can become masters of Italy, by reason of their nearness and our disorders and vile conditions. And because this frightens me, I wish to remedy it . . ." (Gilbert's *Letters of Machiavelli*, no. 134, pp. 137–38).

In the very next extant letter to Vettori, we find a detailed examination of the actions of Lorenzo de' Medici:

> I do not wish to omit giving you notice of the Magnificent Lorenzo's way of proceeding, for he has demonstrated such quality up to now that he has filled with good hopes all this city, and it seems that everybody finds in him happy recollection of his grandfather; because His Magnificence is attentive to business, liberal and pleasant in audience, slow and weighty in his answers. . . . He makes himself . . . both loved and revered, rather than feared, which as it is the more difficult to achieve, so it is more praiseworthy in him. . . . Thus, in all his movements, outside and inside, nothing is seen that offends anybody or is to be censured; at which everybody appears to be much pleased. (*Letters*, no. 135, 138–39).

It appears that he began writing *The Prince* at this time, since the letter of 10 December 1513 contains the famous description of his doffing of his dusty clothes in preference for "garments regal" so that he might "enter the ancient courts of ancient men" and converse on politics with the greatest thinkers; the product of this reading and writing was a "little work *On Princedoms*" (letter no. 137, *Letters*, 139–44).

Nor did Machiavelli ever abandon his hope for the grand family who had rendered him unemployed. In March of 1526, just a few months before the death of Giovanni de' Medici (grandson of Lorenzo), Machiavelli wrote his estimate of his military prowess:

> A few days ago it was said throughout Florence that the Lord Giovanni de' Medici was raising the flag of a soldier of fortune, to make war where he had the best opportunity. This rumor stirred up my spirit to imagine that the people knew what ought to be done. I believe anyone who believes that among the Italians there is no leader whom the soldiers would more gladly follow, and whom the Spanish more fear and more respect; everybody also thinks that Lord Giovanni is bold, prompt, has great ideas, is a maker of great plans. We could then, secretly making him strong, have him raise this flag. . . . (letter no. 204, *Letters*, 224–28).

Finally, the advice he continued to provide the Medici had the ring of his original message in *The Prince:* play the role of Romulus, unify Italy, reduce her people to lawful obedience, and give her institutions that will enable her, after your deaths, to become a free republic. For instance, after giving a detailed description of how to retain the elective apparatus of the *balia* for choosing representatives, Machiavelli details the importance of the institutions he is recommending: "I believe, considering all this organization as a republic, and without your authority, that it lacks nothing necessary to a free government according to what is above debated and presented at length. But if it is considered while Your Holiness and the Most Reverend Monsignor are still living, it is a monarchy, because you have authority over the armed forces, you have authority over the criminal judges, you keep the laws in your bosom" (*Remodeling the Florentine Government,* Gilbert, 113).

There can be no doubt that the myth or idealization of Romulus continued to captivate Machiavelli's imagination and that he continued to hope that the Medici family could be induced to imitate that ancient example.

But what he considered most necessary to the success of this strategy is recognizing the differences in historical situations and responding appropriately: "This brings us to two important considerations: the first, that the means of attaining glory are different in a republic that is corrupt from what they are in a republic that still preserves its institutions pure; and the second, (which is in a measure comprised in the first,) that men in their conduct, and especially in their most prominent actions, should well consider and conform to the times in which they live" (*Discourses,* 3:8, Ricci–Vincent, 439).

In many senses, this is the advice of *The Prince:* to adapt to the corruption Italy was facing and save her from it.

B. Reversing Corruption in a Princely Way

When a society had fallen from its lawful condition to corruption, the greatest challenge was to reclaim it. "It is a great good fortune for a republic to have a legislator sufficiently wise to give her laws so regulated that, without the necessity of correcting them, they afford security to those who live under them" (*Discourses,* 1:2; Ricci–Vincent, 110).[12] But a state not so fortunate required something by way of help. Italy was such a state.

Hence, his advice in *The Prince* must be understood as tied to the circumstances of corruption then existing in Italy. After noting that it is almost impossible that one could reform a corrupt polity incrementally, Machiavelli suggests that the corruption of such a polity's institutions is also hard to correct at one stroke "because to accomplish it the use of lawful devices is not enough, since lawful methods are futile, but it is necessary to resort to unlawful ones, such as violence and arms, and before anything else to become prince of that city and have power to manage it in one's own way" (*Discourses*, 1:18).

Noting that this forcible change to good government assumes a good man while the force itself seems to require an evil man, he concludes that "a good man will seldom attempt to become prince by evil methods, even though his purpose be good; on the other hand a wicked man, when he has become prince, will seldom try to do what is right, for it never will come into his mind to use rightly the authority he has gained wickedly" (ibid.) Ending corruption requires a leader evil enough to perform cruel deeds and good enough to do them for the right reasons; a singular such leader would be a prince.

This is why a prince is sometimes necessary. Keeping in mind Marx's metaphor of the "material conditions necessary" for a particular form of society, we can understand Machiavelli to be saying that a prince may be essential for creating the material conditions necessary for freedom while temporarily depriving the people of exactly that freedom. Experiencing the kind of prince he advocates—a Romulus, say, who gave Rome good representative institutions—arouses in people the need for a Brutus, or someone who would fully realize the potential for freedom in those good institutions. This recognition that peoople must be civilized before they can be freed, coupled with a recognition that civilizing them requires forcible imposition of laws, is why Machiavelli could write a book of advice to a prince when his moral and political convictions committed him to a republic.

A good prince, then, is one whose motivation has shifted from ambition to *gloria* and who seeks to establish good laws that will empower him during his lifetime and work to his glorious reputation after his death. This vision of princedom, inspired by his myth of Romulus, was never lost to Machiavelli, nor did he abandon his hopes for Medicean glory, especially when a member of the family became a pope. In 1520, responding to Pope Leo X's questions about a new constitution for Florence, Machiavelli returned to this theme of the glorious, and not merely ambitious, prince. Continuing to press the princely rulers to reestablish a republic in the city, Machiavelli advised them to reconstitute the *balia* and the council, along with a court of appeal. Advising the pope to be like Romulus, he recommended princely veto power during the lifetime of the pope and his nephew. Even the proposed executive powers that were to grant monarchical status to the Medici were drawn from Roman inspirations: "I believe, considering all this organization as a republic, and without your authority, that it lacks nothing necessary to a free government. . . . But if it is considered while Your Holiness and the Most Reverend Monsignor are still living, it is a monarchy, because you have authority over the armed forces, you have authority over the criminal judges, you keep the laws in your bosom. I do not know anything more to be wished for in a city" (*A Discourse on Remodeling the Government of Florence,* Gilbert, 113; compare this to his description of Romulus's powers, *Discourses* 1:19). Here, as in *The Prince,* Machiavelli continued to invite the Medici to play the role of Romulus—whose mythic figure continued to inspire Machiavelli's vision of glorious princedom, especially in a city lacking laws—so that Italy would some day know her Brutus.

The rectification of corruption requires unusual, and severe, medicine. Unfortunately, the need to use severe and cruel means attracts bad rather than good actors: "And yet nearly all men, deceived by a false good and a false glory, allow themselves voluntarily or ignorantly to be drawn towards those who deserve more blame than praise. Such as by the establishment of a republic or kingdom could earn eternal glory for themselves incline to tyranny, without perceiving how much glory, how much honor, security, satisfaction, and tranquility of mind, they forfeit; and what infamy, disgrace, blame, danger, and disquietude they incur" (*Discourses,* 1:10; Ricci–Vincent, 142).

A prince who seeks to become a tyrant is deceived by a false glory, by ambition, and yet princes, who are necessary to correct corruption, can be good princes. When they abide by the laws, their accomplishments earn Machiavelli's highest praises:

> In the period under the good Emperors he [the reader] will see the prince secure amidst his people, who are also living in security; he will see peace and justice prevail in the world, the authority of the Senate respected, the magistrates honored, the wealthy citizens enjoying their riches, nobility and virtue exalted, and everywhere will he see tranquility and well-being. And on the other hand he will behold all animosity, license, corruption, and all noble ambition extinct. During the period of the good Emperors he will see that golden age when every one could hold and defend whatever opinion he pleased; in fine, he will see the triumph of the world, the prince surrounded with reverence and glory, and beloved by his people, who are happy and secure. (ibid., 144)

A good prince is one who abides by the laws he himself created, laws that will create the conditions for the later glory of his people by making of them a good, law-abiding people now. Sometimes this requires actions that appear to be evil by conventional standards. Machiavelli's point, given his moral theory, is that the apparent evil is not a real evil. Similarly, although "liberality," a willingness to spend the wealth of the kingdom to keep the people happy, appears to be a "good" thing and comes recommended to a prince by no less an authority than Cicero, it is in reality a bad thing: "[A] prince must care little for the reputation of being a miser, if he wishes to avoid robbing his subjects, if he wishes to be able to defend himself, to avoid becoming poor and contemptible, and not to be forced to become rapacious; this niggardliness is one of those vices which enable him to reign" (*Prince*, chapter 16).

Even when he must be cruel, a good prince is cruel for the right reasons: "[O]ne ought to be both feared and loved, but as it is difficult for the two to go together, it is much safer to be feared than loved, if one of the two has to be wanting. . . . Still, a prince should make himself feared in such a way that if he does not gain love, he at any rate avoids hatred; for fear and the absence of hatred may well go together, and will be always attained by one who abstains from interfering with the property of his citizens and subjects or with their women" (ibid., chapter 17).

While a prince should be feared rather than loved, he should prefer to be both loved and feared—but he must never earn the hatred of his people. It is perhaps of note that Machiavelli moves from this topic to the next (eighteenth) chapter ("In What Way Princes Must Keep Faith") before moving to chapter 19 ("That We Must Avoid Being Despised and Hated"). After all, he wants to teach good princes how to survive. And conspiracies, the natural result of the prince's having earned hatred, are a threat to princely survival: "I conclude, therefore, that a prince need trouble little about conspiracies when the people are well disposed, but when they are hostile and hold him in hatred, then he must fear everything and everybody" (*Prince*, chapter 19).

A good prince, then, need fear little, while few things can preserve a bad prince. This precipitates Machiavelli's comments on fortresses: "Therefore the best fortress is to be found in the love of the people, for although you may have fortresses they will not save you if you are hated by the people" (ibid., chapter 20).

However daunting it may be to avoid earning the people's hatred, the tactical problems only seem overwhelming; a quick analysis shows that there are in fact relatively few who would oppose a good prince in his quest to reduce a people to lawfulness:

> For in all republics, however organized, there are never more than forty or fifty citizens who attain a position that entitles them to command. As this is a small number, it is easy to make sure of them, either by having them put out of the way, or by giving them such a share of the public honors and offices as, according to their condition, will in great measure content them. The others, who only care to live in security, are easily satisfied by institutions and laws that confirm at the same time the general security of the people and the power of the prince. When a prince does this, and the people see that by no chance he infringes the laws, they will in a very little while be content, and live in tranquility. (*Discourses*, 1:16)

In this fashion will a prince win eternal glory and the love of his people.

Machiavelli even offers the aspiring prince several models of ancient rulers who accomplished exactly this task:

> For it is much easier to be beloved by the good than the wicked, and to obey the laws than to enforce them; and if kings desire to know what course they have to pursue to do this, they need take no other trouble than to follow the example of the lives of good rulers, such as Timoleon of Corinth, Aratus of Sicyon, and the like, whose lives they will find to have afforded as much security and satisfaction to him who ruled as to those who were governed; which should make kings desire to imitate them, as is easily done. For when men are well governed, they neither seek nor desire any other liberty; as was experienced by the two above-named princes, whom their people constrained to reign to the end of their lives, though they often wished to retire to private life. (*Discourses*, 3:5)

So, by a few wisely chosen acts of cruelty and terror, a good prince can both demonstrate and enhance his power, blazing a path that others will follow, to his and their greater glory.

Of course, cruel acts performed by a good ruler creates a practical and moral quandary. How can actions and actors so cruel be good? The answer seems simply to be: cruelty is good only when the times are unusual. What would otherwise be good may not be good—and what would otherwise be bad may not be bad—under unusual circumstances. At least one analyst, John Leonard, has commented on this connection of goodness (*bonta*) with glory in Machiavelli's thought, concluding that extraordinary and even cruel actions could be an indication of goodness only if it is "consistent with glory" and complements "the needs of the state."[13]

Following this line of reasoning, we might infer that, in conditions of corruption, "Extraordinary action must fill the gap left by the absence of virtue because the majority of men are incapable of internalizing not only virtue but any code of conduct that requires them to define their own good in terms of a wider good. . . . Rather, extraordinary action is a response to a vision of private ties as posing a potential threat to public life."[14] Perhaps the most extraordinary action available to a republican like Machiavelli would be a recommendation that a people who had been free be placed under the severe rule of a prince; so desperate were conditions in Italy that this could be the only recourse to end the corruption of "private ties." The threat to public life, to which Machiavelli referred, was probably the private wealth of the neo-feudal lords who were seeking to resurrect in commercial cities the private ties similar to the oaths of fealty that had bound some people to feudal lords; feudal or private, both divided up a nation into sects. Equally important to Machiavelli as the republic of Florence, then, was the need for unification and modernization of Italy.

PRINCES AS MODERNIZERS AND UNIFIERS OF NATIONS

Although Machiavelli might have preferred a unified and free Italy to one unified under a Medicean prince, he was realist and empiricist enough to recognize that the conditions necessary for a modern republic were lacking. Given the impossibility of freedom, unification under a prince was preferable to division. Hence, the first task of modernizing the nation was to deal with the corruption (that is, to find a Romulus) and rely upon the *virtù* of some subsequent leader (a Brutus) to form the republic. If a nation is not fortunate enough to have such a Romulus to unify and a Brutus to free it at the same time, then it may be necessary to have two distinct *virtuoso* actions, one to create the material conditions for freedom and another to realize that freedom.

Nor is Machiavelli relying on *fortuna* to provide the second action; rather his trust is in a human need for freedom, which will drive us to demand the security of laws we have made to meet our own needs. This requires a leader who appears, on the surface, to resemble a tyrant. This is indeed only an appearance; and given human needs, we can expect that even the appearance of tyranny will not continue indefinitely. We can also expect that any pure form of government, like monarchy, will eventually degenerate into tyranny. Consequently, having experienced the benefits of a Romulus, the people will eventually come to need a Brutus:

> No one ever displayed so much sagacity, or was esteemed so wise on account of any distinguished act, as Junius Brutus deserves to be esteemed for his simulation of folly. [Not only did this simulation secure him, but it afforded him] a better chance of destroying the kings, and of liberating his country whenever an opportunity should offer. And that such was really his thought may be seen, first from his interpretation of the oracle of Apollo, when he pretended to have fallen and kissed the earth, hoping thereby to propitiate the gods to his projects; and afterwards, when on the occasion of the death of Lucretia, in the midst of the father, husband, and other relatives, he was the first to pluck the dagger from her breast and to make all present swear henceforth to suffer no king to reign in Rome. (*Discourses*, 3:2)

Thus, in circumstances of corruption, extraordinary action is needed; traditional morality is suspended, and one's moral obligation was apparently to act in such a way as to end the degradation and bring humans back to nobility. "From all the things explained above comes the difficulty or impossibility of maintaining a government in a corrupt city or of setting up a new government there. Indeed when in such a city one is to be set up or maintained, necessity demands that it be inclined more toward kingly rule than toward popular rule, in order that those men who, on account of their arrogance, cannot be controlled by law may in some fashion be restrained by a power almost kingly" (*Discourses*, 1:18).

Perhaps, then, it should not be surprising that Machiavelli offers different moral evaluations of particular actions in varying circumstances, since one's actions in creating a lawful republic out of chaotic, amoral corruption will be judged differently from identical actions within a lawful republic.

Presumably, after the fall of the republic when he was writing *The Prince,* the former secretary saw—or hoped to see—something in his "noble" overlords, the Medici, that led him to believe that they could provide part of the salvation of Italy, if only their ambition could be transformed into a search for glory. What might this have been? Might it be that they seemed willing and able to employ power when it came into their hands?

One need not speculate nor infer to answer these questions; Machiavelli has explicitly addressed them. It certainly seems significant that so illustrious a Renaissance man of letters as Lorenzo de' Medici is quoted but once by Machiavelli in a chapter (3:29) of *The*

Discourses entitled "The Faults of the People Spring From the Faults of Their Rulers": "And Lorenzo de' Mecidi confirms this idea by saying: 'The example of the prince is followed by the masses, who keep their eyes always turned upon their chief.'"

In short, Machiavelli seemed to continue to consider the Medici as a family who appreciated the role that leaders could play in the reforming of a corrupt people. Unfortunately, however, the reformers of corruption were also corrupters. They did not fully understand how to turn power to the pursuit of glory. They needed a book like *The Prince*.

One problem, of course, was that the wealth of the Medici had enabled them to purchase power, but they had not purchased that power for the sake of the kind of historical glory Machiavelli had in mind. Rather than seeking to free the Italian nation, they had smaller "ambitions" and had to be shown how to direct their vision upward, beyond their familial interests to the interests of the nation. What can you teach a commercial burgher family that will encourage them to raise their sights to the larger good? "The art of war" is Machiavelli's response.

Hence, in devoting so much of *The Prince* to matters of war, Machiavelli is not *simply* the militarist he at times appears to be. Although he is preoccupied with military affairs, this is not for their own sake but for two higher reasons. First, his dedication to the infantry is a method of creating a modern army in two distinct senses: an infantry is both more democratic and more motivated by nationalism and defense of homeland than were the mercenary armies then laying waste to Italy.

Second, encouraging military concerns in a family whose principal goal had been self-enrichment is a way of gearing them up to be concerned with the common good. This is why he teaches the grandsons of Lorenzo the Great that

> A prince should therefore have no other aim or thought nor take up any other thing for his study, but war and its organisation and discipline, for that is the only art that is necessary to one who commands, and it is of such virtue that it not only maintains those who are born princes, but often enables men of private fortune to attain to that rank. And one sees, on the other hand, that when princes think more of luxury than of arms, they lose their state. The chief cause of the loss of states, is the contempt of this art, and the way to acquire them is to be well versed in the same. (*Prince*, chapter 14)

"Forget about your wealth and luxuries," Machiavelli is telling a family whose sole concern so far has been only the amassing of

wealth to purchase luxuries. Indeed, they are advised that the accumulation and consumption of wealth is dangerous for a prince, since
it seduces a prince into believing that it will make him strong:

> And money alone, so far from being a means of defence, will only render
> a prince the more liable to being plundered. There cannot, therefore,
> be a more erroneous opinion than that money is the sinews of war. . . .
> [A story about Solon is recounted here, in which great treasure of a king
> is shown to Solon, who is then asked what he thinks of that king's power.]
> Solon replied "that he did not consider him powerful on that account,
> because war was made with iron, and not with gold, and that some one
> might come who had more iron than he, and would take his gold from
> him." (*Discourses*, 2:10)

Not only will wealth not strengthen a prince militarily, but it will
make him a more obvious target. We can almost hear the former
secretary's unwritten words to the illustrious family of oppressors
who might be capable of unifying Italy: "Turn your attention away
from wealth. Turn your attention instead to concerns of the state.
Become statesmen!" The art of war was the means for achieving
this good end, and his writing *The Art of War* was a means to the
same end.

CONCLUSION

If Machiavelli was seeking to transform Medician ambition into
a desire for *gloria,* then Machiavelli's advice to the Medici in *The
Prince* was indeed revolutionary and it would, as Dietz contends,
undo them; but not in the way that a feudal conspiracy of deception
would. Indeed, in his recommendations to the Medici for a new
constitution for Florence, Machiavelli explicitly recommends that
they follow the lead of Romulus, giving Florence institutions like
ancient Rome's, institutions that would later lead to republican
glory. Rather than wanting to assassinate them immediately, he
wanted to render them powerful in their lives and powerless in
death; as he advises the Medici to leave their country villas and
estates and move to the cities, Machiavelli aims to modernize their
feudal aspirations, to lure them into a different form of using wealth
that would not be detrimental to liberty. As he advises that it "is
better to be feared than to be loved," he is urging them to resist
the temptations of feudal loyalties and the sectarianism that goes
with them and opt instead for a more modern and nationalistic ap-

proach to governance. As he advises them to forgo castles, he aims not to turn them over to republic assassins but to make proper capitalists of them by having them use their wealth in different ways and for different ends. As he advises them to arm the citizens, he seeks the loyalty due a nation-state that grows along with commercial markets. As he advises the Medici to eschew the liberality that worked so well for Cosimo and Lorenzo, he is hoping to substitute a more modern form of loyalty that is less tied to sectarianism and personages, and more tied to a "people." As he advises the Medici to be mistrustful of the *ottimati,* he is suggesting that they create a new regime that moves beyond obsolete feudal arrangements. The advice to the Medici then is that they, as princes, set up a modernizing version of the principality of Romulus.

Similarly, an armed citizenry is recommended as a means of modernizing Italy. The Swiss and other mercenaries will be no match for armies marching under the flag of the king of their own nation. If Italy is to be saved from foreign domination, she must modernize her armies. Similarly, feudal fortresses would have little value in modern warfare; why waste money and human energy upon them? The relentless theme of Machiavelli's advice to the aspiring princes in the Medici family is to seek the glory suited to modern times, to lay the foundations for Italian freedom and glory. "Play Romulus," he keeps insisting, "create the conditions for later freedom and you will be remembered forever in glory." The call of *The Prince* is the call for political modernization.

7

Ambition, Corruption, and Nationalism

AMBITION, THE NATION, AND THE STATE

OPPONENTS and proponents agree that Machiavelli is a theorist of the nation-state. From him more than from most other philosophers—with perhaps Jean Bodin the principal exception outside of the Fascists—one would expect to learn that "Such princes and republics of modern times as have no national troops for defence or attack ought well to be ashamed of it . . ." (*Discourses,* 1:20; Ricci–Vincent, 175). Less certain is the precise meaning he gave to the idea of nationalism, which was just beginning to emerge. Mansfield is almost certainly correct that Machiavelli's use of *lo stato* was too "personal"[1] to be equivalent to our modern usage of the word "state." Even though the notion of *res publica* in the sense of "affairs of state" can be traced to the ancients, the "state" might, in the Renaissance, have been little more than an "estate," the personal patrimony of a prince in some cases, although that notion was fading.

Yet Machiavelli's diplomatic experience as a delegate from Soderini's government obviously imprinted upon him the contrast between the feudal divisions of Italy and the more modern, though still quasi-feudal, unity of, say, the French nation. At the very least, Machiavelli certainly must stand at a point of transition from patrimony to the modern state. The central question concerns the way in which he bridges the ancient and the modern worlds. Mansfield is probably wrong that "the decisive shift was from the personal state in the Aristotelian sense to the *acquisitive* personal state of Machiavelli."[2] While ambition was a topic of some concern for Machiavelli, it was not a positive trait in his moral universe. In his *Tercets on Ambition,* he depicts them as "transgressions" and warns that "Everywhere Ambition and Avarice penetrate. When man was born into the world, they were born too; and if they had no existence, happy enough would be our condition" (lines 11–15; Gilbert,

735). In the private arena, acquisitive ambition led to elevating personal and familial interest to the highest position, even over moral duty and the common good; hence he feared it: "[T]he ambition of the rich, if . . . a city does not crush it, is what quickly brings her to ruin" (*Discourses*, 1: 37). In the public spheres of life, ambition was a perverse desire to employ the resources of the state for personal rather than collective interests.

Even attempting to formulate foreign policy on the basis of ambition was as hazardous as it was tempting: "I say then that there is no easier way to ruin a republic, where the people have power, than to involve them in daring enterprises; for where the people have influence they will always be ready to engage in them, and no contrary opinion will prevent them" (*Discourses*, 1 : 53; Ricci–Vincent, 250).

For a nation to survive, as well as for a republic to survive, ways must be found to limit ambitions.

Machiavelli's use of *ambizione* is exactly opposite to the ancient Roman use of *ambitio* where it referred "mostly . . . to public life."[3] By contrast, "For Machiavelli, *ambizione* is a striving for, or using, office or power to achieve private ends."[4] As Machiavelli viewed it, ambition was corrupting, corrosive. He certainly did not celebrate such ambition; rather it opposed the common good: "Those who are ambitious think more of themselves than of others, and this is why Machiavelli often contrasts actions motivated by *ambizione* with actions motivated by a desire to promote the common good."[5] In Machiavelli's writings, *ambizione* may even be the selfish motivation behind corruptive actions; it must be curtailed or transformed.

It is partly because of their private ambition[6] that Machiavelli denounces mercenaries:

> The mercenaries and auxiliaries are useless and dangerous, and if any one supports his state by the arms of mercenaries, he will never stand firm and sure, as they are disunited, ambitious, without discipline, faithless, bold amongst friends, cowardly amongst enemies, they have no fear of God, and keep no faith with men. Ruin is only deferred as long as the assault is postponed; in peace you are despoiled by them, and in war by the enemy. The cause of this is that they have no love or other motive to keep them in the field beyond a trifling wage, which is not enough to make them ready to die for you. (*Prince*, chapter 12)

Mercenaries are "ambitious" in exactly the sense that they are not committed to any good higher than their own pecuniary interests. For the sake of "a few more dollars" they will fight for you, or against you. Even while in your employ, when they are not fighting an enemy of yours, they will be looking to see how to pillage your wealth, since they are armed and you are not. Such men, unable to rise above their private ambitions, are not to be trusted.

A. Ambition and Aspirations to National Unification

But what about the "ambition" to unify a nation? Is that corruptive and dangerous to freedom, or is it a different type of desire? Apparently, it is not corruptive, or Machiavelli could never have written *The Prince*. But what are the conceptual grounds for distinguishing the two cases? Presumably, expanding a state to its "natural" boundaries, aspiring to national unification, is aimed at a common rather than a particular good.

The desire to incorporate all of one's people into a state, or the "external ambitions" of states expanding to include all of their people, are not corrupted because such expansion works to the benefit of all, as Price notes: "In *Discorsi*, II, 8, Machiavelli maintains that wars are made for two main reasons. One is when a people, constrained either by hunger or war, seeks a new country to inhabit. . . . The other is when . . . its intention is to acquire territory and to maintain it, and so act that both itself and the conquered territory are enriched, not impoverished."[7] Thus, as Machiavelli sees it, wars deriving from external ambition "promote the general good of the community."[8]

But some wars are bad. Wars that arise from the personal and petty ambitions of particular agents are "bad," while those that work to unify a people who are a part of a "nation" are "good" ones. But in an age in which the nation-state was just beginning to emerge, how are we to know how large a nation should be? How far can we legitimately expand? Machiavelli was realist enough to know that world conquest was not possible at this point in history—thus "when he speaks of *il bene comune*, he always has in mind the good of a particular community."[9]

For Machiavelli, then, "external ambition" had limits that were imposed by realities: "It may be concluded, then, that Machiavelli conceives of wars motivated by *ambizione* as being collective enterprises, whose normal purpose is to promote the general welfare of the state that undertakes them. And, lacking any conception of a universal common good, or of a genuine international 'society', he approves of them when the state that undertakes aggression is equipped to conquer and to maintain the conquered territories."[10] So expanding to incorporate all the people of a nation may be permissible; but as soon as an expanding state confronts peoples who

are radically different, problems begin: "when dominions are acquired in a province differing in langauage, laws, and customs, the
difficulties to be overcome are great, and it requires good fortune
as well as great industry to retain them . . ." (*Prince,* chapter 3,
Ricci–Vincent, 8). If the expansion of growing city-states is limited
by the principle of nationalism, then wars of expansion are in effect
wars of national unification and are justifiable. But such expansion
should not usually exceed national limits.

B. *Lo Stato* and the State

Given that *lo stato* is not yet the modern nation state, we can
rightfully ask how close to it Machiavelli has come in his recognition
of the emerging nation-state. Today, a nation is typically seen as an
entity different from the institutions of governance (the state) and
of the geography under its control (the territory or jurisdiction of
the state). Hence, the German "nation" is neither the institutions
nor the geographical territories held by the Germans; it is rather
the people who "belong" to that nation. In other words, nationhood
is more of a social and psychological reality than a physical one.
Any person is part of a nation (say, "is German") by claiming to be
part of that nation ("I am German") and being accepted by others
as such a part ("That person is one of us"). Since Italian unification
was relatively late in coming, one term of endearment in Italian is
paisano or "one from my village," which can carry the connotation
that "you are one of us" or "you are from my country."

What, in quattrocento Italy, would enable an expanding state "to
take and hold" a territory? Here again, the example of the French
unity that he had personally witnessed was part of Machiavelli's
equation: any given city-state could expand as far as the boundaries
of a common nationality extended, or as far as people recognized
their "conquerors" as a part of "them." Just as the success of the
Roman expansion had rested on the ability to make Roman citizens
of those they conquered, so the French unification had been possible
because of a sense of community and belonging that existed among
the French people.

This sense of unity poses both opportunities and risks for leaders.
Because a people can think of themselves as one, warriors ought to
refrain from insulting and threatening their enemies, since taunts
can strengthen their resolve to defeat their tormentors: "I hold it to
be a proof of great prudence for men to abstain from threats and
insulting words towards any one, for neither the one nor the other
in any way diminishes the strength of the enemy; but the one makes

him more cautious, and the other increases his hatred of you, and makes him more persevering in his efforts to injure you." (*Discourses,* 2:26; Ricci–Vincent, 373).

Much of politics is, after all, "mind games." Among a people who see themselves as belonging to a nation, wars of expansion benefit all by unifying that people.

But the exhortations to national unity in both *The Prince* and *The Discourses* would be reduced to mockery if we were to assume that Machiavelli approved of the French interference in Italian politics, of the "external ambition" of the French with respect to the Italians. We may in fact conclude that the limits placed on "external ambition" by Machiavelli were precisely the limits of nationality and that nationalism is a psychological reality based on the commonality derived from a common language, common experiences, a common religion, and a common culture. Machiavelli was at least aware of the emerging nation-state.

NATIONAL UNITY VERSUS NATIONAL HARMONY

How far in fact is it wise to go in order to unify a people? Should we be content to arouse the need for national communal feeling or should we go further, seeking harmony within a people? Is it enough that a people shares a sense of belonging together even though they are divided on a variety of issues? Or does unifying a nation require a homogenization that overcomes the divisions and promotes harmonious perspectives? Lionel McKenzie has argued that Rousseau and Machiavelli disagreed fundamentally on the question of the desirability of harmony in a polity, with Rousseau seeing it as necessary for liberty to be articulated in a general will while Machiavelli preferred a system of checks and balances in a polity with a division between the wealthy and the less well-off.[11] Much of McKenzie's thesis is right; another part is demonstrably wrong. Let us begin with the part he got right.

Rousseau was explicitly aware of Machiavelli's thoughts on faction, and he rejected them. But McKenzie's consideration of both philosophers' evaluations of Rome leads him to conclude that, although Rousseau implied that he had refuted Machiavelli's theory of factions, he had in fact not addressed Machiavelli's argument. His refutation of Machiavelli "was equivocal and arbitrary," since part of the force of Rousseau's argument "depended upon a deliberate confusion of key terms. The reference to 'orders' and to the existence of two 'states,' or estates, in one was calculated to bring to the minds of his audience the orders and estates of the ancien régime instead of the existence of the broadly opposed social interests which Machiavelli's analysis identified."[12] In other words, Rousseau's restatement of the problem of faction in terms of French *états* violated the spirit of Machiavelli's insight. Where Machiavelli was arguing against feudal splits but approving of factions based on other forms of property holding, Rousseau makes it appear that all factions are divisive in the way that feudal classes were and then concludes that, to survive, a republic must reach beyond faction to harmony.

This leads MacKenzie to a fundamental inference about French as opposed to British/American democracy:

> Enough is known about the basic assumptions of political rhetoric in the French Revolution to suggest that Rousseau was successful in winning wide acceptance for his theory that harmony was the norm in a political association constituted by enlightened and uncorrupted individuals. The history of the revolution may be understood in part as the record of how rapidly the circle of virtue narrows when men allow their thought and action to be guided by such a theory. The disillusionment of many [with the Revolution] . . . in both England and America is related to the fact that the republican tradition had taken a different direction in France than it had taken in the Atlantic or English-speaking world, with very different results. In explaining this parting of the ways, Rousseau's role . . . cannot be overlooked.[13]

While McKenzie may be too harsh in blaming the excesses of the French Revolution on Rousseau's desire for a harmonious community, he is right on two points. First, the ambiguity concerning *lo stato, estate,* and *the state* undermines Rousseau's argument. By playing upon the senses of estate that tie it to feudal patrimony, he is also playing upon the emotional reaction against feudal divisions, especially of classes. While Rousseau might have depicted class interests as particular interests opposed to the general interest, Machiavelli saw positive benefits in some types of class distinctions—although not in feudal classes, which *were* divisive. Conflicts, within limits, between the rich and the poor could be beneficial to a polity, as they were to Rome; but conflicts between the landed gentry and the peasants tended to be corrupt and divisive, leading to sectarian ambitions and then to violence. So some kinds of class conflict are beneficial to a republic, so long as there is not too much inequality, while others—especially feudal dissensions—are destructive of freedom.

In addition, McKenzie reasons, while Rousseau valued the har-

mony of a general will, Machiavelli valued the creative conflict
engendered by faction. Machiavelli's observations about factions
are initially startling: "I say that those who condemn the dissensions
[in ancient Rome] . . . seem to me to be finding fault with what as
a first cause kept Rome free . . . ; they are not considering that in
every republic there are two opposed factions, that of the people
and that of the rich, and that all laws made in favor of liberty result
from their discord. . . . It is impossible, therefore, to pronounce these
dissensions injurious . . ." (*Discourses,* 1:4; Gilbert, 202–3).

The dynamic interplay between those with wealth and those without it can keep both factions alert to corruptive abuses of the other.
In quattrocento Florence, a healthy dose of "factionalism" would
have been beneficial to freedom and democracy, instead of which,
as the historical data suggest, one faction had rendered the other
powerless. By the end of the fourteenth century, as Pitkin reminds
us,[14] Florence was no longer a financially stable and successful commercial center, and the republic shared that fate of decline; as the
role of the Medici family came to be one of domination within the
guilds, a small circle of wealthy families came to form a ruling elite.
For this elite, self-interest was far more important than public service, although they continued to pretend that they were serving the
public. The corruption was so extensive that it was the inner circle
of the elite who "decided how much money [the city] needed; they
or their friends who put up the cash for war loans; they who imposed
taxes as security for the sum; they who made sure that repayment
of their loans would be given precedence and at what interest. . . .
The gap between the self-protecting rich and the heavily taxed
majority was growing."[15]

Citing this passage, Pitkin is right to conclude that "In Florentine
politics in the latter half of the fifteenth century, as in the late
medieval Church all over Europe, the gap widened between ideals
and practice."[16] The new commercial elite was not much different
in practice from the old feudal elite; both put their personal and
familial interests ahead of the common good.

How can such an intractable problem be solved? Quentin Skinner's great insight into Machiavelli's theory is that he saw clearly
Machiavelli's solution: "to frame the laws relating to the constitution
in such a way as to engineer a tensely-balanced equilibrium between
these opposed social forces, one in which all the parties remain
involved in the business of government."[17] In such a system of
checks and balances each rival will jealously examine each action
of the other, so that "the resolution of the pressures thus engendered
will mean that only those 'laws and institutions' which are 'conducive

to public liberty' will actually be passed. Although motivated entirely by their selfish interests, the factions will thus be guided, as if by an invisible hand, to promote the public interest in all their legislative acts. . . ."[18]

Seeking to control the factional interests, Machiavelli asserted the desirability of placing the protection of liberty in the hands of the poor, stating that

> because in every republic there are rich men and men of the people, there has been doubt in the hands of which of these the said guardianship is better placed. . . . And, without doubt, if one will look at the purpose of the nobles and of those who are not noble, there will be seen in the former great longing to rule, and in the latter merely longing not to be ruled, and as a consequence greater eagerness to live in freedom. . . . Hence, if the common people are set up to guard liberty, it is reasonable that they will care for it better, and since they cannot seize it themselves, they will not allow others to seize it. (Discourses, 1:5; Gilbert, 205)

Obviously, Machiavelli's point here is not simply that the poor like liberty more or that they are more virtuous; rather, they have good reason to be on guard against the corruptive *ambizione* of the nobles—and constitutional designers need to put them in a position to check the ambition of the nobles. Hence, "faction," the limited conflict between the rich and the poor, is a good thing for a republic, provided that constitutional designers have planned for it and devised a method for controlling it.

Nevertheless, some social divisions were evil. Because Machiavelli distrusted feudal aristocrats with their ambition and saw them as dangers to republics, he came to value the democratic ideal of equality of holdings. Concentrations of wealth, in his eyes, were corruptive: "To a great extent the ambition of the rich, if by various means and in various ways a city does not crush it, is what quickly brings her to ruin" (*Discourses*, 1:37; Gilbert, 274.)

Given their ambitions and their unequal economic power, the rich can corrupt a polity. "Such corruption and slight aptitude for free life spring from inequality in a city; and anyone who tries to bring her back to equality must use entirely extralegal means, such as few can or will use . . ." (*Discourses*, 1:17; Gilbert, 240). If a small portion of a people becomes excessively wealthy, if the gap between them and the remainder of the polity becomes too large, they can turn economic power to political power—and then direct that power against republican freedom. Machiavelli's general outline of this progression reveals two major steps. First, *il grandi* use their economic power to aid those in economic distress, purchasing their loyalty. Second, emboldened by this loyalty, they begin an eroding attack on the laws until they can transform the republic into an oligarchy. To prevent this, a polity should never permit the gap to become too wide; this is why "well-ordered republics ought to keep their treasuries rich and their citizens poor" (*Discourses*, 1:34; Gilbert, 272). So, in *The Art of War* (book 1, Gilbert, 572), as Cosimo asks Fabrizio which of the customs of the ancients he would like to introduce, the response includes a respect for poverty which he defines as a willingness of a people to forgo personal gain for national glory. The proper opposite of a respect for poverty, of course, is ambition.

This advice apparently does not mean that the very poorest members of a republic have to be kept destitute; in elaborating upon the statement that, "We have argued elsewhere that the most useful thing a free state can bring about is to keep its citizens poor," Machiavelli examines the case of Rome and praises her because, whatever the reason, "her people were still in the utmost poverty" (*Discourses*, 3:24; Gilbert, 486). Importantly, this does not mean that anyone was kept from riches, from power, or from the necessities of life: "I cannot believe that any condition was stronger in producing this effect [acceptance of poverty and preservation of liberty] than the knowledge that poverty did not close your road to whatever rank and whatever honor" (*Discourses*, 3:24).

Machiavelli's meaning, then, must be that Rome did not permit a lack of wealth to become a barrier to public life and that Rome prevented massive accumulations of wealth that would enable the very wealthy to corrupt the less well-off by bribes. In short, the constitution prevented the use of wealth to realize effectively one's lordly "ambitions," but neither wealth nor its lack closed the doors of opportunity. Hence, "keeping the people poor" does not mean pushing the most impoverished citizens deeper into penury; rather, it means keeping the rich from becoming too ambitious.

CONCLUSION

No individualist, Machiavelli believed that human freedom was possible only in a properly constituted community. The collectivism he envisioned took the form of nationalism (a concept that has only become more important since then). An examination of Machiavelli's life suggests the significance of this idea for his time; a commitment to the common good of a people held the possibility of liberating humans from the narrow confines of personal and familial interests. Given the social and historical situations that Machiavelli observed, nationalism then promised to be a benevolent force.

It is no longer easy to be so optimistic about this notion. While no superior organizational idea has yet manifested itself, two signal events force us to reconsider the notion of nationalism and to define the limits beyond which pursuit of national interests becomes illegitimate. The first was that peculiar blend of statism and nationalism that brought about the Holocaust and World War II. The racist evils of Fascism may have unfairly tarnished the collectivist idea of nationalism but there can be no doubt that the collectivist notion of the *volk,* or people, contributed, along with Darwinian ideas of inheritable traits and "survival of the fittest," to racism, hatred, suffering, and death on a scale that is almost unimaginable.

The second event was the implosion of the former Soviet empire. Even though much of Stalinist theory ("socialism in one state") and practice (e.g., the purges) may have been more similar to Fascism than to orthodox Marxism, the proclamation of "internationalism" in Marxian theory provided a basis for curtailing nationalistic hatred and exclusion. In the absence of that countervailing force, nationalist excesses in the former Communist states may be writing one of the most tragic chapters in twentieth-century history as "ethnic cleansing" returns to our world.

Nevertheless, anyone sympathetic with Machiavelli's writings could not be so naive as to believe that nationalism is dying and we are about to transcend it. That the Soviet armies could merely constrain, and not eradicate, intense nationalisms is proof of that. Yet challenges to nationalism need no longer be dismissed as extremist rantings. Perhaps the time has come for a twentieth-century Machiavelli to point a way to an alternative basis for the state. One alternative already exists, although its significance is rarely appreciated. Just as the nation-state supplanted the city-state, the multinational state is now edging ahead of the nation-state. While European conquests of colonies frequently aided this movement by forcibly pulling disparate peoples into one administrative unit, the more significant occurrences are of peoples joining a state on a voluntary basis. The experiments of the United States and of Canada are hardly completed enough to be judged successes, but they suggest the power of this alternative. Similarly, but for different historical reasons, the Mexican successes in bringing such diverse peoples as the Mayans, Aztecs, and Europeans together in one state are not trivial. In addition, many African states have diverse peoples (Nigeria is a good example), while Russia and China each bring incredible ethnic diversity under one government. Ethnic or racial purity may be becoming a luxury we can no longer afford.

If such multinational states are to flourish and survive, Machiavelli's call to equality will take on new meaning and significance, and we should examine that call to determine if its philosophical underpinnings can support the weight its demands place upon a society.

8

Economics, Equality, and Justice

EQUALITY AS AN INSTITUTIONAL BARRIER TO CORRUPTIVE AMBITION

ALTHOUGH equality is frequently associated with the idea of socialism, effective moves toward equality have been frequently accomplished in liberal regimes. But the central theoretical question concerns the justification of equality, and the most sound justification may turn out to be the liberal democratic justification. For instance, Amy Gutmann argues persuasively in *Liberal Equality* that equality is implicit in many of the premises of liberal democratic thought. Although Machiavelli is only mentioned passingly in her account, he draws out the equalizing implications of liberal democracy even more than most similar thinkers. But his calls for equality, like most liberal ideals, are not of the leveling sort that would prohibit all inequalities.[1] Even Marx, from a socialist perspective, acknowledged that perfect equality of holdings was impracticable.[2] Given the inequality of human needs, Marx reasoned, even if we were to achieve a perfect equality of holdings and of income, those of us with fewest needs would have "more," relative to what is needed, than the rest.

Like Marx, most egalitarians do not seek to "knock down" those who are "productive" to a level below what they "deserve." Rather, for the most part, they seek to minimize the gap between the very rich and the very poor, between the billionaires on the one hand and the homeless on the other. To the extent that egalitarians are rational and practical, they seek to create a condition of open opportunity where holdings are not radically different, and they aim only to remove the privileged positions of status within society that make productivity unnecessary for some people.

The moral appeal of liberal egalitarianism is rooted in an intuitive idea of moral desert: no persons or groups of persons should have incomes greater than the value of the goods they produce or are

175

responsible for calling into production. By direct inference, if the incomes of some exceed their productive contributions, the incomes of others must be lower than the value of their productive contributions. From this egalitarian perspective, the deficiency of unregulated markets is that they can permit moral inequities of this sort. This perception of inequity feeds the egalitarian resentment of the wealthy few who exploit the less fortunate but more-productive many. In such a context, arriving at equality requires rewriting the rules so that the market allocates to the various parties an income more commensurate with the contribution each actually makes to the collective wealth. Our "rights" to an income come to be defined by these new rules: under rules written with an eye to equality, none of us would earn more than we have created in value, whereas, under rules written without regard to equality, one person could earn more than the Gross National Product of some countries.[3]

An advocate of equality in this liberal sense, Machiavelli was committed to a comparatively narrow gap between the richest and poorest within a democratic society. But unlike many other egalitarians, his commitment was not the result of a moral preference for equality as a moral good or right. Rather he became committed to equality as a result of realizing that it is a necessary condition for freedom in a democratic republic. Nor was this equality to result in the elimination of factions or classes; as we have seen, he believed that the factious classes of Rome had made freedom possible. In what way, then, is inequality seen as a problem in his theory? Why is inequality an enemy of freedom? Why does freedom thrive in equality's presence and shrivel in its absence?

One way of establishing Machiavelli's beliefs—that inequalities of wealth, whether feudal or capitalistic, were all inimical to democratic freedom—is by considering an alternative hypothesis; we can render one hypothesis more plausible by showing the deficiencies of the other. Both perspectives recognize that Machiavelli was committed to equality; they part on the nature of that commitment. The alternative hypothesis, that Machiavelli was opposed to feudal inequalities but not to capitalistic inequalities, has been powerfully presented by Lionel McKenzie. For the sake of convenience, let us call his hypothesis the *particular* or *feudal* hypothesis; the alternative will be called the *general* hypothesis. Either Machiavelli believed that the corrosive and corruptive wealth of the feudal nobility (*uomini grandi* or *nobili*) in particular was and remains inimical to freedom, or he believed more generally that any excessive inequalities of wealth, whether feudal or capitalist, would be inimical to freedom.

Let us first indicate what is not in question, so that these can become premises in the later argument. Clearly, for Machiavelli it is no problem that people hold wealth and hold it differentially; if he believed otherwise, the differences between poor and wealthy could not have been seen as helping Rome to preserve her liberty. If, for instance, he were a rigid, utopian egalitarian, then any and all disparities in wealth would be bad, whereas he found the disparities between rich and poor to be good, insofar as they are conducive to liberty or can be made conducive to liberty by a good constitution. Thus, he could not be a rigid egalitarian, and for him the problem of inequality is not merely that people have different amounts of wealth or income.

The problem, then, appears to be in the *manner* in which people hold property. What are the different ways that people hold and use property unequally, and how might these differences support or oppose freedom under democratic laws? Let us examine the rationale for each hypothesis in turn.

The "Feudal Wealth" Hypothesis

The *particular* hypothesis offered by McKenzie about unequal property is that Machiavelli recognized that feudal property was opposed to democratic freedom and so Machiavelli came to oppose feudal property. McKenzie's Machiavelli beat Marx to the punch, noting the corrosive impact of differential wealth and classes at the very beginning of the modern era. Unlike Rousseau who had argued that "money and finance," presumably capitalist wealth, enabled people to "pay others to discharge their political and military duties in the form of parliamentary representation and a standing army," Machiavelli apparently shared Montesquieu's "belief in the neutral or benign political consequences of commerce compared with the malignancy of jurisdiction over land and castles."[4]

Before criticizing this thesis, let me note what its strengths are. It focuses on Machiavelli's political economy; it highlights his democratic impulses; and it avoids some of the petty and polemical interpretations. An even greater advantage is that this thesis enables one to make sense of passages—Machiavelli's ravings against "gentlemen" near the end of the first book of *The Discourses,* for instance—that escape the alternative interpretations.

By this interpretative hypothesis, what is the problem of inequality or wealth? If we take as a guide the ways that the Medici, especially Cosimo, used their wealth, then we might begin to suspect that the corruptive defect of their wealth was that it was *feudal* wealth. Thus McKenzie reasons that the feudal and patrimonial holdings of wealth corrupted a republic's freedom. Even though commerce was "scarcely a typical theme of civic humanist thought," Machiavelli had seen firsthand the impacts of commerce and the new types of property holding that were characteristic of commercial urban centers like Florence, and he "never condemned commerce; quite to the contrary, he seemed to give it his approval in the case of Venice, to which he referred in the course of his examination of the effects caused by the disproportionate ownership of landed property."[5]

Indeed, Machiavelli was explicit that those cities with remnants of the feudal aristocracy were unlikely to become free—feudalism's elite was incompatible with democratic freedom. So he may be criticizing feudalism and its aristocratic elites as he writes that "those republics which have thus preserved their political existence uncorrupted do not permit any of their citizens to be or live in the manner of gentlemen, but rather maintain amongst them a perfect equality, and are the most decided enemies of the lords and gentlemen that exist in the country; so that, if by chance any of them fall into their hands, they kill them, as being the chief promoters of all corruption and troubles" (*Discourses*, 1:55).

In other words, one solution to the problem of inequality is to kill off those who have more. It should not surprise us that Machiavelli would not shrink from this—if that were required for human freedom. For him, there is no natural right to own feudal property that is used to destroy the freedom of others. Equally importantly, achieving "perfect equality" means prohibiting "gentlemen" from achieving excessive wealth. McKenzie's plausible thesis is that such striking down of the feudal elite might make democratic freedom possible.

Although it would be premature to proclaim on the basis of this evidence that Machiavelli was a theorist of capitalism, we can probably consider him a witness to the preliminary changes of society that ultimately gave rise to the free market economies of Europe. He also appears to have been cognizant of the changes occurring in property holding even though he lacked the vocabulary for articulating the insight. He also seems to have approved of this new method of holding property, Mckenzie rightly reasons, since it was conducive to free republics. Republics could not be established in Naples, Rome, Romagna, and Lombardy because the "concentration of landed wealth in the hands of a few 'gentlemen' or nobility produced inequality and increased the growth of political corruption."[6]

Things were different, though, in cities like Venice. Here a democratic tradition was alive, although there were also families of great
wealth. But Venice did not count as a counterexample to Machiavelli's theory, according to Mckenzie, because the nobility who controlled that city were gentlemen in name only: "they derived their
wealth from commerce and movable property, not landed estates."[7]
Further, feudal property was so inimical to democracy that it corrupted a city almost beyond repair, making necessary an almost
kingly power to end the corruption. Machiavelli writes that "From
all the things explained above comes the difficulty or impossibility
of maintaining a government in a corrupt city or of setting up a new
government there. Indeed when in such a city one is to be set up
or maintained, necessity demands that it be inclined more toward
kingly rule than toward popular rule, in order that those men who,
on account of their arrogance, cannot be controlled by law may in
some fashion be restrained by a power almost kingly" (*Discourses*,
1 : 18).

So arrogant were some of the feudal nobility that they knew
neither law nor authority, or so McKenzie's Machiavelli reasoned.
They could be constrained only by a power greater than themselves.
For dealing with such people, monarchy becomes a necessity. Further, aristocratic types become so involved in their sectarian feuding
that they render law and order an impossibility. Their privileged
position, which almost immunizes them from the law, is actually
inimical to life under laws. In fact, one important piece of evidence
reinforcing McKenzie's thesis is the fact that the position of *gonfalonier of justice* was created to attack exactly this lawless status of
the nobles. Needless to say, creating a position to bring law to the
aristocracy was an important first step toward democracy.

Since democracy can only grow in an environment where there
is at least a rough kind of equality, feudal property, in its obvious
inequality, is inherently hostile to self-rule. "Such corruption and
slight aptitude for free life spring from inequality in a city; and
anyone who tries to bring her back to equality must use entirely
extralegal means, such as few can or will use . . ." (*Discourses*, 1 : 17).
If force must be used to create equality, only a good constitution
can preserve it. To prevent the massive inequalities that corrode
liberty, as we have already seen, we need appropriate constitutional
safeguards. In particular, the poor must be empowered to guard
their own liberty:

And because in every republic there are rich men and men of the people, there has been doubt in the hands of which of these the said guard-

ianship [of liberty] is better placed. . . . And, without doubt, if one will look at the purpose of the nobles and of those who are not noble, there will be seen in the former great longing to rule, and in the latter merely longing not to be ruled, and as a consequence greater eagerness to live in freedom, since they can have less hope of taking possession of it than the great can. Hence, if the common people are set up to guard liberty, it is reasonable that they will care for it better, and since they cannot seize it themselves, they will not allow others to seize it. (*Discourses,* 1:5; Gilbert, 204).

Finally, McKenzie's reading of Machiavelli rightly depicts the holding of property as essential to the success of any constitution. Whether a Legislator wants to create a democracy or a principality, property holding must be arranged to support the desired constitution:

We may then draw the following conclusion from what has been said: that if any one should wish to establish a republic in a country where there are many gentlemen, he will not succeed until he has destroyed them all; and whoever wishes to establish a kingdom or principality where liberty and equality prevail, will equally fail, unless he withdraws from that general equality a number of the boldest and most ambitious spirits, and makes gentlemen out of them, not merely in name but in fact, by giving to them castles and possessions, as well as money and subjects; so that surrounded by these he may be able to maintain his power, and that by his support they may satisfy their ambition, and the others may be constrained to submit to that yoke to which force alone has been able to subject them. (*Discourses,* 1:55; Ricci–Vincent, 256).

As Mckenzie's Machiavelli saw it, then, the way that the landed gentry held land posed a danger to liberty because they were able to build castles and armies, creating dependency among the people. So although Mckenzie is wrong to think that "History and contemporary experience gave him [Machiavelli] no evidence for linking the same forms of corruption with ownership of banking houses, shops, and warehouses"[8] (see next section), he concludes that "both Machiavelli and Montesquieu believed that commercial wealth was compatible with political freedom whereas the concentration of landed wealth inevitably brought tyranny. If commerce was not preferable to civic virtue based on the individual citizen's possession of land and arms, it was nevertheless preferable to 'feudalism.'"[9] The great advantage of commercial wealth over feudal wealth was that the latter prevented democratic freedom while its successor seemed to permit such freedom.

The "Excessive Wealth" Hypothesis

The alternative and more general hypothesis here being proposed is that it is excessive wealth, whether feudal or commercial, that corrupts liberty. The case for this alternative arises from a deficiency in one factual premise of the first hypothesis: although McKenzie thought otherwise, "history and contemporary experience" had indeed given Machiavelli cause to pause and reflect upon the ways that the new, commercial wealth could corrupt republics. Since the democratic republic of Florence had been corrupted twice by wealth, the empirical question then concerns the kind of wealth that had corrupted Florence.

McKenzie's thesis is threatened by the fact that Florence was among the Italian cities where commerce had revived. If Florence was a commercial city, the wealth that undermined liberty may not have been feudal wealth. Most importantly, there is no evidence to controvert the empirical finding that Florence was a commerical city. McKenzie himself notes that Florence was among the new, commercial cities, not part of the older, feudal order ("Rousseau's Debate with Machiavelli," 213). By Vilari's account, quattrocento Florence had become "exclusively a city of traders," no longer divided between noble and peasant, nor even between "nobles and burghers, but between *fat* people and *small* people, into major and minor arts or guilds."[10] By Machiavelli's account (*Discourses* 1:55), Florence was one of the commercial cities where democracy was possible. If Florence was a new, commercial city, then why was the new democratic order, begun under the auspices of Savonarola and later led by Soderini, not able to survive?

Part of the answer is obviously external—the interference, from Rome, by the Cardinal de' Medici, later to be Pope Leo X. But equally damaging was the internal weakness of Soderini's government, capitalized upon by its opponents, who rallied around the Medici. For the loyalties of the Florentine people were divided between its democratic government, on the one hand, and the magnificent Medici family, on the other. Hence, our original empirical question is now transformed: what was the origin of Cosimo de' Medici's wealth? Was it commercial or feudal?

Vilari reports that as far back as 1378, "Salvestro di Medici . . . although belonging to the greater guilds, assisted and spurred on the lesser to overthrow their power, thus achieving great popularity."[11] His son Vieri, abandoning politics, led a life "always devoted to money making."[12] Upon the death of Vieri in 1429, his son Cosimo became head of the family at the relatively young age of forty;

"He had largely increased his paternal inheritance by commerce, and he used his means so generously, lending and giving on all sides, that there was hardly any man of weight in Florence who had not sought and received help from him in moments of need."[13] In a more recent and more scientific history, Schevill concurs that Cosimo had "inherited his father's solid burgher qualities."[14] These data are conclusive: the wealth that had corrupted the democratic republic of Florence was not feudal, but commercial, in origin. In sum, McKenzie is almost right about Machiavelli's view of property: he was not hostile to commerce and had seen that, in some cities of Italy, commerce provided the economic foundation for liberty. But liberty had not survived in Florence; further, the fault was not to be found in feudal wealth but in the commercial wealth of the Medici.

How did McKenzie come to this error? Some confusion was undoubtedly created by the inadequacies of Machiavelli's conceptualization of the problem. Consistency is not his strength; as Pitkin points out, sometimes there are two classes, upper and lower, while there are three at other times (nobles or *il grandi,* the "people" or *il popolo,* and the plebs or *la plebe*).[15] Finally, the terms he uses are inherently ambiguous: "In Italian as in English the term people is ambiguous, meaning sometimes a particular social class, sometimes the entire membership of society, or all but the singular ruler. . . . Only the nobles or grandi are intrinsically ambitious, crave glory, and desire to dominate others. The people at large intrinsically want only security in their privacy, the absence of oppression."[16]

For Pitkin, these ambiguities are a barrier to clear understanding, leading Machiavelli himself to inconsistencies. While in *The Discourses,* for instance, he had argued that the inequalities and even factions of Rome had contributed to her freedom, he then appeared, in his *Florentine Histories,* to condemn the "bourgeoisie precisely for having largely eradicated the city's aristocratic class and forced those few nobles remaining to adopt or pander to the 'spirit' and 'ways of living' of the common people."[17]

This ambiguity leads Pitkin to misunderstand Machiavelli's position on equality, interpreting his message to mean that "The Roman Republic fared well because its conflicts always increased social inequality there, while the Florentine Republic did poorly because of ever increasing social equality."[18] It becomes necessary for Pitkin to then account for the contradiction between this conclusion and other passages where Machiavelli was explicitly arguing that a society needs enough inequality for the existence of classes and factions but not so much that the gap between the very rich and the very poor becomes too wide.

In any case, we must ultimately reject Pitkin's conclusion since it flies in the face of what Machiavelli had explicitly said (*Discourses*, 1:37) about equality in Rome: during the times prior to the debate about the agrarian law—which would limit inheritances of land and divide up conquered lands among all and not just the nobles—when rough equality of wealth and parity of power prevailed, Rome "fared well." But the patrician nobles were so offended by the egalitarian impact of the agrarian law that they mobilized against it, "and renewed conflict over the law destroyed the Republic" (*Discourses*, 1:37). When the factions lined up with the rich behind Sulla and the plebs behind Marius, "civil war broke out, during which the nobility gained the upper hand" (ibid.). This led Machiavelli to conclude that "the ambition of the nobility is so great that it must be checked in various ways if a city is not to come to ruin" (ibid.). He found that rather than faring well when inequalities increased, the Roman republic was destroyed when the nobles' ambition prevailed over the interests of the poor and the inequalities increased.

What Machiavelli lamented in his *Histories* was not "too much equality" in Florence, but the absence of military ardor and valor that had been characteristic of the feudal nobles. The ritual pastimes of the nobles, like the hunt, were useful not only as practice to improve marksmanship, he wrote, but also to learn the "lay of the land," geographical knowledge that could be useful from the perspective of military strategy and tactics. The rising bourgeoisie lacked these traditions and so lacked knowledge necessary for the defense of the city—truly a lamentable situation. *The Prince* was written to alleviate, in part, this inadequacy on the part of the bourgeoisie.

Hence Machiavelli concludes (*Discourses*, 3:1), not that faction caused beneficial inequalities in Rome, but that the "enmities that at the outset existed in Rome between the people and the nobles were ended by debating, those in Florence by fighting; those in Rome were terminated by law, those in Florence by the exile and death of many citizens." Prior to the Gracchi, Rome was blessed with factions; after that, the corrosion of the constitution permitted sectarian violence.

Most importantly, then, it was an appropriate constitutional arrangement in Rome that provided a rough parity of power between the classes which in turn prevented the factionalism from degenerating into civil war, pitting class against class. Of course, a case could be made that the demands of the Roman plebs were less extreme than those of the poor in Florence; but the reason for this was to be found in the laws, not in a moral superiority of one over the other.

If the corruptive danger of property is that it can be turned to feudal ends of domination, then the new, commercial property must not be permitted to be turned to those ends. But massive accumulations of even the new wealth made possible exactly that corruption. Hence, prevention of such accumulations becomes necessary, and creating or preserving equality is a duty connected to preserving liberty.

We can now see that it was not the feudal origins of the wealth of the Medici that corrupted Florence; it was the ends to which they turned their money. Unlike proper burghers who strive for profits so that they might expand their commmercial empires (thereby increasing productivity and conquering scarcity), the Medici, like so many of the "nouveau riche," had sought to turn their commercial wealth to feudal purposes, trying to purchase status and respect, seeking social approval and acceptance of the privileged status afforded by their new wealth, intermarrying with nobility and becoming infected with their *ambizione* to "lord it over" the people. Small holdings of wealth can only rarely tempt their owners with this ambition, since it is not self-perpetuating. But excessive wealth is different. It was, then, not the origins of Medicean wealth that corrupted Florence; the danger came from the size of the fortune and the purposes to which it was turned.

Even so, Machiavelli discerned that it might prove to be possible that the very ambition that destroyed Florentine freedom could be turned to a good purpose. If the corruptive *ambizione* could be transformed into noble *ambitio* (a quest for *gloria*), the agents of Florentine destruction could become the agents of Italian salvation. If their goals could be moved beyond familial interest, enrichment, and power, to historical glory, then their power might be the basis for Italian unification. Perhaps the Medici could do for Italy what Cesare Borgia had done fleetingly for the Romagna: "reduce" it to civility and law.

THEORETICAL IMPLICATIONS

For Politics

If Machiavelli's analysis of the corruptive potential of excessive wealth is valid, then many larger questions are raised about property and freedom. First, contrary to McKenzie, Machiavelli is much closer to Rousseau than to Montesquieu on this central question, and he did oppose massive inequalities in wealth, regardless of kind, because of the corruptive tendencies of inequality.[19] The problem is not simply that wealth is held unequally but that defective rules of distribution foster the creation of an elite who are able to usurp the functions of self-government from the lower class, rendering them dependent. The *ambizione* of the wealthy corrupts a republic by enabling the rich to seek and attain public office while turning its powers to the benefit of private, familial interests.

Second, if Machiavelli's analysis is correct, then the modern social welfare state is, in the circumstances of the twentieth century, crucial to the maintenance of a free and independent people. In moments of hardship and need, the poor will, of necessity, become dependent upon someone. It is better that they should become dependent upon the state than upon the wealthy, to whom they then become indebted. Making people indebted and dependent is exactly the method for creating partisans that corrupters of democracy have regularly employed.[20] In this sense, relying on private charities is dangerous to a republic, fostering in the poor independence from government but dependence upon the wealthy, a most unhealthful condition.

The third question raised by Machiavelli's insight raises major concerns for modern theories of moral justification. While it would be unwise to attempt to answer here the *empirical* question, "has capitalist wealth been corrupted?" it is instructive to note the implications for contemporary *theory* if Machiavelli is correct. For example, John Rawls (one of this century's most important moral and political philosophers, whose *Theory of Justice* offered a justification of the modern social welfare state) employs a device called "the Original Position" to develop a kind of social contract theory of justice.[21] In this position, prior to the constitution of society, the creators of society are to deliberate about notions of justice that will define moral obligations in the emerging society. Persons deliberating in this position are to be devoid of all threat power and false appeals to authority; instead, they are to rely almost exclusively upon their rationality.

They are also to be devoid of all knowledge of personal placement in society, but while deliberating behind this "veil of ignorance," they are to be fully cognizant of the facts of social organization.[22] In this fashion, they are to be charged with arriving at a notion of justice that is fair. Rawls argues that it would be rational for them to pick what has been called the Maximin Principle, a principle urging that in conditions of great uncertainty with high stakes, the rational agent seek to maximize the worst case outcome.[23] In this way, he makes a case for the social welfare state: no rational agent, deliberating behind the veil of ignorance in the "Original Position," would prefer the laissez-faire versions of capitalism to the social welfare variant. If I did not know whether I would be rich or poor, I would opt for constituting a society with programs to prevent starvation, for instance, even if I knew that this would reduce my wealth somewhat should I turn out not to be impoverished.

Now we are to imagine that the store of information about the workings of societies includes Machiavelli's claim that some holdings of wealth corrupt republican societies and deprive them of liberty. They might also consider what could be called a Minimax Principle: rational agents deliberating in great uncertainty about constituting society should opt to minimize massive holdings of wealth so as not to undermine liberty. Since such a minimizing of the wealthy could create the preconditions for liberty, rational agents seeking to order their own lives as they see fit would be inclined to accept this requirement and to reject any society that failed to include this requirement in its constitution. This Machiavellian recommendation of equality has revolutionary theoretical significance and recommends itself to liberal democratic theory on its own merits.

Finally, Machiavelli's analysis of quattrocento Italy provides another form of theoretical insight. This analysis, almost Marxian in its scientific spirit, aims to understand the material conditions in which a given kind of society becomes possible. Marx asked what would make possible both revolutionary change and a socialist society in Germany, and he answered that it would require the creation of a proletarian class.[24] Machiavelli had already asked parallel questions about what would make possible revolutionary change and a democratic republic in Italy, and his answer was that it would require the unification of the nation and the elimination of certain kinds of property—and perhaps even the elimination of the landed gentry. Both agree on one central point: the desired social and cultural ways of life would be impossible without first creating the material conditions to make it possible.

For Economics

Given Machiavelli's contention that feudal property failed to provide the necessary, material conditions for freedom, might capitalist property similarly fail? If capitalist property can be turned to feudal ends, would socialist property provide the only alternative institutional arrangement to guarantee human liberation? As attractive as such a possibility might be, there are several reasons why this may not be the case. The perspectives of Hayek and Friedman[25] on this subject are familiar enough: until a superior alternative is invented, the mechanism of the market is unsurpassed in its efficient allocation of resources and the consequent satisfaction of existing human desires. But Oliver Williamson now offers an alternative that not only reinforces their insights but also begins with assumptions that are essentially Machiavellian.[26] As we shall see his political economy in fact reveals the full power of Machiavellian assumptions.

Economists traditionally make few assumptions about human virtue—if people were saints, we would need the allocative functions of markets even less than the authoritative institutions of politics. The "typical" assumption is said to be "minimal": that we are merely rational calculators of self-interest. Assuming more—say, attributing altruistic feelings to them—about people would render a theory incapable of explaining real human behavior. Williamson makes these minimal assumptions even more minimal. When one is deliberating about the structures of institutions, so as to prevent human corruption, he is convinced that one must assume the worst about human nature. The worst is not simply that people will seek their own ends, but that they will do so ruthlessly, without regard to the duties or obligations they might have under the laws of politics or morals. Not only do humans seek self-interest, but they do so "with guile." Williamson calls this assumption "opportunism"[27] and ties opportunism explicitly to Machiavelli's view of human nature.[28]

In addition, in this imperfect world, one rarely knows, as Platonic rulers must know, all that is necessary. Human rationality is not perfect but limited or, in Williamson's terms, "bounded."[29] Hence, people rarely know all that they need to know even to be perfectly selfish, let alone all that they need to know to seek the common good. This assumption of "bounded" rationality is a kind of recognition of the limits of human knowledge.

Employing these Machiavellian assumptions about human nature, Williamson examines "transaction costs," especially risks in contracting, in an attempt to resolve some long-standing difficulties in economics. One such problem is the apparent de facto limit upon the size of firms: why do they not keep growing ever bigger, until only one firm remains? In Williamson's words, "Why can't a large firm do everything that a collection of small firms can do and more?" After noting the "transaction costs" to large firms that render them relatively inefficient in the "start-up" stages of some industries, he goes on to examine earlier efforts to resolve this quandary—including his own earlier claim that information "distortions" provide an absolute limit to firm size—and he finds them inadequate.[30]

Finally, in an attempt to simplify the problem so as to reveal the disincentives to perpetual growth, he creates an imaginary scenario of proposed "vertical integration," in which the buyer (say, an automobile manufacturer) of an intermediate product (say, tires) "integrates backward" by purchasing its former supplier (the tire manufacturer). Assuming that the former owner received a fair price and was asked to stay on as manager, we turn our attention to his/her incentives to manage the firm efficiently.

Here the new owner of the now integrated tire firm faces a dilemma: (a) if the incentives to the former owner/new manager are not "high powered," the new manager will not have the same incentive as before to produce the good as efficiently, and tires will now cost the larger firm more than they had before integration; but (b) if the incentives are high-powered, then the two internal management teams will have institutional imperatives to enter into a counterproductive rivalry. On the one hand, (tire) management has an incentive to maximize short-term profits at the expense of plant maintenance, so as to maximize its compensation at the expense of the larger entity. On the other hand, the management of the larger firm has an incentive to "cook" the books to minimize the nominal profits of the supply branch—so as to minimize the expense of compensating the manager of that supply branch. Either way, the new, larger firm experiences inefficiencies.[31]

Nor is the problem eased by separating ownership and management prior to the merger, since the managerial team must still be retained or dismissed. In short, larger, integrated firms are not always—nor even usually—as efficient as a collection of smaller firms operating in an open market.[32] Williamson's argument, of course, is equally applicable to the "single-firm economy," a centralized socialist economy. Machiavellian assumptions about human nature and behavior can help us to understand, then, the inefficiencies of centralized economies.[33]

For Populism

If Williamson can be seen as a legitimate descendant of Machiavelli, as he claims to be, the point the two make now appears to be this: since feudal and socialist property are not conducive to freedom in a democracy, then if we are to be free, we must find constitutional means to direct capitalist property away from the excessively hierarchical and autocratic goals of feudal nobles.

Here is where the metaphor of populism can do the most good. (Populism usually refers to the body of thought articulated by the Populist party as well as by the movement that surrounded and supported that party.) There are at least four good reasons to use populism as an *introductory metaphor* to explicate and defend, before criticizing, Machiavelli's thought: first, since the move from theocentric to human-oriented worldviews coincided with a shift from autocratic to democratic governments, serious questions were raised in *quinquocento* Florence about hierarchy and wealth. Anticipating the populists by several centuries, Machiavelli linked these questions about democracy and equality to his fear of the economic power of the upper classes. For Machiavelli, as for the populists, the economic foundations necessary for democratic freedom, whether for the Renaissance guild republics or for modern mass democracies, were rooted in an egalitarian vision at odds with Social Darwinism of the nineteenth century—as well as with the Social Darwinism in vogue today.

Second, while I add no precise meaning to populism and can offer here no new insights into its historical origins and development, the archetype (stereotype?) operative in the "collective unconscious" of Americans can help focus our attention upon otherwise neglected aspects of Machiavelli's thought. For example, the populist hatred of the privilege and economic power attendant to wealth may or may not have intellectual origins in *The Discourses;* but the raw emotional power of that hatred is certainly as alive there as in any populist propaganda. After all, the economic elite of quattrocento Florence—the Medici—had used wealth to destroy the government of the petit bourgeois led by Piero Soderini, whose republican government Machiavelli had served. Not only did this cost the secretary his public career, it also led to his arrest and torture. Why should he resent their wealth any less than small farmers hated the "Big Capital" of the American East? In short, there is an emotional linkage, well articulated in the secretary's descriptions of "gentlemen" as "parasites" (*Discourses,* 1:7, 1:55, and 3:28).

Third, Machiavelli's commitment to democratic equality, like that of the populists, raises fundamental questions about the role of rights generally and property rights particularly in republican politics. To the extent that populist hatred of the rich inspired the populists to attibute illegitimacy to the property of the rich, this sentiment challenged the traditional role of property rights in American culture. Insofar as that culture is Lockean,[34] Americans will be tempted to see the issue of wealth in terms of "rights" and to ask if the "extremist" position of egalitarians violate the rights of the rich. The response to this question by those on the conservative right is that the rich have earned their rights to their property and proposals to equalize wealth violate those rights; the response of the liberal left is that the poor too have rights and these rights are not adequately respected in political and legal practice. Although Americans may agree upon what John Rawls would call the *concept* of rights, they employ different *conceptions* of rights.

Hence, there are two notions of "rights" or "liberty" operative in the American as in the European tradition: the "negative" tradition of liberty insists upon protecting individuals from governmental power by granting them legal protections, while the "positive" tradition insists upon expanding governmental power so that government can help to make more "real" the rights individuals are supposed to have.[35] If classical liberalism was "too negative" in its insistence upon only formal and legal liberty, Machiavelli's "autonomy," "freedom," and "liberty" share many affinities—as well as weaknesses—with Green's and Hobhouse's "positive liberty" and Kant's "autonomy." What is needed, but beyond the scope of this work, is a theory of liberty that is neither negative nor positive; the best of both can be captured in a notion of "purposive" liberty, the freedom to conceive of—and live for—one's own purposes. The ambiguities in Machiavelli's notion of liberty suggests the need for such a shift.

Fourth, in approving of and advocating violence in "class warfare," Machiavelli, like the populists, would not, in principle, object if cruel deeds were necessary to secure the economic foundations for their shared vision of democratic freedom and equality. Where he saw the constitution as depriving the lesser guilds of the power needed to secure their, and the public, interests against the sectarian interests of the rich, Machiavelli urged surgical violence to destroy the base of economic power of those who would use the law against the law. Ironically, Machiavelli's celebration of the judicious use of power conceals the need to recognize the limitations of coercion. However useful coercion can be in establishing "law and order" or a "new order," it is not enough to establish the kind of civility that is really necessary to create a community. What is ignored by the believers in the creative power of power, who may purport to find inspiration in Machiavelli, is the need to move beyond coercion to justice, beyond "law and order" to peace and cooperation.

It is not clear, then, whether Machiavelli's message is radical or moderate. But few have accused Machiavelli of moderation. Grant Mindle, for one, is suspicious precisely of Machiavelli's lack of moderation and criticizes him for the radical changes his democratic regime would require. Noting that Machiavelli directed most of his advice to new princes, Mindle cannot help but sense that Machiavelli's intention is "far more radical" than national unity.[36] Noting Machiavelli's mistrust of excessive inequalities, he infers that "'the aristocratic principle in particular' is gradually undermined, thereby permitting a more equal struggle between hereditary right on the one hand and raw natural ability on the other. Since the equalization of the aristocratic principle is . . . tantamount to its destruction, even the hereditary prince will soon find himself in need of Machiavelli's counsel."[37]

Regarding the securing of equality, Machiavelli knew little moderation.

In this sense, Rousseau was almost right: Machiavelli was being exactly true to his own republicanism in writing *The Prince*. The establishment of a republic in conditions of corruption requires creating the material conditions in which freedom becomes possible; creating the material conditions, in turn, may require a principality, even though it might be possible to create these material conditions for freedom while not providing freedom itself. Those who desire stable democracies may even—consistently—demand the creation of a principality at one point in history if that principality is necessary for the future success of democracy. What would make such a monarchy necessary? The material conditions that interfere with the creation of democracy—the existence of a nobility, lack of capitalist property, inequality, disunity—are the extremes that require a power almost kingly. One can almost imagine Machiavelli chortling at this unmasking—his task was most probably exactly to so revolutionize and modernize Florentine and Italian reality.

A Summary and Critical Perspective

In summation, Machiavelli may have been among the first to describe corruption accurately, but it remains today what it was then: dangerous to freedom. His descriptions of corruption enable us to see and define it in a variety of ways, for it remains a multifaceted evil arising from unfettered ambitions. Each facet reveals a new dimension and requires a separate definition. Metaphysically, corruption constitutes an opportunity for people of valor (*virtù*) to engage in activity to change/remake the world. Psychologically, corruption is the absence of the conditions necessary for humans to develop their higher potentials, especially their potential for *gloria*. Legally, corruption is depriving a people of the power to make its own laws and to live in lawful and just order. Morally, corruption is the absence of obligations, a condition in which we have not chosen to create our obligations. Politically, corruption means the elevation of personal or familial interests over the common good. Economically, corruption is a condition caused by a turning of modern (capitalist or commercial) wealth to the pre-modern (feudal) and aristocratic goals of domination and oppression—an ambition that has turned many heads away from the *gloria* of living under laws that a people makes for itself in a democratic republic and from the *gloria* of creating one's own obligations. There are few actions so noble as battling corruption; there is no value higher than glory. That Machiavelli was a proponent of such a vision should require our reexamining his place in the Western tradition; this task is reserved for the final chapter.

9

Machiavelli's Place in the History of Western Political Thought

MACHIAVELLI'S CONTRIBUTION

As Machiavelli surveyed the emergence of the modern world, he realized that certain parts of Italian reality would have to be changed if the Italian people were to become and stay free. The political and social changes, already begun, would require other fundamental changes in our views of the world and of ourselves: an open antideterministic view of the cosmos would provide room for humans to create their own criteria of right and wrong; this moral voluntarism would in turn validate the processes of political democracy, in which humans create laws for themselves.

But it is ironic that an open world-view, which opens the possibility for political democracy, also precludes any cosmic guarantees that people *will* be free. Since an open world provides us with the space to be free without guranteeing that we will be free, the responsibility for our being free becomes totally our own. If this humanism places the responsibility for freedom squarely on our shoulders, realism also demands that we recognize that no city can be free in a new world composed of nations. Consequently, if Italians were to know stable freedom, the unification of the nation was mandated. Finally, given that class relations have such an impact on the maintenance of freedom, a rising commercial class in each nation—rooted in the commerce that defines it—would have to emerge without committing the errors of the (old) feudal barons, without giving in to the corruptive ambition that destroys freedom by creating positions of privilege above the law.

Destroying privileged positions above the law has the effect of creating equality before the law. Machiavelli's egalitarian convictions went further, though, requiring that the gap between top and bottom must be narrow enough to keep economic elites from making their "inferiors" dependent upon their largesse. The strength of this insight constitutes firm theoretical grounds for a defensible egalitarianism. Since excessive inequality makes democratic freedom impossible and restoring equality to a society that has lost it requires the use of force that is undesirable for other reasons, the best way to avoid such violence is by preventing the growth of inequality.

Machiavelli's philosophical commitment to autonomy, equality, and empiricism remains a challenge to the elitist and rationalist portions of Western rationalism. As an early modern thinker who saw the emerging new world—and the minimal freedom possible in a guild democracy—and created a vision of human glory fit for it, he left a rich legacy. Although he was not the first to give expression to all of these ideas, he can be credited, at least minimally, with articulating or rearticulating and advancing them—reviving them and offering original insights in each area along the way, merging them into an almost coherent whole:

- the belief that constitution makers must begin with the defective raw materials of human nature—taking "men as they are"—and compensate for them with wiser constitutional mechanisms (political realism);[1]
- the revival of the notion that humans are the authors of meaning and purpose for life (humanism);
- the scientific recognition of the laws of human social and moral evolution and devolution (psychological causation);
- the belief that we create our obligations (moral voluntarism);
- revival of the ancient Roman ideal of liberty (positive liberty as autonomy);
- the belief that liberty was possible only in certain economic contexts, including factional or competitive conflicts between classes (populism);
- the belief that factional conflict must be fostered but also limited by constitutional provisions for rough equality of wealth and political power (economic democracy or egalitarianism);
- the belief that a just and stable government requires both adequate power to deal with problems and a structure including elements of democracy, aristocracy, and monarchy ("mixed" constitution and positive government);
- the belief that a factionalism that divided rich from poor could be brought to the benefit of liberty if each were empowered to veto actions of the other (a system of checks and balances); and
- the definition of corruption as the elevation of personal or famil-

ial interest over the common good and over the restraints of law, destroying civility and order.

MACHIAVELLI'S AFFINITIES WITH OTHER THINKERS

Before we criticize Machiavelli's notion of liberty, we should consider the connections between his thought and later political perspectives. In particular, (1) his belief in the need for a solitary great founder is mirrored in Rousseau's dedication to a great Legislator; (2) his notion of corruption may have provided raw material for Hobbes's "state of nature" and Locke's "state of war;" and (3) his views on humanist activism, factional conflict and its constitutional resolution, and the need for strong but limited executive power were inspirations for Madison, while his preference for an executive strong enough to deal with threats to a constitution may have inspired Locke's "executive prerogative." In addition, his belief that civilian militias are conducive to democracy, national loyalty, and liberty may also be the theoretical foundation for the modern idea of a nationalist citizen militia and, by implication, for America's Second Amendment with its requirement that citizens have a right to the arms necessary for a citizen militia.

Nevertheless, despite these similarities to other great thinkers, there remain deficiencies in his theory. For instance, although he discerns that the application of force is often inadequate to secure civility, he fails to recognize the need, implicit in his view of human nature, for a system of rights (negative liberty). If he is right that we humans are capable of being free and need to be free, but are susceptible to the temptation of ambition, then an institutional solution is required to secure our freedom. For his notion of freedom in a guild democracy to become an adequate, modern theory of freedom, we must move beyond "negative" and "positive" liberty to a more inclusive theory of "purposive" human liberty.

A. Machiavelli and Rousseau

Machiavelli, then, is "modern" in very much the same way that Rousseau is; not surprisingly, there are a number of similarities, stylistic as well as substantive, between the philosophies of the two. Both used language powerfully and cryptically to shock the reader into a new perspective. Both deliberately employed language that appeared to be self-contradictory, like Rousseau's dictum about "forcing people to be free" and Machiavelli's "cruelties well used," in order to reveal deeper truths. Both had great faith in the human transformations created by "legislators." Both recognized human depravity but saw the possibility of human nobility.[2] Both believed in the ancient ideal of republican freedom, but sought a modern justification for it.

Central to this modern justification of the ancient ideal of republican liberty in both Rousseau and Machiavelli are several ideas. First, like Rousseau's, Machiavelli's dedication to democratic liberty grew out of a distinctively modern and empiricist view of the nature of reality. Their common epistemological convictions would not be shared by any Platonist or Aristotelian—nor by most elitists. Second, Machiavelli's opposition to the prevailing medieval view of the cosmos as a place ordered by the will of the creating deity led him to see the world as at least partly open to human exertion; the existence of chaotic *fortuna* makes possible human *virtù*, while a similarly modern view of the world led Rousseau to oppose passivity and propose the general will, a criterion of right (deontology) that is a product of human creativity (moral voluntarism).

Third, Machiavelli's view of human potentials for depravity and nobility mark his philosophy as more akin to Rousseau than to, say, Hobbes. Although one must assume that people will be bad and that this badness will be realized in action unless something or someone prevents it, still a great legislator can provide a republic with a system of laws that makes possible a more noble existence. Humans have the potential for being good and for living freely. This, of course, is akin to Rousseau's idea of the noble savage, although less idealistic (more realistic?). In sum, the similarities of their beliefs about human nature are both structural (both are developmentalists) and substantive (both see developmental potentials for good and evil), though Rousseau is more sanguine about human possibilities than is Machiavelli.

Similarly, for Machiavelli, ethical voluntarism, the belief that our obligations are *created* instead of *discovered* in, say, the laws of god or nature, led to the belief that one has no moral obligations in the absence of the conditions of justice created by legal institutions, a condition we have already labeled as "corruption," while Rousseau's ethical voluntarism made of him a social contract theorist. But both believed that neither god nor nature provided a law that prohibited us from doing what was necessary to be free. In short, although the ideal of both is ancient liberty, the grounds for justifying it (metaphysical, epistemological, psychological, and moral) are in both cases peculiarly modern and opposed to the rationalist tradition.

B. Machiavelli and Hobbes

If any of the major Western theorists deserves the reputation, usually ascribed to Machiavelli, of the scientist of power for the sake of personal security; if any theorist's egoistical calculation of self-interest can be said to be the foundation of statist authoritarianism; that theorist is Hobbes. Yet, even though Hobbes is an unreconstructed autocrat and authoritarian, he is usually more closely assimilated to the liberal-democratic tradition because of his individualism than is Machiavelli, who, ironically, was a democrat who believed in at least a type of freedom. The similarities and differences are telling and imply that we should switch the places occupied by Hobbes and Machiavelli in the iconography of the Western tradition, assimilating Machiavelli more closely to the democratic tradition and placing Hobbes outside of it.

Let us begin the comparison by attending to the similarities. Like Machiavelli, Hobbes is very much committed to a modern view of the world. Empirical science is very close to his heart, his friends and heroes include Bacon and Galileo, and he begins the *Leviathan* with a rather long section on free will, language, and determinism. There is little in his account of reality that directly contradicts Machiavelli's, but his metaphysical theory is less poetic (certainly *fortuna* is not invoked in its metaphorical sense), more precise, and more philosophically sophisticated. Hobbes's world is a physical world characterized by "random" motion, by motion not mandated by a determinist force nor aimed at any natural goal. Both are moral voluntarists, with Hobbes endorsing the social contract variant of that tradition.[3]

It is in his thinking about human nature that Hobbes is most significantly different from Machiavelli. Although both see the evil in human hearts, Machiavelli sees considerably beyond that evil to detect our potential for nobility, under the appropriate or lawful circumstances. Here Hobbes's account is again less poetic, but also more severe. Seeing humans as natural objects in which the random (i.e., nonteleological) but lawful movement of physical particles creates aversions and attractions, he is never able to see the democratic glory of freedom as a human possibility. Not only does he cheapen us in asserting that "The value, or worth of a man, is as of all other things, his price,"[4] but he cannot see beyond our need for security to our need to be free. Hence, he opts to settle merely for security, the best his humans could hope for. And it is this sentiment that closes the door on democracy for him, since a strong authority, such as Machiavelli would see as *sometimes* necessary, is for him the *only* means to secure humans from one another.

The great strength of Hobbes's moral philosophy is his demonstration that, even for perfectly egoistic calculators of self-interest, creating moral obligations can make human life better than living outside of civilized society. Yet the weakness of this perspective is closely related: he equivocates on the issue of obligations, sometimes suggesting that we create these when we contract out of the state of nature into the Leviathan or a state of authorized rule (as in chapter 15), other times suggesting that we have obligations under the eternally binding laws of nature (as in chapter 27). Although Machiavelli may commit other errors, he is at least free of this inconsistency, opting to depict obligations as consistently created by humans.

Machiavelli, Madison, and Liberty

Three final tasks remain before we can move to a critical appraisal of Machiavelli's place in Western thinking about politics. First, there is the fascinating possibility that his constitutionalism may have influenced the Founding Fathers of the United States, especially that American democratic theorist of factions, James Madison. Second, since Machiavelli's theory of liberty is different from, say, Jefferson's,[5] it is worth ascertaining exactly what sort of liberty he advocated. Central to this exposition is a recognition that Machiavelli defended a version of liberty closer to the "positive" tradition than to the classically "negative" variant. This dedication to positive liberty is a strength of Machiavelli's thought, but it may have blinded him to the need for a fuller vision of liberty; this criticism will be developed in the following section. Third, the related charge that Machiavelli was a proponent of egotism must be examined and rejected, for this collectivist cannot be guilty of such extreme individualism.

If truisms are true, then the constitution makers of the United States were well versed in the classics of Western political thought. Much has been made, for instance, of the influence of John Locke and his theory of natural rights upon Thomas Jefferson and the Declaration of Independence.[6] It is even easy to see Alexander Hamilton as concerned with the strong executive authority necessary for national security, in the spirit of Hobbes. But relatively little has been done by way of tracing the impact of Machiavelli upon the democratic tradition of America. The most significant exception is the last section of Pocock's *The Machiavellian Moment*, where our attention is directed to the influence of Machiavelli upon the North Atlantic (i.e., Anglo-American) tradition of democracy.

But this North Atlantic tradition of democracy is not monolithic; there was and is a great deal of difference among Anglo-American proponents of democracy. And, despite the myth of solidarity of purpose among them, the fact remains that the writers of the American Constitution were radically, almost violently, divided about the future course of the nation. Many, mindful of Montesquieu's idea of how to preserve liberty, were committed to confederalism and negative government; they feared that a large union and a strong government were antithetical to their negative liberties. Others were equally convinced that the shortcomings of the Articles of Confederation "proved" that a stronger government, along with a stronger executive, was essential to national survival. Still others were wondering what the fuss was all about: they reasoned that the Articles of Confederation had provided us with a working government and we were a people living under our own democratically enacted laws. We were free of the monarch of England, and we retained our sovereignty. What was there to be concerned about?

There clearly were "factions" among the founders of the American nation. Identifying the opposing viewpoints dividing them may cast light upon what liberty requires of a modern nation-state.

If Jefferson was the theorist of natural rights[7] and Hamilton was the autocrat desirous of the strong, central authority[8] needed for economic development, it was Madison, as well as Washington and Jay, who were the democrats for whom autonomy was everything. Madison was the theorist of factions, the proponent of checks and balances, the devotee of a mixed constitution—Madison was, in short, the Machiavellian.[9] Dedicated to the ideal of positive liberty, Madison initially saw relatively little need for a bill of rights, since the crucial concern of "liberty" was that we would be living under our own laws. Hence, there was considerable irony in his being chosen to craft the first ten amendments from the hundreds of suggestions from the states. Like Machiavelli, Madison was an advocate of positive liberty in the autonomous sense; at least prior to the Constitutional Convention, he considered the concerns of rights or negative liberty relatively less important than the need for autonomy or positive liberty.[10]

Central to the analyses of both theorists was the problem of faction. While they agreed on the general importance of faction, they disagreed on a number of details. Machiavelli, for instance, provided a perspective on faction as basically benign, although it can degenerate into sectarian violence. For Machiavelli, faction is basically good, provided it is restrained by appropriate constitutional barriers. Indeed, a constitutional balancing of factions can secure liberty and thus accomplish a great good. By contrast, as Madison undertook to defend the proposed constitution in his contribution to *The Federalist Papers,* he took a different view of faction: "The friend of popular governments never finds himself so much alarmed for their character and fate, as when he contemplates their propensity to this dangerous vice."[11]

In the middle 1780s, the American union was in trouble. Conflicts like Shay's Rebellion indicated a dangerous possibility that America was to be split into two warring sectarian interests, with big-moneyed interests opposed to small farmers and other debtors; the history of the Renaissance was threatening to repeat itself on another continent. Although he hoped otherwise, Madison acknowledged that "the evidence of known facts will not permit us to deny" his fears "that our governments are too unstable, that the public good is disregarded in the conflicts of rival parties, and that measures are too often decided, not according to the rules of justice and the rights of the minor party, but by the superior force of an interested and overbearing majority."[12]

In other words, corruption—conquest of the common good by sectarian interests—threatened the American experiment in republican government. Much as Machiavelli had, Madison traced these troubles to excesses of faction: "These must be chiefly, if not wholly, effects of the unsteadiness and injustice with which a factious spirit has tainted our public administrations."[13] The crucial issue in the ratification battles, as Madison saw it through Machiavellian eyes, was the need to prevent factions from degenerating into sectarian violence that would destroy the republic.[14] Even his definition of the cause of trouble sounds Machiavellian, provided that we translate his use of "faction" to Machiavelli's sense of faction-turned-to-sectarianism: "By faction, I understand a number of citizens, whether amounting to a majority or a minority of the whole, who are united and actuated by some common impulse of passion, or of interest, adverse to the rights of other citizens, or to the permanent and aggregate interests of the community."[15] Madison's factions, like Machiavelli's sects, were arrogantly placing themselves above the law, assuming that the interests for which they fought were of more value than lawful freedom itself.

Also like Machiavelli, Madison ties the causes of faction to human nature: "The latent causes of faction are thus sown in the nature of man; and we see them everywhere brought into different degrees of activity, according to the different circumstances of civil society."[16] Given the frailty of human nature, this "evil" will be made manifest unless good laws prevent it. Dealing legally with faction requires our understanding of these causes, since we must either destroy the causes or control the effects of faction, Madison reasons.

Since Machiavelli saw factions as benign—it was their degeneration into sects, leading to sectarian violence, that was bad—the destruction of the causes of faction never became an issue for him to consider. For Madison, however, faction was evil and one must *either* destroy the causes of faction or control its consequences. But the causes of faction are found in the foibles of human nature and Madison felt powerless to alter our nature. Preferring, like Machiavelli, to "take men as they are," Madison opts to create institutions based on the assumption that "men are evil." So Madison rejects two methods of destroying the causes of faction: "the one, by destroying the liberty which is essential to its existence; the other, by giving to every citizen the same opinions, the same passions, and the same interests."[17] Both of these "solutions" are as bad as the problem in that they both destroy liberty and violate human dignity.

There is one other, more important, cause of faction that Madison does not even consider destroying: "But the most common and durable source of factions has been the various and unequal distribution of property. Those who hold and those who are without property have ever formed distinct interests in society. Those who are creditors, and those who are debtors, fall under a like discrimination."[18] This inequality, which Machiavelli denounced as preventing freedom, is here accepted by Madison as a "natural" fact of life that cannot be altered. Although he considered and rejected proposals to remove the other causes of faction, this cause goes unchallenged. By contrast, Machiavelli was unrestrained by assumptions that elites had any "rights" to their wealth if its abuse were to destroy freedom; he also saw the institutional restriction of wealth and consequent creation of equality as a necessary condition for democratic freedom.

How then might the undesirable consequences of "faction" be prevented, if we cannot eliminate the causes?

> If a faction consists of less than a majority, relief is supplied by the republican principle, which enables the majority to defeat its sinister views by regular vote. It may clog the administration, it may convulse the society; but it will be unable to execute and mask its violence under the forms of the Constitution. When a majority is included in a faction, the form of popular government, on the other hand, enables it to sacrifice to its ruling passion or interest both the public good and the rights

of other citizens. To secure the public good and private rights against the danger of such a faction, and at the same time to preserve the spirit and the form of popular government, is then the great object to which our inquiries are directed. Let me add that it is the great desideratum by which this form of government can be rescued from the opprobrium under which it has so long labored, and be recommended to the esteem and adoption of mankind.[19]

In republics, then, there is little reason to fear factions of minorities; the danger is tyranny of the majority. In a reversal of Machiavelli, since the masses are the poor, it is they who are the greatest threat to liberty according to Madison.

Further, institutional safeguards against this tyranny are difficult to create. In the case of "pure" or direct democracies, institutional protection is impossible: since decisions on matters of public policy are made directly by majority votes of the citizens, there is little to protect minorities against unwise and unfair infringements upon their rights. "From this view of the subject it may be concluded that a pure democracy, by which I mean a society consisting of a small number of citizens, who assemble and administer the government in person, can admit of no cure for the mischiefs of faction. A common passion or interest will, in almost every case, be felt by a majority of the whole; a communication and concert result from the form of government itself; and there is nothing to check the inducements to sacrifice the weaker party or an obnoxious individual."[20]

Democracy without representation fails to protect against this sort of tyranny of the majority and may not even be able to so protect no matter what institutional tinkerings are attempted.

But a republic or a representative democracy differs from a direct democracy in exactly this respect: it can interpose a group of people, the representatives, between the majority faction and its preferred policy. "A republic, by which I mean a government in which the scheme of representation takes place, opens a different prospect, and promises the cure for which we are seeking. . . . The two great points of difference between a democracy and a republic are: first, the delegation of the government, in the latter, to a small number of citizens elected by the rest; secondly, the greater number of citizens, and the greater sphere of country, over which the latter may be extended."[21]

The Madisonian solution[22] to the problem of faction is thus two-fold: a democracy must be relatively large and it must be representative.

Extensive size works to reduce the intensity of faction by spreading loyalties out, so that there are crosscutting cleavages in the society, making more difficult the emergence of a dominating but lasting majority: "The smaller the society, the fewer probably will be the distinct parties and interests composing it; the fewer the distinct parties and interests, the more frequently will a majority be found of the same party; and the smaller the number of individuals composing a majority, and the smaller the compass within which they are placed, the more easily will they concert and execute their plans of oppression."[23]

Tyranny of the majority is more likely in smaller societies than in bigger ones, if Madison is right.

The advantage of size is also related to the limits of divisive leaders; the "charismatic" appeal of demagogues can only extend so far:

> The influence of factious leaders may kindle a flame within their particular States, but will be unable to spread a general conflagration through the other States. A religious sect may degenerate into a political faction in a part of the Confederacy; but the variety of sects dispersed over the entire face of it must secure the national councils against any danger from that source. A rage for paper money, for an abolition of debts, for an equal division of property, or for any other improper or wicked project, will be less apt to pervade the whole body of the Union than a particular member of it; in the same proportion as such a malady is more likely to taint a particular county or district, than an entire State.[24]

Size mitigates faction in two ways: weakening demagogues and requiring larger groups for majorities. The more extensive the polity, then, the less intensive should be factional strife.

Finally, an appropriate scheme of respresentation can mitigate faction. Here Madison's concern[25] is with the unlettered masses, those who lack the wisdom to govern well. The effect of representation, he writes, "is to refine and enlarge the public views, by passing them through the medium of a chosen body of citizens, whose wisdom may best discern the true interest of their country, and whose patriotism and love of justice will be least likely to sacrifice it to temporary or partial considerations."[26] In short, with a representative democracy, a nation can achieve a mixture of democratic rule with elite knowledge and judgement.

Of course, this benefit could be "inverted" so that a few factious men could, "by intrigue, by corruption, or by other means," win election and then "betray the interests of the people."[27] This, in turn, directs our attention back to size: "The question resulting is, whether small or extensive republics are more favorable to the election of proper guardians of the public weal. . . ." So faction can be mitigated by removing day-to-day politics from the hands of the untrustworthy masses and by constituting larger republics.

Let us pause to note the differences in emphasis between the Machiavellian and the Madisonian solutions to the problem of faction. Where Machiavelli had urged a state to keep its coffers full and its citizens poor by narrowing the gap between the rich and the poor, Madison associates proposals for more equal property holding with "other improper and wicked projects," referring to them collectively as a "malady." Where Machiavelli was a democrat with confidence in the people, even in all-important military matters, Madison is careful of the masses, not trusting their judgment. There is then this fundamental difference of perspective separating the two theorists: the danger of sectarian violence arising from inadequate constitutional checks and balances between factions for Machiavelli has become, for Madison, the danger of faction understood as fear of rule by the inferior but numerous masses.

More seriously, the difference between these methods for mitigating violent disputes arising from factional divisions within a society draws attention to two deficiencies of Madison's solutions, from the Machiavellian perspective.

First, we must ask if the Madisonian solution of size is an appropriate institutional barrier to sectarian violence. At first blush, Madison's argument is plausible. However, Machiavellian empiricism requires confirmation by data, and it is far from clear that the differences between the Roman and the Florentine experiments in freedom can be traced to size. The Roman experiment had been more successful over a longer period than the Florentine, it is true. But it is not clear that this was so *because* Rome was the larger society. One might even argue that Rome grew to be great and large because hers was a good constitution, rather than believe that she had a good constitution because it covered a large area. In other words, understood as a problem of causation, the stability of the republic may have caused its growth rather than its size having caused its stability.

Further, although Rome had been considerably larger, still her size did not prevent the two factions from degenerating into two warring sects. Alternatively, it is not clear that the Indian democracy today has any inherent institutional advantage over the smaller British variant. Size may have some influence upon the corruption of a society, but it is certainly no fail-safe protection against corruptive faction.

Equally problematic is the Madisonian solution of representation.

Although his argument is persuasive in the abstract, it again lacks empirical confirmation. Whatever the other merits of representation, there is little empirical proof that it defuses factions. The direct democracy of the New England town meetings, for instance, offers little evidence of heightened sectarian conflict that is any more troublesome than in other parts of the country. California, a continent away geographically and in terms of direct democracy, seems far more explosive at the end of this century, in terms of the factions based on race and length of residence.

Further, the concreteness of the Machiavellian solution of checks and balances demonstrates a firmer grasp of reality. Where Machiavelli insisted that the factions within a society must be institutionally represented, and sufficiently empowered to prevent their rivals from dominating them, the American opted to let the inferiors select one of their superiors to represent them. Rather than guaranteeing that the less advantaged will be equally represented, the American solution was to permit both factions to be represented by delegates chosen in an electoral system dominated by landowners and the educated. In the Madisonian—but *not* the Machiavellian—solution, very wealthy males, like the Kennedys, could come to represent the downtrodden and oppressed. Since poverty effectively "closed doors" upon ownership and education, and thence upon power, the Madisonian system was not Machiavellian.

Finally, since the Madisonian solution could degenerate into an electoral system dominated by wealth, some wealthy persons would represent the interests of the wealthy while other wealthy representatives were to articulate the interests of the poor. If that degeneration occurs, ours becomes a system of government "of the poor, by the rich, for the rich."[28] Given the Madisonian institutional solution to the problem of faction, it is no surprise, from the Machiavellian perspective, that we have prevented stealing of a Robin Hood type from the rich to give to the poor. The wonder, from the egalitarian perspective of Machiavelli, is that the looting and pillaging of the poor by the rich has not occurred on a more massive scale. In the absence of strong constitutional checks and balances between the poor and the rich, only good fortune is left to protect "liberty."

Identifying Machiavelli's Notion of Liberty

There can be no doubting that, although both theorists sought to protect liberty from the corrosive effects of faction, their solutions are radically different. One possibility, though, is that Madison and Machiavelli were each attempting to protect a *different* notion of liberty, in which case, although both were concerned with faction, and although both sought to preserve liberty, their solutions to the problem of faction would be different.[29] It is possible that Machiavelli was committed to the preservation of the autonomy of positive liberty while Madison was committed to the "natural right to property" so characteristic of negative liberty. If this is so, then, *on this issue,* Madison was closer to Jefferson, and so to Locke, than to Machiavelli; this may also have been the intellectual basis for the two Americans' lifelong cooperation despite their differences.

In this simplifying light, Madison was more committed to the "negative" liberties like the property rights of the wealthy that appear to mandate a constitution more appropriate for a classical capitalist economy. By contrast, Machiavelli was a proponent of the "positive" part of the liberal tradition, more concerned with the freedoms requiring vigilance by the poor, with the autonomy that is possible only in conditions of equality, and with the notions of liberty inherent in the democratic tradition. While Madison's commitment to liberty is somewhat more complex, this simplification of his views is essentially valid.

Machiavelli's republican liberty is the ancient ideal of liberty as democratic, participative self-governance, adopted and adapted for modernity. Thus his is not our contemporary notion of liberty as a system of legal protections of individual rights. Pitkin notes the relevence of his historical situation as she depicts his notion of liberty in these realistic terms:

> He was a republican for hard times, seeking to encourage men to action, but to action that would not be destructively self-interested or blindly self-defeating. . . . To begin with the theme's most obvious form, Machiavelli poses autonomy as a goal for states. . . . Machiavelli's advice to states merges, particularly in *The Prince* with his advice to new rulers who want to maintain their power. . . . While Machiavelli does urge the prince to seek the support of the common people, this is precisely because such support allows the ruler to stand "solitary"; he can "command" and "manage" his popular support at will, while a ruler relying on a few rich nobles is dependent on them.[30]

As we have seen, there were other reasons why Machiavelli advised the Medici not to rely upon the *ottimati,* reasons related to modernizing a nation-state and preserving equality. But there can be no doubt that Pitkin is right in suggesting that Machiavelli urges rulers to become autonomous or self-ruling. To be free, then, is to be ruled by no other than oneself.

Fascinatingly, incorporating this Machiavellian view of liberty into Berlin's historical perspective, which depicts "negative" liberty as the "older" or "classical" version, turns many of our preconceived notions upside down. In this age of ideology, we tend to see tyranny and/or oppression as the proper opposite of liberty; by contrast, Machiavelli, the advocate of "positive liberty," saw corruption as its proper opposite. This is possible only given his notion of liberty as autonomy. Corruption is a kind of heteronomy, a willingness to let others rule us because of the position purchased by their wealth.

The first preconceived notion challenged by Machiavelli's notion of corruption is connected to the linguistic intuitions of contemporary Americans. After all, corruption is a characteristic of actions that typically occur in private—not many officials would take a bribe, sell a vote, or steal an election in public. Consequently, it appears to be simply a characteristic of perverse actors, a lamentable but private and personal abuse that turns a system away from its good purposes. While it is to be deplored morally, its principal effect appears to be providing salacious headlines for the tabloids.

One defending this perspective might buttress the validity of contemporary usage by reasoning that America has gone through periods of corruption with its liberties, as enshrined in the Bill of Rights, more or less intact. Whatever President Nixon may have done in Watergate, or however much money former Vice President Agnew may have extorted while governor of Maryland, we still have the constitutional right or negative liberty, say, not to incriminate ourselves in criminal procedures. Corruption, seen in this light, is more or less a private concern, unconnected to our liberties. Unlike public affairs, corruption appears related to the personal morals and principles of particular agents; for these isolated abuses of liberal politics, isolated agents are to be punished in accordance with the law and morals. In this contemporary and American view of it, corruption becomes a personal and moral issue rather than a public and political concern.

A second preconceived notion, the assumption that negative liberty is a logical and chronological precursor of positive liberty, is also called into question by Machiavelli's commitment to positive liberty. Prevailing Anglo-American wisdom has it that we first secured our "negative liberties" in basically Lockean societies, which need not have been democratic, and then discovered that egalitarian pressures pushed us toward first extending suffrage and later toward the social welfare state with its programs to protect the indigent and dependent. The logical outgrowths of Locke and Jefferson, therefore, are Andrew Jackson and then Hobhouse and T. H. Green.[31]

But if Machiavelli can be seen as an advocate of positive liberty in its autonomous sense, then the tradition of positive liberty not only precedes Locke and Adam Smith by a century or two, but can also be traced back to the ancient Roman republic, where the distinction between "free man" and "slave" centers on the legal rights to inherit the position of head of household and so the right to a voice in public affairs. Positive liberty, then, in its many senses, is both ancient and modern.

Nevertheless, if the *ideal* of positive liberty is ancient, Machiavelli's *justification* of it remains peculiarly modern. In fact, he seems to have been convinced that the older notions of the world and of our place in it were inhospitable to democratic freedom. In this sense, Strauss is exactly right to see Machiavelli as marking a threshold separating antiquity, which possessed a sense of "natural right," from modernity, which lacks that sense—a threshold separating an autocratic, aristocratic world from a free, democratic world. In one sense, in a world without natural right, there is room for the "dirty" politicking of democracy, where the compromising of interests replaces the inflexibility of ancient verities. If there is no one right way for humans to live, then we should be free to find a way of living that meets our particular needs.

Egoism and Collectivism

The "evil" that Machiavelli is supposed to have taught is presumably the error of elevating egotistic pursuit of power and self-interest over moral obligations to others. The reality is more likely that the "evil" he taught was the egalitarian "evil" that Madison denounced in the Federalist discussion of faction: "A rage for paper money, for an abolition of debts, for an equal division of property, or for any other improper or wicked project." The irony of this misperception of his "egoism" is that he is far from the philosophical doctrine of egoism or even individualism. Since egoism is an extreme form of individualism, Machiavelli cannot be accused of egoism if he cannot be shown to be an individualist. In fact, if one were pressed to place him on a continuum between collectivism (the commitment to the common good even at the expense of individual interests) and individualism (the commitment to individual rights even over the common good), textual evidence would mandate placing him closer to collectivism than to individualism.

For he is almost a quintessential collectivist, in his commitment both to democracy and to the nation: "for it is not individual prosperity, but the general good, that makes cities great; and certainly the general good is regarded nowhere but in republics, because whatever they do is for the common benefit . . ." (*Discourses*, 2:2). Even democracy is valued for its social rather than individual worth. In *The Discourses*, he eulogizes those who have contributed to the common good, and criticizes those too individualistic to see beyond personal ambition to societal glory: "And truly, if a prince be anxious for glory and the good opinion of the world, he should rather wish to possess a corrupt city, not to ruin it wholly like Caesar, but to reorganize it like Romulus. For certainly the heavens cannot afford a man a greater opportunity of glory, nor could men desire a better one" (1:10).

Nor can the individual's well-being be secured without securing the common good, not even if the individual is a prince: "And, in fine, let him to whom Heaven has vouchsafed such an opportunity reflect that there are two ways open to him; one that will enable him to live securely and insure him glory after death, and the other that will make his life one of constant anxiety, and after death consign him to eternal infamy" (ibid.). For the higher good of his nation and its freedom, he was personally prepared to make great personal sacrifices and to demand similar sacrifices from others. In *The Discourses* (2:2) he notes the intimate connection between private and public wealth. Finally, although he is an advocate of "liberty" in the sense of autonomy, his commitment to liberty is not born of a respect for the rights of individuals. In fact, if one is to criticize him, it must be for a too weak rather than a too strong commitment to individualism. He cannot be an egoist recommending selfish pursuit of interest against the collective good when he is a collectivist recommending submission of the individual in the collectivity or the nation.

Deficiencies in Machiavelli's Thought

It is not surprising that many of Machiavelli's positions are implicitly critical of contemporary American political practice, which is hostile to many of the goals of positive liberty, especially egalitarianism. But if contemporary practice is blind to many goals of positive liberty, so too is Machiavelli's theory silent about many concerns raised by negative liberty. In his celebration of the liberty of a people in a republic, Machiavelli shows little evidence of fearing what Mill and Tocqueville were later to call "tyranny of the majority." Given his preference for decisive governmental action, Machiavelli believed that a government should have whatever power is necessary to solve the problem at hand—that is, he was an advocate of positive government. Flush with electoral victories, a majority in Florentine democracy would have few institutional barriers—only a long-term calculation of self-interest—to prevent their trampling upon the rights of minorities.

Nor was restraint a hallmark of the Florentine republic. When one sect met military or electoral defeat, its members were frequently expropriated and/or tried and convicted of treason in absentia. Nor, finally, is there any sign that Machiavelli was distressed by this, except for the fact that the competing sects were unrestrained by any law. He exhibited little or no sense that his opponents were possessed of any "natural" rights to hold their political beliefs. Political strife had become a fight to the death, and Machiavelli was intent on teaching those on his side that, if they desired to win, they should not be any more restrained than their opponents. Thus, those trained in the Lockean tradition of negative liberty will find cold comfort in the "liberty" that so fascinated Machiavelli.

In the language of this century, especially as Sir Isaiah Berlin developed it, Machiavelli was so much committed to positive liberty that he failed to see—at least with the clarity needed—the demands of negative liberty. Hence, he valued autonomy or self-rule so highly that he was blinded to the more important demands that the individual be protected from governmental intrusions. Almost all of Berlin's concerns about the illiberal tendencies of some versions of positive liberty[32] apply to Machiavelli, for whom a dose of negative liberty would have been beneficial. Although Berlin overstates the case by saying that negative liberty is "a truer and more humane ideal" than positive liberty,[33] it seems safe to say that a sound theory of liberal democracy requires elements of both.

What was Machiavelli's vision of liberty? Was it viable? Three points remain to be made: first, that Machiavelli should have included elements of negative liberty in his theory,[34] second, that he failed to see the "dark side" of nationalism, and third, that he failed to perceive clearly the limits of coercion in politics.

MACHIAVELLI AND NEGATIVE LIBERTY

The central deficiency of Machiavelli's defense of liberty is that it incorporated too few legal protections. If his dedication to positive liberty was so strong that he was inadequately committed to negative liberty, then we might look to a synthesis in which we draw inspiration for the protection of rights from the negative tradition while aspiring to the democratic ideals of equality and participation in democratic politics articulated by proponents of positive liberty. It would be easy to argue for a theory of natural rights or negative liberty by assuming different premises from those that Machiavelli began with. But then one would have to prove that those other assumptions are better than his assumptions, which would require other assumptions, and so on into an infinite, or potentially infinite, regress. Fortunately, that is not necessary; instead we need only begin with Machiavelli's own assumptions, especially his assumptions about human nature, for they lead inexorably to the conclusion that governmental power should be restrained and circumscribed by our rights.

Given the Machiavellian assumption that humans are capable of both glory and corruption, it is easy to infer that we have a moral obligation to foster the potential for glory. Note, though, that Machiavelli is sophisticated enough to resist this easy temptation. For glory is a complex goal, involving more than just licentious anarchy. Glory is the freedom to live under our own laws, the freedom to define our obligations for ourselves under a constitution designed to preserve that very freedom. Prior to our defining what is right, the only appropriate moral evaluation concerns the efficacious reaching of this goal; after that definition in law, one is obligated to obey one's own laws.[35] The "we" in his formulation is presumably the "we" of a "people" or a "nation." Yet those people are "only human" in exactly the Machiavellian senses that they do not know all that could be known, say, by a god, and that they are "evil." Hence the laws they make will not always be "good" laws, by Machiavelli's own assumptions.[36]

Since any particular people may live under bad laws at any particular time, even under democratic institutions, the glory that is positive liberty for my "nation" may strip my "faction" of liberty. The disintegration of the Balkans in the post–Iron Curtain era is some evidence that this potential is not merely theoretical. Alternatively, even though the Italian nation, say, might not be subject to, say, German domination, corrupt wealth within the nation may destroy liberty for the poor, creating an oligarchical government.

Hence, the Machiavellian defense of liberty is too skeptical, rooted as it is in a theory that denies the existence of moral obligations.[37] It is not enough to say that there are no "eternal" laws of right and wrong, leaving people to choose whatever they might arbitrarily want. Some choices, like the German choice of Hitler in the 1930s or the democratic decision of Forsythe County, Georgia in the 1980s to bar Black Americans from the county after dark, are simply bad choices. Although humans can define what is right and wrong, they are not free to do so whimsically.[38] Yet this "higher standard" to which human choices must conform need not be a divine standard. If it is "natural," it is "humanly natural" in the sense that it derives from human nature. Following Machiavelli's lead, then, we might conclude that the human need to be free arises from deep human needs and sets limits upon what human legislation can define as right and wrong.

But a barrier seems to block such a move: Is there not an unbridgeable chasm between the facts of "what is" and the "oughts" of moral obligations? How can we discover moral valuations in observations of what humans are or could be? Nor is this objection trivial. After all, the fact that humans *are* one thing or another, say, selfish, does not mean that we *should* be that thing; it certainly is *not* the case that we should be selfish. Nor does the fact that we are *capable* of becoming something imply that we should become that thing, say, corrupt or sadistic.

Two lines of response are open to a Machiavellian. First, the gap between the "is" and the "ought" is not quite so wide as it first appears. There are, after all, many different kinds of facts and they connect differentially to obligations. Some facts, like the fact that the earth is 93 million miles from the sun, are quite distant from any knowledge of what I should do. On the other hand, the fact that I made a promise is not neutral with respect to what I must now do. Other things being equal, the fact that I promised to do something is a reason—and a rather strong one—for doing it.[39] More generally, the fact, if it is one, that I have an obligation to do something is a reason for doing it, a reason why it ought to be done. Hence, the fact that I took part in the democratic process by which we created a binding law is not indifferent with respect to my obligation to obey that law.

Second, at its best, Machiavelli's claim is not simply that we are capable of being free; it is that we have a need to be free.[40] The facts of human needs are much more closely tied to human obligations than are the facts of the physical world. Perhaps the fact that humans need something might even imply that we have an obligation not to deprive others of it. Yet this will not do either. The fact that one has a sexual need does not imply that any one else has an obligation to satisfy that need. Putting this hypothesis in the negative (that one has an obligation not to deprive someone else of what they need) provides no assistance in saving the idea: that it would be wrong to deprive a person of what that person needs is as easily disproved by the sexual counterexample as was the first articulation of this idea. The connection between human needs and our moral obligations must be more complex than this.

Nevertheless, there *is* a connection between human needs and moral obligations. Consider Marx's formulation of a categorical imperative to do what is necessary to "end all conditions in which man is an abased, enslaved, contemptible being."[41] Machiavelli himself supplies us with this premise: the fact is that humans cannot achieve the dignity and nobility of which they are capable in the absence of laws. Perhaps if we make a distinction, then, between the things a human can need generically and what humans need to retain their dignity as individual persons, we can make another stab at determining our obligations: we have an obligation not to deprive others of what they need, as a matter of psychological fact, to retain their dignity as human persons.

Now, phrased slightly differently, this amounts to a claim that we have rights to those things necessary for our dignity as persons. Thus, Machiavelli's assumptions about human nature provide us with a very strong argument for a kind of liberty that is neither negative nor positive. This liberty can best be called "purposive" liberty in that it is the liberty to be, or become, a purposive person, to conceive of a life plan: we can then take steps to achieve what we want in our lives.

The "Dark Side" of Nationalism

Machiavelli witnessed the early stages of the emergence of the modern era, with its emphasis on the nation as the basis of political organization. In these early stages, nationalism must have appeared to be, on balance, a positive and benevolent force in world politics. Further, as a form of collectivism, it would be easy to see it as providing a kind of "glue" to hold people together. In this sense, the "inclusiveness" of nationalism can be seen as its great benefit, its "light side."

Less obvious, in this early stage of its development, was the "darker side" of nationalism. Not only could it provide the glue to hold a people together and get it through adversity, but nationalism was also capable of a less beneficial impact. First, as Herder and romantics like Coleridge best understood, there is a strong emotional power associated with nationality. Great emotional strength aimed at inclusion, or any good end, can provide great benefits to a political system. But such strength aimed at evil only magnifies the evil. In short, the emotional power of nationalism makes it a force to be handled with a great deal of care. Second, while nationalism may lead me to recognize my immediate neighbor as a fellow citizen, it can also stimulate me to depict a less immediate neighbor as "one of them," or one of "the others." This exclusion is the dark side of nationalism's great force.

Turned to such exclusion, one of the most powerful emotions known to humanity can become a great evil. When this form of collectivism is turned against "the others," it can unleash great hatred and destruction. Extended from "the others" of a nation to "the others" of a race, it can provide the early stages of racism with a powerful beginning. When people of one nation hate the people of a neighboring nation intensely, that hatred can bubble into genocidal policies, which are all the more unjust because personal worth and commitments are of no consequence next to the accidents of birth. If Machiavelli saw this potential for evil and still advanced nationalism, he is guilty of a great moral vice; if, more plausibly, he failed to see the danger, then his failure is one of insight.

The Limitations of Coercion

Our final concern, while related to the idea of nationalism, is more general, applying to international concerns as well: Machiavelli was inadequately aware of the limits of coercion or force in politics. As Bertrand Russell reminded England, after Germany's "frightful" Zeppelin attacks on London in 1914 evoked a British desire to deter future attacks by responding equally barbarically, realist belief— that, to survive, the "good guys" must be prepared to stoop as low as the "bad guys"—can remove all scruples, can dehumanize us all. The full power of Russell's admonition can be felt in Alan Ryan's summary of it: "Those inclined to sneer would do well to ask themselves how well they have lived up to the injunction not to follow a multitude in doing—or assenting to—evil."[42]

Although Machiavelli recognized that coercion could not unify peoples with different cultures and languages into a nation (*Prince,* chapter 8; *Discourses,* 2:8 and Price, "Machiavelli's Thought," 395), there were, in his mind, few problems facing a corrupt nation that a healthy dose of force—or shrewdness—could not address. While most of his concerns with military affairs can be legitimately attributed to the needs of defense, national unification, and democratization of the army and society, it is also possible that, in his celebration of war, he crossed the thin line to militarism. Much like the Fascists, with whom he differed in so many other respects, Machiavelli seemed almost to glory in warfare,[43] where an individual with valor might find a hero's reward. As the events of the twentieth century have demonstrated, too strong a dose of militant nationalism can be a threat to stability and peace, perhaps even to national survival.

To borrow a military metaphor, the "war" that Machiavelli fought was the fight for human freedom. To fight such a war effectively, a general needs an overall strategy as well as a series of particular tactics to deal with exigencies. In this case, the immediate exigency was the corruption of the Medici; the goal of the overall strategy was to unify and liberate the Italian nation by modernizing it. The strategy, we might say, was sound. But the Medici must also be turned to this goal; the tactical question was "how?" It was an ingenious but risky tactic to substitute the glory of war for the more egoistical goal of enrichment of the family; but that tactic was evidently Machiavelli's choice. One is almost tempted to judge it in Machiavellian terms: had it succeeded, everyone would have thought that it was a great and glorious scheme. But it failed. Even worse, to borrow another Machiavellian evaluative criterion, it established a precedent for invoking bad means to reach a good end. One must conclude, I fear, that his subscribing to war as a substitute for self-interest was a mistake; but it was a grand and glorious gamble that might have proved useful under other, somewhat similar circumstances.

In defense of this tactic, I can find only two arguments. First, given the violent epoch in which he lived, Machiavelli can hardly be accused of inventing the idea of committing the resources of democratic nations to militant ends, nor is it clear that the world is worse off because of armed and militant democracies, given the existence of armed and militant dictatorships. Second, I cannot think of any alternative technique for transforming the Medici into statesmen that had as good a chance of success with lesser risks. The imperfection of the tactic, when it appears the best alternative in a bad situation, is no reason for calling the tactic bad. Nevertheless, orienting nationalist politics in violent, military directions for the sake of securing liberty may or may not succeed and should be the tactic of choice only under the worst of circumstances.

The use of domestic violence for good ends is similarly flawed. Although Machiavelli gave his advice to Soderini under some of the worst circumstances a democracy can face, and although he intended the violence he proposed as a kind of surgical removal of a poisoned growth from the body politic, still he should have realized the limitations of violence. Even conjoined with shrewdness, it cannot solve all domestic problems. Further, seeking a goal like modernization without "moral side-constraints" on governmental action[44] is conducive to paternalism, the "greatest evil imaginable" for believers in liberty like Kant and Berlin.[45] The danger of such paternalism is exactly that it reduces persons from their ontological status as "ends in themselves" to that of "means to my ends." It is this paternalism that has created the image of Machiavelli as a "manipulator" of people: the fact that the empirical desires of empirical Italian citizens did not square with his vision of the future of development, however accurate it might be, was never a deterrent to Machiavelli's desires for unification, commerce, and liberty. That a people are too benighted to know their own long-term interests and will never understand what they must do is all the more reason for the Machiavellian modernizer to scheme to get them to do what they should.

Here again Machiavelli drew the wrong inferences from his own premises. Note that he drew a distinction between beneficial factions and detrimental sectarianism. One of the bases for this distinction was that sectarian divisions knew no limits in violence. This implies that factional conflict must have limits imposed upon its violence. Whether those limitations originate in divine commands, natural law, or political culture is, in practical respects, of little consequence. What is crucial is that his premises require some kind of limitation upon violence.

As a corrective to this perspective on the creative use of power, the notions of "negative liberty" and "negative government" arose in the seventeenth century. Thus, focusing less centrally on *The Prince* in Machiavelli's thought (shifting it from figure to ground) enables us to make a similar shift in viewing Western thought more generally: rather than seeing "negative" liberty as the "classical" or older variant supplanted by its "positive" variant in the twentieth century, we can now see the idea of "republican freedom," which Bernard Crick believed had not survived the eighteenth century,[46] as the "positive" liberty predecessor of Locke's negative variant and as a powerful modernizing idea. In short, each arose as a corrective of deficiencies of the earlier variants. This reinforces the need, discussed in the preceding chapter, for a new notion of liberty, neither negative nor positive but incorporating the best of both. Hence, after examining the strengths and weaknesses of Machiavelli's defense of positive liberty, we turn to the notion of "purposive" liberty as a respect for the ability of persons to conceive their own purposes as a way of correcting the deficiencies of the dichotomy of negative and positive liberty.

What this discussion of his thought is meant to demonstrate is the sanguine hope that a theory of rights and liberty can be expanded to cover the various competing but legitimate positions—but not in

its current conceptual form. Hence, the inadequacies of Machiavelli's "autonomy" are symptomatic of the inadequacies of "positive
liberty" more generally, as developed by Berlin and others; taken
together with the shortcomings of "negative liberty," as articulated
by Hobhouse, Green, and other opponents of positive liberty,[47] the
deficiencies of each type of liberty in isolation constitute evidence
of a need for a new theory of rights that avoids the deficiencies of
each while preserving the strengths of each.

The realization that violence cannot solve all political problems
is hard to come by. The tragedy of Tiananmen Square, like the
collapse of the Eastern European socialist economies, can be tied
to a failure on the part of the leaderships of those nations to accept
the fact that coercion can only be successful to a point; after that,
people do need to be free. Similarly, many American proponents of
"law and order," especially those who are inclined to remove limitations of police power imposed by the Bill of Rights, fail to see that
additional governmental coercion provides little guarantee of
achieving their purposes, no matter how noble they may seem. To
reiterate, coercion provides only a weak foundation for civil unity.
While it may be imprudent never to use coercion, it is also imprudent to employ it except as a last resort.

CONCLUSION

Despite his errors and shortcomings, the challenge of Machiavelli,
the disturbance he has caused in Western thought, resonates still.
His problems remain our problems: how to create a stable democracy? how to preserve liberty? how to unify nations? how to improve
commerce? how to keep the rich and powerful from dominating
the poor? how to forcibly create the conditions of freedom? how to
modernize and improve human society? Perhaps most importantly,
how can we achieve all of these without compromising our moral
integrity?

When all is said and done, a careful reading of the Machiavellian
corpus, especially *The Discourses,* poems, and plays, at the very
least reveals that this man was no protofascist, no teacher of evil,
no apologist for totalitarianism. One can find fault with his errors
and oversights: he was not adequately respectful of the role that
rights can play in securing individuals, limiting violence, and meeting the human needs he identified; he failed to see the darker side
of nationalist collectivism; and he failed to see the limits of coercion
as a creative force. Nevertheless, his is a theory from which all ages

can learn much. A very consistent and modern dedication to the ideals of positive liberty led him to a comprehensive theory of corruption (the opposite of autonomy or positive liberty), to a recognition of the necessity of national unity for liberty, to a recognition of the role that property can play in making liberty possible, and to a celebration of faction as conducive to liberty.

The Prince was indeed a revolutionary book that aimed to "trap" the Medici—but its intent was not to trap them in a feudal conspiracy that would eventually expose them to republican assassination. Its intent was rather to trap them in a modernizing conspiracy that would destroy the remnants of feudalism and its corruption in the emerging commercial cities of Renaissance Italy—to trap them into transforming their corruptive ambition into a socially beneficial quest for glory and reputation by attending to affairs of war and state rather than familial gain.

One must wonder how things might be different for the Italian nation had Lorenzo de' Medici not received a distracting gift of greyhounds on the same afternoon Machiavelli presented his Prince in manuscript form.[48] Without the distraction, would that illustrious family have taken more seriously the invitation to unite Italy? One must also wonder what the course of human history would have been had the forces of inequality and status not been able to malign Machiavelli's efforts to free humans, had his egalitarian vision of democracy achieved the same respectability as Locke's less egalitarian version, had Madison followed his lead and seen elitism of property as an "evil." But, temporarily, fortuna robbed Italy of its chance for modern glory and defeated Machiavelli's hope for modern liberty.

Machiavelli was not a great man—not in the sense that historians typically mean that—but he was a great thinker. His contribution to humanism was enormous; his articulation of the doctrine of moral voluntarism must count, whether or not one agrees with it, as a tremendous accomplishment; and his devotion to, and advancing of, republicanism should earn him eternal esteem. He also had flaws, as we all do; he made errors, miscalculations, and mistakes. Judging a person's contribution to the philosophical tradition of the West, however, requires a balancing of these strengths and weaknesses. If his advice to the Medici in The Prince created an illusion that his doctrines were damnable, this study should show the error of that illusion. Having shown us the path to modern freedom, along with the perils we would have to overcome, Machiavelli has earned the right to be redeemed. If we cannot fully secure his redemption, we can at least be thankful that his sharp intelligence has helped show us the way to freedom and modernity—and honor his memory.

Chronology of Events Shaping Machiavelli's Thought

I. Antiquity

753 B.C. This is the legendary date for Romulus's founding of Rome; he reputedly created a monarchy assisted by a senate of old men (*senes*); the origins of patricians (nobility) and plebians (commoners) can be traced to these institutions.

509 B.C. Rome was transformed into a republic; by legend, the rape of Lucretia by a son of the king, coupled with her frustration in seeking justice, led to her suicide; this in turn inspired Brutus to lead the uprising that overthrew the Tarquin monarchy. When Brutus' own sons were implicated in a counterrevolutionary conspiracy, he oversaw their trial and attended their executions.

450 B.C. The Plebian Revolt resulted in the codification of the laws (Laws of the Twelve Tables) by the Council of Ten (*decemvir*); a council of ten elected officials of plebian birth was created to protect their interests in legislation; these tribunes, charged with protecting plebian interests, could negate patrician legislation by uttering *"veto"* ("I forbid"); in Machiavellian terms, class interests had become factions.

Note on sources: This chronology was constructed from a variety of sources, since no single source provided all of the chronology to put Machiavelli's life and writings in context. At least the following sources were consulted, although none of them is responsible for any errors or omissions:

Boak and Sinnigen. *A History of Rome to A.D. 565,* Fifth Edition (New York: Macmillan, 1965).

Ebenstein, William and Ebenstein, Alan O. *Great Political Thinkers: Plato to the Present* (Fort Worth: Holt, Rinehart, Winston, 1990).

Pitkin, Hanna Fenichel. *Fortune Is a Woman: Gender and Politics in the Thought of Niccolò Machiavelli,* (Berkeley and Los Angeles: University of California Press, 1984).

Pocock, J. G. A. *The Machiavellian Moment* (Princeton: Princeton University Press, 1975).

Porter, Jene M. *Classics in Political Philosophy* (Scarborough, Ontario: Prentice Hall Canada, 1989).

Schevill, Ferdinand. *History of Florence* (New York: Frederick Ungar, 1961).

Vilari, Pasquale. *Life and Times of Niccolò Machiavelli* (London: Ernst Benn, 1891).

287 B.C. A mutiny by plebian soldiers resulted in laws providing for debt relief and the Hortensian Law, which presumably established legislative supremacy of the tribal assembly over the senate (which nevertheless continued to dominate Roman politics) and increased the power of the tribunes.

197 B.C. The *cursus honorum* (the ladder whose steps lead to higher office) was prescribed by law; the growth of the latifundia began to drive small farmers into the cities, creating an urban mob.

133 B.C. Factionalism degenerated into sectarian violence, with the aristocrats called *Optimates* and the commoners *Populares*. When Tiberius Gracchus, as a tribune, focused on "land reform"—aiming to re-create a class of free peasants by disbursing public lands—the interests of the wealthy represented in the Senate were threatened.

132 B.C. When Tiberius Gracchus resolved to run for the tribunate a second time, his opponents were pushed to assassinate him in a public meeting in the Forum.

124 B.C. Gaius Gracchus, younger brother of Tiberius, was elected tribune and enacted the Grain Law (which required the state to sell grain to the urban poor at a fixed, low price) and the Agrarian Law (which set a fixed limit on the amount of land one could own). His followers, drawn primarily from the *Populares,* became known as the Gracchans.

121 B.C. Gaius was to be tried before a hostile senate, but sensing an unfair trial, he decided to resist arrest. In the resulting battle, the *Optimates* won a decisive military victory over the Gracchans and Gaius committed suicide.

104 B.C. Gaius Marius, a soldier with sympathies for the *Populares,* rose in power and influence; after opening the army to men of no property, he became a popular hero and leader of the Marian party, which was opposed by Sulla, leader of the *Optimates'* party.

82 B.C. The army of Sulla won a decisive victory over that of the younger Marius; Sulla promptly sought revenge by confiscating the property of his former enemies and denying them legal protection, so that they were killed with impunity. Thousands were said to have died, along with ninety senators; in Machiavellian terms, factional strife had become sectarian violence.

77 B.C. Pompey rose to prominence as the leader of armies against Sertorius, who led the army of the *Populares* in a guerilla war in Spain.

73 B.C. Spartacus led a revolt of gladiators and slaves which was crushed by Crassus, a rival of Pompey.

70 B.C. Cicero, of the *Populares,* prosecuted Verres for provincial mis-government under Sulla, forcing Verres into exile and weakening the *Optimates,* who had profited from Sulla's reign.

67 B.C. The pirate scourge prompted the passage of the Gabinian Law, which granted extraordinary *imperium* (power) to Pompey.

64 B.C. Cicero was elected consul and allied himself with the *Optimates* by advocating a "concord of the orders."

63 B.C. Second Catiline conspiracy resulted in forceful action by Caesar and extralegal executions. In Machiavellian terms, sectarian violence corrupted the glory of Rome.

62 B.C. Pompey returned from the East victorious, but the Senate humiliated him by rejecting his proposed land bill (to reward his veterans) and refusing him permission to celebrate his triumph. Cicero's hopes for a concord of the orders were dashed by this snubbing of Pompey.

60 B.C. Pompey allied with Caesar to neutralize their opposition. Together they exiled Cicero and sent Cato on a special mission to Cyprus, neutralizing his influence.

58–51 B.C. Caesar's military conquests added to his, and Rome's, "glory."

52 B.C. Violence in Rome led the Senate to confer a special consulship upon Pompey, prompting him to ally with the *Optimates* against Caesar, whose wealth and power were feared by the *Optimates.*

49 B.C. Caesar and Pompey broke their alliance; Pompey pushed through a law requiring Caesar to resign his military command in Cisalpine Gaul. Caesar refused and instead marched on Rome, pushing Pompey into exile. By 46 B.C., Caesar was master of the Roman state, a king (*rex*) in all but name because he ostentatiously refused that honor in public.

44 B.C. (15 March) The assassination conspiracy against Caesar succeeded, including among the conspirators descendants of the earlier Brutus (who had been instrumental in the demise of the Tarquin kings).

43 B.C. Octavian, adoptive son of Caesar, became the leader of the Caesarian party.

27 B.C. The Senate conferred the title of Augustus upon Octavian.

Roman Emperors

The Caesars: 27 B.C.-A.D. 14 Octavian; 14–27 Tiberius; 27–41 Gaius (better known as Caligula); 41–53 Claudius; 53–68 Nero; 68–79 Vespasian; 79–81 Titus; 81–96 Domitian.

The Five Good Emperors: 96–98 Nerva; 98–117 Trajan (who extended relief to children of the poor); 117–38 Hadrian; 138–61 Antoninus Pius; 161–80 Marcus Aurelius (who shared his imperium with his adoptive brother Lucius Verus).

Military Despotism: 180–93 Commodus; 193 Pertinax; 193 Julianus; 193–211 Severus; 211–17 Caracalla; 217–18 Macrinus; 218–22 Elagabalus; 222–35 Alexander Severus; 235–38 Maximinus; 238 Gordianus I, Gordianus II, Pupienus, and Balbinus; 238–44 Gordianus III; 244–49 Philip; 249–51 Decius (responsible for the first effort to abolish Christianity); 251–53 Gallus; 253 Aemilianus; 253–60 Valerian (renewed Christian persecution); 260–68 Gallienus (temporarily halted persecution); 268–70 Claudius II; 270–75 Aurelian; 275–76 Tacitus; 276 Florian; 276–82 Probus; 283 Carus; 283–84 Carinus and Numerian; 284–305 Diocletian (who renewed persecution of the Christians) and Maximian; 305–6 Constantius I and Galerius; 306–37 Constantine the Great (who issued, in 311, an edict of toleration for Christians; he was baptized on his deathbed); 337–61 Constantine II, Constans, and Constantius II; 361–63 Julian the Apostate (renewed Christian persecution); 363–64 Jovian.

Roman Emperors of the West: 364–75 Valentinian I; 375–83 Gratian; 375–92 Valentinian II; 392–95 (379–95 in the East) Theodosius the Great; 395–423 Honorius; 425–55 Valentinian III; 455 Maximus; 455–56 Avitus; 457–61 Majorian; 461–65 Severus; 467–72 Anthemius; 472–73 Olybrius; 473 Glycerius; 474–75 Nepos; 475–76 Romulus Augustulus; 476 Odoacer deposes and banishes Augustulus, ending the Empire.

II. The End of Antiquity

430 St. Augustine, who had argued in *The City of God* that Christian morals were a logical extension of Roman morals and so were not responsible for the weakening of Rome, died.

455 As the Vandals plundered Rome, the destruction of the Roman order began.

493 Italy was conquered by Theodoric, the Ostrogoth.

536 Belisarius conquered Italy for Justinian, ruler of the Byzantine half of the Empire (ruled 527–565).

III. The Middle (or Dark) Ages

568 Italy was conquered by the Lombards, who began the Lombard kingdom.

774 The Lombard kingdom passes to Charlemagne, who was crowned in 800.

899 The attempted invasion by the Magyars drew Otto I of Germany into Italian politics.

962 Otto I of Germany was crowned king of Italy; to rule the country-side, he depended upon feudal lords called *margraves*.

IV. The Later Middle Ages

1069–1115 Margrave Matilda, forced to choose between loyalty to the pope and loyalty to the Holy Roman (now Germanic) Empire, presided over the demise of feudal authority in Tuscany, leaving remnants of greater lords (*nobili* or *grandi*) and lesser lords or knights (*milites,* or mounted soldiers, core of the cavalry) to do battle with the emerging commercial traders (*popolani grassi,* or fat burghers). Normal citizens who joined the army became *pedites,* or part of the infantry.

1107 Commercial Florence began an aggressive policy of conquest by destroying the Pistoian city of Prato, which had been created by the noble Alberti family.

1200 The factions of the Ghibellines (favoring imperial German forces) and Guelphs (favoring papal powers) became evident in Tuscany; this tension is historically rooted in the margravial choice between emperor and pope.

1207 Nobiliary sectarianism and violence led to a reform of executive power, creating the *podesta,* an antecedent to the *gonfalonieri.*

1216 The Buondelmonte murder intensified nobiliary sectarianism between Guelphs and Ghibellines and baffled the *popolani* (the people), who began to view sectarian violence as a silly preoccupation of nobles.

1225–74 The life of St. Thomas Aquinas marked the height of Medieval Rationalism and of the Aristotelian teleology incorporated in his thought.

1248 The Guelphs were driven from Florence.

1250 Guelphs returned amid cries of *"viva il popolo"* and created the First Democracy (*il primo popolo,* 1250–60) with the assistance of the foot soldiers (*pedites,* of the infantry); they also created the office of the *capitano del popolo.* Blood feuds continued among the lesser lords (*milites*), but the nobility proper (the *margraves*) were in decline.

1260 The Ghibellines, under Count Uberti, returned to power in the name of the German empire and destroyed the First Democracy.

1265 The birth of Dante presaged the end of the Middle Ages.

1270 Collusion between the Pope and the King of France brought about the fall of the Hohenstaufens and, with them, the Ghibelline government of Florence. Returned to power, the Guelphs sought final vengeance by expropriating the Ghibellines.

1282–93 The Second Democracy was created by the merchant guilds, along with the post of *gonfalonier of justice* to carry out sentences against nobles. The nobles (now called the *magnates*) are excluded from elective office. (Later, Machiavelli would draw parallels between the gonfalonier and the Roman tribunes, while the magnates would be depicted as similar to the order of the patricians in the ancient republic).

1289 The merchant-dominated Second Democracy liberated the serfs, further damaging the power base of the remnants of the feudal lords.

1293 Guelph sects emerged, with the Donati and the Cherchi at their heads. (These conflicting sects among the *grandi* also came to be known as the Blacks and the Whites.) As the Cherchi came to prevail, they learned that, as the price of returning to power, they must do the bidding of the pope; when they proved reluctant, papal intervention brought the Blacks back again to power and vengeance.

1304–74 Petrarch was the first of the famous Florentine humanists.

1311 Ghibellines returned to power again when the pope (out of fear of French supremacy) changed sides, becoming an ally of the German emperor, Henry.

1312 Henry was crowned emperor of Italy and unsuccessfully laid siege to Florence.

1313 Threatened by Uguocione of Pisa and Castruccio Castracane of Lucca, Florence appointed Raymond the Catalan war captain—and learned a difficult lesson about despotism.

1328 After the death of the despot Charles, Florence was reconstituted as a guild democracy; *il popolo grasso* (fat burghers) came to power in the Third Democracy.

1342—43 Walter of Brienne became war captain; when his palace was attacked by conspirators, he was deposed. The priorate—a representative body now with a wider base in the guilds—and the office of gonfalonier were reinstated in the Florentine republic.

1348 The Black Death devastated Europe.

V. The Renaissance

1362 The expanding economic empire of Florence brought it to war with Pisa.

1378 Those without guild representation rose in revolt against the guild system, creating a government of the minor guilds. This was in turn swept away and two new guilds of workers were recognized. Two families with famous names, Guicciardini and Medici, were observers or participants.

1382 In a counterrevolution, the major guilds forced the calling of a new council with the *balia* (the authority to reorganize government): the guilds of workers were disbanded and a new oligarchy was created (in the guise of a democracy based on twenty-one guilds), which guaranteed itself a majority by controlling the selection of the priorate.

1387 and **1393** So-called "reforms" to the *balia,* or electing council, secured again the oligarchy and settled old feuding scores.

1414 Giovanni de Bicci de' Medici became an official in the oligarchical government.

1421 Giovanni de' Medici rose to the position of gonfalonier of justice.

1433 Albizzi, succeeding Uzzano as gonfalonier of justice, arrested Cosimo, son of Giovanni de' Medici.

1434 Cosimo de' Medici was called back to Florence by *il popolo* and awarded control of government.

1469 Niccolò was born of Bernardo Machiavelli.

1476 Niccolò's education began with Latin, Dante, Petrarch, and Livy as subjects; later, Pliny was added.

1478 The Pazzi conspiracy to assassinate the Medici brothers failed, but Giuliano de' Medici died.

1492 Lorenzo the Great, scion of the Medici family and major Renaissance figure, died.

1494 A new republic, the Fourth Democracy, was born. Piero de' Medici, great grandson of Cosimo, was expelled from Florence; with the aid of inspiration from the holy monk, Savonarola, the new republic was instituted, with a new gonfalonier of justice. Soderini was elected to this office of chief executive.

1498 Machiavelli sought the position of secretary, or second chancellor; after failing on his first try, he succeeded later in the year.

1499 Machiavelli was sent on a mission to the Countess of Forli (Catherine Sforza).

1502 Machiavelli was sent on a mission to Cesare Borgia; Piero Soderini is made gonfalonier of justice for life.

1504 Machiavelli wrote *The First Decennale*.

1506–12 Machiavelli oversaw the creation and training of a new Florentine militia, composed primarily of infantry because it is a more democratic and nationalistic organization of the military than are mercenaries.

1508 Machiavelli was sent on a mission to Emperor Maximilian.

1509 Machiavelli supervised the savage Florentine siege of Pisa; he began to work on the *Second Decennale* and probably on the poem *On Ambition*.

1512 The Spanish army invaded Tuscany, restoring Medicean autocracy. This undoing of Soderini's government rendered Machiavelli unemployed. In exile from the city and confined to his small estate, he began work on *The Discourses* and *The Prince*.

1513 (February) After an assassination conspiracy against the Medici failed, Machiavelli was implicated by being included on a list of names in the possession of one of the conspirators. He was interrogated and probably tortured with the rope. (His arms were tied behind his back, he was raised to the ceiling, and then dropped until the taut rope pulled his arms out of their sockets.)

1513 (March) Giovanni de' Medici was elected Pope Leo X. In an ensuing general amnesty of political prisoners, Machiavelli was released; his life may have been saved by the amnesty.

1513 Machiavelli completed *The Prince* and presented it to the Medici.

1519 Cardinal Giulio de' Medici requested Machiavelli's advice on constituting the government of Florence. In response, Machiavelli penned his *Discourse on Remodeling the Government of Florence*.

1520 Machiavelli's visit to Lucca on Florentine business inspired him to write *The Life of Castruccio Castracanni*.

1521 Cardinal Giulio de' Medici commissioned Machiavelli to write his *History of Florence*.

1523 Giulio de' Medici became Pope Clement VII.

1525 Machiavelli was sent as papal emissary to Guicciardini in Lombardy and as the Florentine emissary to Venice to negotiate damages for Florentine citizens.

1526 Machiavelli finally became a regular in the Florentine administration under the Medici. He worked diligently to prepare the city walls for the impending assault by the imperial forces of Maximilian and raised another citizen army to help defend the city.

1527 (16 May) The Medici family was again ousted from power, rendering Machiavelli unemployed again. More damagingly, the new Republican government viewed him with suspicion because he had collaborated with the Medici.

1527 (22 June) Machiavelli died.

1530 An alliance of pope and emperor reduced Florence to submission to the Medici once again.

Notes

PREFACE

1. Sir Isaiah Berlin, "The Originality of Machiavelli," originally in *New York Review of Books* 4 (November 1971): 20–32. Also reprinted in *Against the Current,* Henry Hardy, ed. (New York: Penguin Books, 1982).

2. Since the works of Machiavelli are cited so frequently in this work, I have opted to cite them parenthetically so that the reader can have a sense of where to find Machiavelli's words without flipping to the endnotes. Citations to the *Prince* are typically by chapter; to the *Discourses,* by book and chapter, with colons separating the two; and to the plays, by act and scene. Unless otherwise noted, quotations are from the three-volume collection by Allan Gilbert, *Machiavelli: The Chief Works and Others* (Durham, North Carolina, Duke University Press, 1965). Because the Gilbert selection is not easily available at all college libraries and/or book stores, I have, on occasion, employed quotations from the more readily available paperback version edited by Max Lerner: *The Prince and the Discourses* (New York, The Modern Library, 1950). When that source is quoted, it is designated, by the names of the translators, as the "Ricci–Vincent" version. All other works are cited in traditional endnotes.

3. I have attempted to organize these events, along with those of antiquity, to which Machiavelli frequently refers, in a chronology to be found at the end of the book.

4. Pasquale Vilari, *The Life and Times of Niccolò Machiavelli* (London: Ernst Benn, 1891). Although limited by the level of development of nineteenth-century historiography, it remains a fascinating biography that sheds much light on the motivations of a complex man in extremely convoluted times. Vilari's account is not the most objective and impartial, but reading it will transform your views of Machiavelli irretrievably. It is also consistent with many of the findings that led De Grazia to place the Florentine in a corner of Heaven called "Hell."

5. John W. Chapman, "Political Theory: Logical Structure and Enduring Types," *Annales de Philosophie Politique,* Paris (1966), 57–96.

INTRODUCTION

1. Edmond Beame, "The Use and Abuse of Machiavelli: The Sixteenth Century Adaptation," *Journal of the History of Ideas* 43, no. 1 (January–March 1983): 33–54. With extensive historical detail, Beam argues that Machiavelli's bad reputation began in the religious strife of sixteenth-century France, where participants accused each other of being "Machiavellian" for performing evil deeds.

2. Frederick II, King of Prussia (1712–86), *Anti-Machiavel: The Refutation of*

Machiavelli's Prince, (Athens: Ohio University Press, 1981). No stranger to realpolitik, Frederick II fought several wars to acquire and retain Silesia, manipulating a series of alliances along the way. An autocrat and hereditary monarch whose actions appeared so "Machiavellian," he found it necessary to repudiate Machiavelli's ideas and to denounce their creator. It is unclear whether he was a Romulus or an Agathocles.

3. Quentin Skinner, *Machiavelli* (New York: Hill and Wang, 1981), 1. Skinner is apparently referring to the third part of Shakespeare's *Henry VI* trilogy, where Richard, Duke of Gloucester, son of Richard, Duke of York, says, "I can add colours to the chameleon, change shapes with Proteus for advantage, and set the murderous Machiavel to school." Shakespeare also mentions Machiavelli in the first part of the trilogy, as well as in *The Merry Wives of Windsor*.

4. Leo Strauss, *Thoughts on Machiavelli* (Seattle: University of Washington Press, 1958), 12–13.

5. Mark Hulliung, *Citizen Machiavelli* (Princeton: Princeton University Press, 1985).

6. Skinner, *Machiavelli*. On economic issues, especially on the issue of Machiavelli's commitment to equality, Skinner's analysis broke new ground in emphasizing the centrality of Machiavelli's preoccupation with economic equality to his entire analysis.

7. Sebastian de Grazia, *Machiavelli in Hell* (Princeton: Princeton University Press, 1985). De Grazia develops his theme of Machiavelli in hell from Machiavelli's alleged deathbed story that he would rather spend eternity speaking with the ancients about politics in hell than to spend eternity with the ignoble who do not read and think.

8. Berlin, "The Originality of Machiavelli," *Against the Current*, 26.

9. This school of thinkers, trained by or sympathetic to Leo Strauss, is known colloquially as the "Straussians." They are the closest thing in American political philosophy to a coherent school of thought and have deeply influenced academic thinking as well as political practice. The perception of Strauss and the Straussians as anti-Machiavellians is not fully accurate, but the fault is not fully that of readers and interpreters. For instance, the first line of Strauss's *Thoughts on Machiavelli* begins: "We shall not shock anyone . . . if we profess ourselves inclined to the old-fashioned and simple opinion according to which Machiavelli was a teacher of evil." Although this has been taken as a condemnation of Machiavelli as a teacher of evil, this troublesome passage may mean something rather different than it first seems to mean. The implicit use of "were" is central to understanding that this is a counterfactual conditional, positing as a condition something that is not—or may not be—true. Consider, for instance, the difference between "if the sun is shining in August, then it is warm" and "if the sun were shining in August, then it would be warm." The first asserts that it becomes warm anytime the the antecedent is true while the second asserts that, even though the sun is not now shining, it would warm up if it were to start to do so. Hence, although it should surprise no one if I were to do something, I still may not do so. Similarly, although it should surprise no one if Jesse Jackson or Colin Powell were to run for the presidency, neither may have any intention to do so. So although it should surprise no one if Strauss were to condemn Machiavelli, he may not be doing so. Given Strauss's insistence upon the distinction between "esoteric" and "exoteric" messages in texts, and given a much more equivocal assessment of Machiavelli in the footnotes, caution in interpreting this passage is called for.

Nevertheless, Strauss and the Straussians, in fact, are troubled by Machiavelli's abandonment of "Natural Right."

10. Leo Strauss, *Natural Right and History* (Chicago: University of Chicago Press, 1951). Strauss develops this theme of natural right as an objective body of moral truths evident to premodern thinkers but lost in modern thought; Machiavelli is depicted as one of the first to be guilty of having lost this notion of right.

11. Harvey Mansfield, *Machiavelli's New Modes and Orders* (Ithaca: Cornell University Press, 1979). While Mansfield's account of Machiavelli differs from Strauss's in details and emphasis, he too responds to the "disturbance" by contending that Machiavelli was wrong about morality, adhering to Strauss's notion of Natural Right and implicitly criticizing Machiavelli for rejecting it.

12. See the fourth chapter for a more detailed analysis of why it is wrong to depict Machiavelli as a relativist. To anticipate that argument, we may here note that any one who passes firm moral judgment, condemning some actors and praising others from a moral point of view—as Machiavelli does—is either not a relativist or an inconsistent one.

13. Berlin's thesis, that Machiavelli is so disturbing because he makes us face choices between moralities, is at least partly right. But Berlin's further point, that Machiavelli in some way anticipated the doctrine of moral pluralism, is less likely; credit for the notion of moral pluralism is more accurately placed with Berlin himself.

14. Gabriel Almond and G. Bingham Powell, *Comparative Government: A Developmental Approach* (Boston: Little, Brown Co., 1966): throughout.

15. Alexis de Tocqueville, *Democracy in America* (New York: New American Library, 1956); especially in chapter 18 of the first part.

16. Tocqueville did not literally mean that the process was "inevitable." If he had meant that, he would have become a determinist. But we know from his correspondence with Gobineau (*Selected Letters,* 297) that he objected strongly to Gobineau's racism exactly because of its determinism. Hence, although the language of *Democracy in America* seems deterministic, the message of the work is more akin to Aristotle's belief that everything in nature moves toward its own goal (or *telos*). Since Aristotle's doctrine is commonly called *natural teleology,* Toqueville's vision of modernization should be described as teleological to contrast it with real determinism.

17. Nevertheless, it may be too extreme to describe him as irreligious. First, many themes of religion, including rational reflections upon humanity's place in the cosmos and upon right action, were themes in his writings. Second, he was frankly impressed with the civilizing and legalizing influence of religion, praising Numa for bringing religion to the Romans (*Discourses,* 1:11). Finally, his criticisms of the Christian church (1:12) were for failure to renew itself, for failure to return to the spirit of its founder.

18. The principal exceptions to this are his almost adulatory comments on Moses, Romulus, and (more problematically) Cesare Borgia. But this exception may prove the rule, for it is not simply the power of these men that is admired by Machiavelli, but their status as "Legislators"; similarly, the problem with including Borgia in that company is that he did not succeed in creating a legal system. In the same vein, in *The Prince,* where Machiavelli is reputed to be currying favor with the Medici in order to win a job, he cannot avoid depicting authority as a tool for achieving the good of glory (chapter 8)—and he reminds the Medici, destroyers of the Republic of Florence, that those who destroy republics are likely to be de-

stroyed by republicans in the name of their liberty (chapter 5). With the exception of legislators, then, it remains true that Machiavelli approached authority as an instrument to be aimed at a goal, and that goal is republican glory.

19. Mansfield, *New Modes and Orders*. Mansfield makes much of Machiavelli's use of the expression "new order," but stops short of recognizing the implication that Machiavelli was beginning or attempting a theory of modernization.

20. Tocqueville, *Democracy in America*, 3.

21. It is conceivable that the line of causation may point in the opposite direction, with his humanism causing his commitment to democracy; but that matters little to the current point, which is that the two are integral parts of a coherent whole.

22. This analysis begins with Berlin's assertion that there is something peculiarly disturbing in the Machiavellian corpus, but the source of the disturbance is here attributed to Machiavelli's moral voluntarism rather than to his moral pluralism.

23. H. G. A. Pocock, *The Machiavellian Moment: Florentine Political Thought and the Atlantic Republican Tradition* (Princeton: Princeton University Press, 1975), and Ferdinand Schevill, *History of Florence* (New York: Frederick Unger, 1961). Pocock's work best articulates the interconnection of worldview, epistemology, and politics, while Schevill's history brings to the fore the connection between the reemergence of commerce and the reemergence of democracy.

24. Aristotle had arranged constitutions along two dimensions: respect for law and number of rulers. Since there could only be lawful and lawless constitutions, and those governed by a single ruler, by an elite few, or by the masses, six constitutional variants emerged: monarchy and (its lawless variant) tyranny, aristocracy and oligarchy, and the *polis* along with mob rule.

25. Skinner, *Machiavelli*, 65–67. More than most others, Skinner emphasizes the importance of a mixed constitution to Machiavelli, along with the democratic stability it makes possible by means of checks and balances.

26. Berlin, "Two Concepts of Liberty," in *Four Essays on Liberty*, 118–72.

27. L. T. Hobhouse, *Liberalism* (Oxford: Oxford University Press, 1964). Hobhouse is probably as responsible as any one for helping to get this terminology widely accepted.

28. Berlin, "Two Concepts of Liberty," in *Four Essays on Liberty*, 122.

29. Ibid., 131.

30. The technical trail of this amendment is even more tortuous than this. A Congressional Act of 1790, presumably a good source for discerning the original intent of this amendment, provided for governmental funding of counsel. In *Powell v. Alabama*, 287 US 45 (1932), the Supreme Court first gave judicial approval to this positive liberty reading, directing the state of Alabama to provide Powell with *effective* representation. This right to have counsel at the expense of the state was then narrowed to capital cases in *Betts v Brady*, 316 US 455 (1942). Finally, in *Gideon v Wainright* 372 US 335, (1963), the Warren Court reverted to the Powell precedent, removing the narrowing effect of Betts, and establishing the positive liberty to have government provide counsel as a legal right.

31. For those fortunate enough to remember or to have heard of the radio show, "the Shadow" is here credited.

32. The single work most obviously addressed to the problems of constituting a new state was his piece for the Pope, a member of the Medici family, on the constitution of Florence. Less obviously, *The Discourses* are explicitly devoted to a consideration of the difficulties of properly constituting a republic or, when that

is not possible, of properly constituting a principality. Similarly, his *Tercets on Ambition* are a warning about the dangers to a constitution posed by that class with ambitions. Finally, *The Prince* can also be read in this light, as advice to a prince who may desire—or may be led to desire—to modernize a nation.

33. Rousseau, Jean-Jacques. *The Social Contract* (London: Dent, 1973). The "General Will" is the general theme of book 2 of *The Social Contract*, but especially of chapter 3.

34. Carl Cohen, *Communism, Fascism, and Democracy: The Theoretical Foundations*, 2d ed. (New York: Random House, 1972). While this book is quite useful for pedagogical purposes, it is also quite guilty of portraying Machiavelli as one of the "statist" predecessors of Fascism.

CHAPTER 1. HUMANISM AND EMPIRICISM: A WORLD OPEN TO HUMAN EFFORT

1. Ernst H. J. Gombrich, *Art and Illusion: A Study in the Psychology of Pictorial Representation* (Princeton: Princeton University Press, 1969), and Sheldon Wolin, *Politics as Vision, Continuity and Vision in Western Political Thought* (Boston: Little, Brown, & Co., 1960). The role of perception in social change is a larger, more general subject than can be adequately addressed here. Gombrich points to the relations between art and perception, suggesting that worldviews are expressed in the visual arts and changed by them. Similarly, Wolin argues that political theory (from the Greek, *theoria*, or way of looking) creates and conveys a vision of the world.

2. The primary sources for this summary of social conditions are two histories: Vilari, *The Life and Times of Niccolò Machiavelli* and Schevill, *History of Florence*. This summary is also consistent with the account given by Hanna Fenichel Pitkin in *Fortune Is a Woman: Gender and Politics in the Thought of Niccolò Machiavelli*, (Berkeley and Los Angeles: University of California Press, 1984).

3. Pocock, *The Machiavellian Moment*, passim, but especially chapter 1: "Experience, Usage, and Prudence."

4. Many devout Christians will be tempted to read this as implying that Machiavelli is opposed to all that is good, true, and sacred. Although Strauss described him as a diabolical and antireligious thinker, his position on Machiavelli is considerably more complex than this, although I suspect that he would continue to assent to this proposition that Machiavelli is an anti-Christian thinker, even in its bald-faced expression. (Imagine, though, the difference in meaning this would have if the description were written by, say, a Jesuit rather than someone of Jewish descent.) In a similar vein, Steven Smith argued at the 1989 Northeastern Political Science Association convention that Strauss had written on why he remained Jewish, expressing concern about Christianity's lack of tolerance for earlier religions. Add to this the high praise Strauss gave to Machiavelli when Machiavelli criticized Christianity for its efforts to blot out the earlier pagan religions, and Strauss may not be criticizing Machiavelli in calling him anti-Christian. Of course, Machiavelli had the Roman religion in mind, but context suggests that as far as Strauss was concerned, Christianity was deserving of criticism for its intolerance of the Jewish faith as well. What seems at first blush to be a ringing denunciation of Machiavelli, then, is somewhat less so when context is considered.

5. This devotion to monarchy is a characteristic of much of medieval christian thought. One implication of Augustine's *City of God,* drawn by later Christian monarchs, was that the pagan Roman Empire could eventually be resurrected as a Holy Roman Empire; hence, the political institutions appropriate to Augustine's worldview are monarchical, rather than democratic. Similarly, Aquinas was no enemy of monarchs nor friend of democracy; his essay *On Kingship* shows a strong commitment to leadership that, like God, is singular. "(W)e must now inquire what is better for a province or a city: whether to be ruled by one man or by many. . . . Now the welfare and safety of a multitude formed into a society lies in the preservation of its unity, which is called peace. . . . Now it is manifest that what is itself one can more efficaciously bring about unity than several—just as the most efficacious cause of heat is that which is by its nature hot. Therefore the rule of one man is more useful than the rule of many" (reprinted in Ebenstein and Ebenstein, *Great Political Thinkers: Plato to the Present* [Fort Worth: Holt, Rinehart, Winston, 1990], chapter 11, 262).

6. Mao Zedong, *Five Essays on Philosophy* (Peking: People's Republic of China: Foreign Languages Press, 1959), chapter 2.

7. Formally, modern or empiricist epistemological theories are radically different from the older, rationalist theories Machiavelli was trying to replace. Rationalist theories of knowledge posit the existence of an eternal, unchanging truth to be accessed through reason. Those who possess this truth have the best claim to rule. When coupled with Christian teleology, such theories could preclude, in principle if not in each theorist's case, the possibility of valid historical knowledge. Like optical illusions, empirical data are almost beside the point. You could not, say, define justice by conducting a public opinion poll; opinions, rooted in mere facts, need not be true. By contrast, modern empirical theories rely primarily upon the knowledge we can gain from daily, sensual experiences, viewing these as the only things of which we can be sure.

8. In many ways, this thesis resembles Pocock's in the introductory sections of his *Machiavellian Moment.*

9. In Aristotelian language, there is no disagreement in the two Christian views about the *efficient* cause of being, who remains the creator, but there is a question as to the *final* cause of being, as to whether God had any purpose in mind when creating this world, as to whether God gave to each being any particular purpose. In the first view, God gave meaning and purpose to everything, including us, at creation; we are viewed as purpose takers. In the other, God left the meaning open for us to create, letting us become purpose makers.

10. Stephen J. Gould, *Ever Since Darwin* (New York: Norton, 1977), 23.

11. Of course, his fear was quite different from what a scientist today would experience over publishing a heretical idea in the professional journals: he had no fear of being denied tenure or of missing a great career opportunity at a prestigious university because he had published a controversial idea. His fear was of a different sort: that he would be ostracized, that he would no longer be welcome in polite company, that "gentlemen" would no longer associate with him. In nineteenth-century England, this was a serious worry—as the captain and his companion on the HMS *Beagle* would both well know. As Gould argues (23–24), the reason for Darwin's being invited on the cruise was that he was a respectable gentleman with whom the captain, also a gentleman, could dine. Without another gentleman on the ship, the captain would have been condemned to eating alone, for he could not dine with the common men. Similarly, if Darwin were no longer acceptable among

the gentlemen of his home, he would be damned to living alone, to foregoing the pleasures of polite society.

12. Gould, *Ever Since Darwin,* 12.

13. Ibid., 14.

14. This view of Machiavelli as a modern empiricist owes much to Berlin's interpretation of him—the great power of Berlin's reading in fact lay in his seeing the modernity of Machiavelli's thought. Machiavelli's insights into human nature and the nature of reality anticipate, for Berlin, much of the modern romantic tradition. Further, he depicts this romanticism as a collection of several discordant strains of modernity, strains that culminate in existentialism. Berlin's Machiavelli realized that existential choices had to be made, that although Western philosophers had disagreed profoundly about moral issues," what none of these thinkers, not even the skeptics, had suggested was that there might exist ends—ends in themselves in terms of which alone everything else was justified—which were equally ultimate, but incompatible with one another, that there might exist no single universal overarching standard that would enable a man to choose rationally between them" ("The Originality of Machiavelli," in *Against the Current,* 69). Berlin's Machiavelli made his choice between conventional morality and republican virtue and committed his life to that choice—"there was no problem and no agony for him" (ibid., 70). This is what upset so many commentators: "I should like to suggest that it is Machiavelli's juxtaposition of the two outlooks—the two incompatible moral worlds, as it were—in the minds of his readers, and the collision and acute moral discomfort which follow, that, over the years, has been responsible for the desperate efforts to interpret his doctrines away. . . ." (ibid.).

15. Hanna Fenichel Pitkin, *Fortune Is a Woman,* 10.

16. This reference to the need to apply force in order to "conquer" women reveals a blatant sexism. There is much that could and should be said in criticism of Machiavelli's sexism in this passage; but little can be added to Pitkin's articulation, and criticism, of his sexism in *Fortune Is a Woman.*

17. This does not, however, require a repudiation of Christianity; in fact, it is similar to the nonteleological Christian view that God has not so infused the world with meaning and purpose as to take care of all our needs and deprive us of the chance to bring meaning and purpose to our lives. Humanism need not be secular, though it can be.

18. *Shorter Oxford English Dictionary,* vol. 2, 1926.

19. Pocock, *The Machiavellian Moment,* 31.

20. Ibid., 35.

21. Ibid., 47.

22. Although Pitkin (*Fortune Is a Woman*) makes a similar argument, it appears that she takes Machiavelli's references to *fortuna* a bit more seriously and literally than do I.

23. Although it is generally true that Machiavelli's world view is secular and empirical, there are still some relatively mystifying passages, like those near the end of *The Prince,* where Machiavelli refers to the presence of, and interference in human events by, spiritual beings. What one is to make of these is not completely clear. Of course, they may be metaphors; they may also be mere remnants of superstitious lessons of childhood that were not completely removed from his adult mind. Or they may literally be references to active, divine beings.

24. Aristotle, *Metaphysics,* book 1, chapter 10, in *The Basic Works of Aristotle,* McKeown, ed. (New York: Random House, 1941).

25. Pitkin, *Fortune Is a Woman,* 165.

26. Ibid.

27. Donald McIntosh, "The Modernity of Machiavelli," *Political Theory* 12, no. 2 (May 1984): 190.

28. Harvey Mansfield, "Machiavelli's Political Science," *American Political Science Review* 75, no. 2 (June 1981): 303. All quotations in this paragraph are from this page of Mansfield's text.

29. Pitkin (*Fortune Is a Woman*); McIntosh ("The Modernity of Machiavelli"), and Pocock (*The Machiavellian Moment*) provide insightful and detailed discussions of the sexuality, and sexism, in Machiavelli's writings.

30. Pocock, *The Machiavellian Moment,* 41.

31. Berlin, "The Originality of Machiavelli," in *Against the Current:* 84–85.

32. Pitkin, *Fortune Is a Woman,* 11.

CHAPTER 2. CORRUPTION AND NOBILITY: MAXIMIZING HUMAN POTENTIALS

1. I have opted to capitalize this usage of "Legislator" to emphasize the similarity of Machiavelli's notion to Rousseau's idea. Rousseau, who also capitalized the word when used in this sense of a "constitution giver," strongly emphasized the need for such an extraordinary giver of laws to make possible the emergence of the general will, an artificial but nonarbitrary standard of right.

2. This noting of Machiavelli's relative originality and sophistication does not imply that emphasizing human nature today would be similarly innovative or sophisticated. The discipline *has* known progress since the Renaissance, and this assertion is to be taken as an historically relative claim. Nor does this imply that his predecessors had ignored the subject of human nature. Indeed, from antiquity to Machiavelli's generation, thinkers had reflected on what it means to be human. Rather, Machiavelli's originality is twofold: first, his approach to human nature was fundamentally empirical rather than rationalist or theological; second, he rooted social philosophy in data about human nature, viewing the institutions of governance as artifacts rather than natural facts and so amenable to changes that conform better to human needs. This is partially definitive of modernity.

3. This emphasis on human development is consistent with Leonid Batkin's similar assessment of the importance of lawful changes in Machiavelli's theory of human nature. Batkin writes that Machiavelli shares the "conviction that any political situation can be appreciated starting from a knowledge of human nature: this does not change 'in order, movement or style' any more than the 'sky, the sun and the elements'" ("Machiavelli: Experience and Speculation," *Diogenes* 107 [fall 1979]: 32).

4. Consequently, this perception of the "evil" within human nature is not exactly a repudiation of Christian thought. To the contrary, this is the essence of that portion of Christianity derivative from the works of St. Augustine, especially his *Confessions* and *The City of God.* It was Augustine, whom Machiavelli here imitated, who had believed that human nature, originally illumined, had been radi-

cally transformed by original sin. What is non- (but not necessarily anti-) Christian in this passage is the belief that human volition can compensate for this evil *without Divine intervention* in the form of grace.

5. By way of preparing for my later argument about the relationship between *The Prince* and *The Discourses,* let me note here that the significance of laws is that they neutralize evil; as Machiavelli notes, there cannot be good laws where there are not good arms. Thus, one of the central themes of *The Prince* is the need for good defense. In context, this is less a fascination with militarism (although one could argue that later in history, militarism evolves from just this concern) than it is a concern with keeping decent states as strong militarily as corrupt ones, so that human decency can survive. In addition, the advice to the prince is set exactly in the context of human depravity and corruption. Under these circumstances, a decent person's advice is different from what it would be under happier circumstances.

6. Pitkin, *Fortune Is a Woman,* 46–48.

7. Ibid., 47.

8. Arthur Boak and William Sinnegen, *A History of Rome to A.D. 565* (New York: Macmillan, 1965), 20.

9. In addition, Machiavelli no more approves of Callimaco than of Ligurio. After all, Callimaco's desire to conquer his Lucretia is little more than *ambizione,* certainly not a type of glory. It is hard to imagine Machiavelli rewarding such behavior, since it is so obviously "corrupt." So, although Machiavelli was a sexist, reading *Mandragola* as a macho celebration of the violation of women may be going even further than he would have gone. Moreover, although the play resembles a comedy on the surface, I believe that Machiavelli infused it with a deeper, tragic meaning: although individuals have sacrificed much, even their virtue, still society has not changed and corruption of authority still prevails.

10. Chapter 8 will provide a more detailed examination of the notion of *gloria* and of the relationship between *The Prince* and *The Discourses.* For now, let us merely note that the description of Agathocles in chapter 8 of *The Prince* was meant to illustrate a point basic to Machiavelli's political thought: the difference between maintaining oneself and achieving glory. Agathocles may have known how to commit the terrible deeds, but he didn't know how to free his people. He missed the central point of acquiring and keeping power—power is but a means to the constitutionalizing of a state, a means to decency and glory, and not itself *virtù.*

11. The origin of this duty to obey good laws is a bit mysterious; Machiavelli articulates it most strongly, but not very clearly, in *The Discourses* (1:34): "Yet it is not good that in a republic anything should ever happen that has to be dealt with extralegally. The extralegal action may turn out well at the moment, yet the example has a bad effect, because it establishes a custom of breaking laws for good purposes; later, with this example, they are broken for bad purposes. Therefore a republic will never be perfect if with her laws she has not provided for everything, and furnished a means for dealing with every unexpected event, and laid down a method for using it." Hence, we may conclude obedience was not due in the case of laws that were defective; see the later comments (*Discourses,* 3:3) on Soderini on what good laws must provide. More evidence for this understanding of Machiavelli's message is provided in the chapters on his moral and legal philosophy.

12. Skinner, "Machiavelli on the Maintenance of Liberty," *Politics* 18, no. 2 (November 1983): 8.

13. Ibid.

14. Ibid., 30.

15. Pocock, *The Machiavellian Moment*, 207. This view of an "evil" human nature is doubly ironic when one remembers that it was St. Augustine, in the *City of God*, who had argued that Original Sin had transformed human nature into something evil. Although Machiavelli creates an appearance of being anti-Christian, he seems here to be providing the secular, empirical, and scientific base for an almost identical view.

16. Russell Price, "Ambizione in Machiavelli's Thought," *History of Political Thought* 3, no. 3 (winter, 1982): 209.

17. Technically, Machiavelli's argument against inequality is more complex than this. At this point, the causal claim advanced here—that unequal property corrupts—is not yet fully established. It may be that it is feudal property to which Machiavelli was objecting, or it may be that he opposes all unequal property holdings, whether capitalist or feudal. See chapter 5 for a fuller exposition of these possibilities. For now, it is enough to note that some cause, like inequality, can provoke the corruptive process.

18. H. L. A. Hart, *The Concept of Law* (Oxford: Oxford University Press, 1961), 33–35.

19. This combination of a developmental psychology with moral voluntarism is especially obvious in Rousseau and, derivatively, in John Rawls, *A Theory of Justice* (Cambridge, Mass.: Harvard University Press, 1971).

20. The "need" that is operative here is not a kind of metaphysical need or determinism. Machiavelli is not here referring to the "necessity" that was so common in *The Prince*, but rather to the psychological, a deeply-felt human need to be free.

21. A Machiavellian observing the transformations of Eastern Europe in the late twentieth century would say that Stalin's harsh and excessive one-man rule made necessary the democratic reforms of Gorbachev. Ruler of the former Soviet Union while it was governed by the Communist Party, until he died in 1952, Stalin was reputedly responsible for the "purges" that resulted in the deaths of millions of Russians; he became a symbol of oppression to his opponents outside of Russia. By contrast, Gorbachev became a symbol of democratic reform in the former Soviet Union, until he was deposed. The Machiavellian point is that democracy grows as a desire under repressive regimes, until they must respond to popular demands or face extinction. Unfortunately for the memory of Stalin, he was only an Agathocles, from this Machiavellian perspective, lacking the vision of glory that would make the democratic reforms redound to his credit. Equally unfortunately, Gorbachev, for all of his good intentions, was not up to the task of rebuilding (renewing) the polity. Hence, Stalin was not a Romulus and, although he sought to be, Gorbachev was not a Brutus.

Similarly, a Machiavellian would predict that democratic reformers will continue to repeat Tiananmen Square until they succeed, and give them advice for less tragic outcomes—Tiananmen Square being another great symbol of democracy in the late twentieth century. Fueled by the democratic discontent of students and workers, this movement promised to remake China—until then, a Communist regime reforming itself in capitalistic but not democratic ways—as a Machiavellian democracy. But the military bloodily and ruthlessly crushed this movement in a showdown. The Machiavellian point is that "in the name of liberty" these demonstrators would return, demanding their freedom and killing their oppressors, until China became free.

22. Price, Russell, "Ambizione in Machiavelli's Thought," *History of Political Thought*, III, no. 3 (winter, 1982), 397–98.

23. Skinner, *Machiavelli*, 69.

24. Ibid., 70.

25. Skinner, *Machiavelli*, 71.

26. Ibid., 72.

27. Textual proof of this hypothesis—that one has a moral duty to obey the law in Machiavelli's theory—must await the development of other premises in the argument. See the next chapter and *The Discourses*, 1:34 and 1:45.

CHAPTER 3. CREATING OUR MORAL OBLIGATIONS

1. Skinner, *Machiavelli*, Introduction, 1.

2. It is worth noting again that Rousseau is most like Machiavelli on this point. Much as Rousseau would write that people could be "forced to be free" (Jean-Jacques Rousseau, *Social Contract*, chapter 7, in *The Social Contract and Discourses* [London: Dent, 1973]; 177), Machiavelli could write that a good prince knew well how to be bad (*The Prince*, chapter 8).

3. Taken together, chapters four and five imply that Machiavelli's moral philosophy combines consequentialism and deontology, so that our duties are defined consequentially in corruption and deontologically in glory.

4. The last chapter of this work is devoted to a discussion of the relationship between Machiavelli and social contract theorists like Hobbes and Locke; the implications of the connection noted here will be more fully developed there.

5. Vilari, *Life and Times of Niccolò Machiavelli*, 14.

6. Madison, who follows Machiavelli's views on faction so closely in *The Federalist Papers*, (New York: Bantam Books, 1982) couldn't disagree more with his proposals for equalizing wealth. Chapter Nine of this work is partly devoted to exploring more fully this comparison and contrast of Machiavelli and Madison.

7. Edmond Beame, "The Use and Abuse of Machiavelli: The Sixteenth Century Adaptation," *Journal of the History of Ideas* 43, no. 1 (January–March, 1983): 33–54.

8. Hobbes, *Leviathan* (New York: Collier Books, 1962), book 1, chapter 13, 101.

9. It is not unusual for a natural law thinker to believe that the laws of nature bind us even in the state of nature, as Locke, for instance, did. It is unusual, though, to assert or imply that moral obligations are dependent upon social institutions and then to imply that moral values nevertheless place moral requirements upon us.

10. The similarity of this belief—that we must seek the goal of civility when among the corrupt—to the moral philosophies of both Karl Marx and John Stuart Mill is quite remarkable. For Mill, of course, our basic duty is to maximize the quantity and quality of human pleasure, or to maximize the developmental potentials of humans. (See his "Utilitarianism," in *Utilitarianism, On Liberty, and Considerations on Representative Government* [London: Dent & Sons, 1972], 6–11.) Marx similarly wrote of a categorical imperative to maximize human potentials: "The criticism of religion ends with the doctrine that *man is the supreme being for man*. It ends, therefore, with the *categorical imperative to overthrow all those conditions* in which man is an abased, enslaved, abandoned, contemptible being. . . ." (Intro-

duction to *The Contribution to the Critique of Hegel's Philosophy of Right,* in Tucker, *Marx-Engels Reader* [New York: Norton, 1972], 60.; emphasis in original). Machiavelli, Mill, and Marx believed that our fundamental moral obligation is to maximize human developmental potentials.

11. Not surprisingly, a great deal of sexist animosity to females is to be discerned in Machiavelli's treatment of *fortuna,* such ideas hardly being unique to the twentieth century, it appears. The sexuality—and sexism—in Machiavelli's depiction of fortune has been dealt with by several scholars. Examples include: McIntosh, "The Modernity of Machiavelli"; Pitkin, *Fortune Is a Woman;* and J. G. A. Pocock, "Machiavelli in the Liberal Cosmos," *Political Theory* 13, no. 4 (November 1985).

12. Pitkin, *Fortune is a Woman,* 9.

13. Mansfield, "Machiavelli's Political Science," 295.

14. We must also keep in mind the fact (to be argued in a subsequent section) that, although Machiavelli was a moral consequentialist in times of corruption, he firmly believed that a people must abide by their own laws in times of republican glory.

15. I deviate from the Machiavellian practice of using the masculine pronoun here. Even though using the masculine pronoun would have been closest to Machiavelli's original meaning, it is also unnecessarily demeaning to women. Ironically, as Machiavelli himself must have known, the passage is as applicable to female as to male rulers, if his comments on the competence of Catherine Sforza can be trusted.

16. This is the philosophical notion of the "performative." That language can perform actions is at the root of most legal language (in which one can, by using language effectively, create wills or marital obligations, to take but two examples). This insight is also the kernel of truth behind many human "superstitious" beliefs in magic. If language can provide us with this power in the social arena, might it not also extend this power over nature? Such a belief is also the key to understanding the almost magical (and so, to nonbelievers, superstitious) power of the Christian sacrifice of the Mass, in which the priest believes he has received from God the power to make God present by reciting His (performative) words: "This is My body." (The *Oxford English Dictionary,* however, cautions that the familiar phrase "hocus-pocus" is *not* derived from the Latin formula "Hoc est . . . corpus Meum.") The magical power of language in any case is not to be underestimated.

17. The other major possibility is that one's supposed or prima facie obligations under one institution (like promise-making) is overridden by a stronger obligation under another, more significant institution (like the family). Thus, if I promise a student to review outside of class a puzzling passage in Machiavelli, say, but encounter on my way an automotive accident in which my mother is seriously injured and needs my help, my stopping to help my mother is my real obligation and I do nothing wrong in breaking my promise. For a related discussion, see W. D. Ross, *The Right and the Good* (Oxford: Clarendon, 1930).

18. Our concern in this section is with that peculiarly modern idea, voluntarism, more precisely, Machiavelli's rejection of the rationalism of the natural law tradition. Later, we will examine the extent to which he rejects—and sometimes endorses—the deontological commitments of natural law. Along similar lines, a discussion of "modernity" understood in Weberian and economic terms is provided by McIntosh in "The Modernity of Machiavelli," 184–202. Mansfield also discusses another dimension of the meaning of "modernity" in the context of Machiavelli's thought, but stops short of describing the theory as modernizing ("On the

Impersonality of the Modern State: A Comment on Machiavelli's Use of *Stato*," *American Political Science Review* 77, no. 4 (December 1983): 849–57).

19. Hobbes, *Leviathan*, 1: 13; 100.

20. Pocock, *The Machiavellian Moment*, 6.

21. McIntosh, "The Modernity of Machiavelli," 186. McIntosh is right in reminding us that Stoic morality was primarily deontological, while the portion of Machiavelli under scrutiny here seems to be primarily consequential. Of course, there is another portion of Machiavellian morality, still to be examined, that is almost as deontological as the Stoics.

22. Ibid., 187.

23. Actually, this theoretical recognition of conflicting duties is a more powerful alternative than it first appears, and more sophisticated than I have here given it credit for. Later, I shall return to. it and attempt to defend it against Machiavelli's arguments. But note that the minimal implication of recognizing this empirical fact is that morality is not a coherent, consistent whole; by prima facie implication, rationalist views of morality are inconsistent.

24. However, we must bear in mind the limits of the metaphor; ethologists might remind us that many beasts—like bears and dogs—would not abandon their children in danger.

25. McIntosh, "The Modernity of Machiavelli," 187.

26. Skinner, *Machiavelli*, 40–46.

27. Hobbes, *Leviathan*, book 1, chapter 13; 100.

28. It is difficult here to resist the temptation to note the surreptitious intention of Machiavelli in giving a princely pretender this particular advice. The advice is to be a good, even great, prince like the "moral" Roman emperors. Not only is this an appeal to the vanity and ambition of the Medici, it is also a clear device to demonstrate to them that it is prudent (i.e., clearly in their self-interest) to be moral.

29. Hart, *The Concept of Law*, 101–2.

30. In a sense, Machiavelli's interests in law are concentrated in the subset of law typically taught in a course on constitutional law. That is, his interest is not in the laws of torts and contracts but in the design of a political system where powers are balanced and freedom is secured.

31. But we must also caution against the temptation today of interpreting this "natural necessity" as a type of "biological determinism." For, even though Aristotle was a biologist by training, he was no determinist, and his assertion that humanity is "by nature a political animal" should not be misinterpreted as asserting that our destiny is set by our genes. "Natural teleology" is a more accurate description of Aristotle's beliefs than is "biological determinism."

32. The Aristotelian assumption of a natural order to things includes a belief that everything in nature has within it a principle of motion impelling it towards its *telos* or natural end. John Cooper has called this "Natural Teleology" (personal communication).

33. Aristotle, *Politics*, book 1, chapter 2.

34. Ibid., *Physics*, book 2, chapter 1.

35. Ibid., *Nicomachean Ethics*, book 1, chapter 2, and *De Anima*, book 2, chapter 4.

36. Actually, as I will argue later, Machiavelli's target is larger than the Christian

or medieval tradition of natural law. Even the natural law doctrine of the Romans, especially Cicero, is subject to his scorn.

37. Berlin, "Two Concepts of Liberty," in *Four Essays on Liberty*, 172.

38. Mansfield, "Machiavelli's Political Science," 293.

39. Kent Brudney, "Machiavelli on Social Class and Class Conflict," *Political Theory* 12, no. 4 (November 1984): 507. Ironically, there is some truth to this claim that Machiavelli with his opposition to Christian and Roman moral thinking, tinged as it was with natural law, would goad moderns into an assault on traditional morality. But to be involved in a "conspiracy" against medieval and Roman versions of natural law is not to be Mephistophelian.

40. Mansfield, *Machiavelli's New Modes and Orders*, 305.

41. Vilari, *The Life and Times of Niccolò Machiavelli*, 517.

42. Ibid., 515.

43. While Machiavelli's commitment to voluntarism (the belief that we create our moral obligations) is what most disturbs Vilari, he here objects not to the voluntarism but to the consequentialist rejection of deontological principles of right/wrong. Even though my heart is with Vilari, it is not clear, at this stage of the argument, that he can carry the day on the strength of this argument alone.

44. What Vilari's interpretation missed is exactly Machiavelli's voluntarism and modernity—republican freedom requires the material conditions of national unity, a system of laws, and the elimination of the excesses of feudal wealth that corrupt democratic politics. Further, creating these material conditions may require actions that would be wrong in other contexts.

45. Terence Ball, "The Picaresque Prince," *Political Theory* 12, no. 4 (November 1984): 521.

46. Ibid., 522.

47. After all, he praised the moral Roman emperors in *The Discourses* 1:10, and went on in chapter 11 to praise Numa, successor to Romulus, who brought decency and morality to a "savage people" by introducing religion. In short, he had a great respect for morality as a civilizing force while scorning particular moralities. By extension, something similar is true of religions: he had great respect for the general category, but contempt for particular instances, especially when they were corrupt.

CHAPTER 4. THE END JUSTIFIES THE MEANS—IN CORRUPTION

1. Skinner, *Machiavelli*, 47.

2. Later, we shall see that Machiavelli was not one to celebrate this trait as the Romans had celebrated *ambitio*. Rather, ambition (especially among "gentlemen," the noble or the rich) is tied to, and perhaps equated with, corruption, to the elevation of personal or familial interest over the common good and the disregard for law that accompanies such striving.

3. See the discussion of the difference between Agathocles and Romulus in the introduction.

4. Vilari, *The Life and Times of Niccolò Machiavelli*, passim.

5. This effort to transform the evil of ambition into the good of glory seeking was to occupy Machiavelli for years. In 1520, writing to the Medicean Pope Leo

X, he resurrects the vision of Romulus as a Legislator (who gave to Rome laws that later made her free) to advise the pope to do the same for Florence.

6. Is it merely a coincidence that the founders of the American Republic three centuries later were to create an executive with virtually the same powers? And that, like the consuls of ancient Rome, this executive was to be elective? It is a truism that the American founders were well educated; I suspect that they were aware of Machiavelli's ideas and that there is some borrowing here. See my comments in the last chapter for the apparent connections between Machiavelli and Madison.

7. The distinction between "esoteric" and "exoteric" significations in a text is typically associated with the Straussian tradition in American political philosophy. While the interpretation of Machiavelli offered here is not Straussian, it would be an error to read it as anti-Straussian. Rather, it is meant as a complement to that tradition. For while we disagree about the value of Machiavelli's voluntarism and modernity and about whether he seeks to undermine or renew moralities, we agree that he marks the transition from antiquity to modernity and that his modern version of voluntarism is a serious challenge to the rationalism of antiquity and of the middle ages.

8. This is a preliminary statement of the central legal proposition—that we have an obligation to obey good laws—and will have to be modified in the light of what Machiavelli has to say about Soderini's respect for a defective constitution. (Soderini was the chief executive of the republic that Machiavelli served, and he was criticized by Machiavelli for not being brave enough to do what was necessary to preserve that republic, even if such preservation required violating the laws.) Apparently, for Machiavelli, the duty to obey laws does not extend to defective laws or legal systems. If the legal system, for instance, prevents the executive from doing what must be done to preserve legal order, that legal limitation is defective and should not be legally binding. But this assertion that one generally should obey the laws is not misleading as a first formulation of a complex idea.

CHAPTER 5. OBEYING LAWS UNDER A GOOD CONSTITUTION

1. More specifically, the deontological aspects of these two theories of duty are different. For Locke, as an advocate of natural law and right, deontology is primary and consequentialism is derivative or secondary, at best. By contrast, Machiavelli is a deontologist only under certain circumstances. In corruption, he is a consequentialist; only in lawful republics does he become a deontologist.

2. The assertion that violating a constitution is *always* wrong needs qualification. Actually, Locke's notion of the executive prerogative is a perfectly Machiavellian calculation of the appropriateness of granting a leader the right and the power to battle threats to the rule of law. Of course, that such violations of rights are almost always wrong does not imply that one has permission in Lockean theory to rebel at all such violations.

3. The belief that criteria for valuing actions emerged from the creation of authority is further evidence for Machiavelli's voluntarism, if any be needed. In other words, Machiavelli discerned that from this primitive political foundation emerged moral evaluations; put yet another way, political action forces us to make moral evaluations. His respect for the creative powers resulting from the formation of a polity separates him from the natural law tradition. Yet, it does not make a moral

relativist of him. Rather, in somewhat different language, it almost seems that he subscribed to some sort of a theory of things as "good in themselves" and that he valued glory in such a way.

4. One does well to keep this commitment to lawfulness in mind when reading *The Prince* and when considering the establishment of a unified Italy under a Medicean prince. Given a good constitution, the unification of a nation under a tyrannical prince will unleash psychological forces that will eventually destroy the tyranny and move the nation toward freedom. Creating the appropriate material conditions will create material forces (emotional needs) that push a people forward, in effect impelling them toward (political) modernization.

5. Gilbert's translation does not use "check," preferring to suggest that one branch "keeps watch over another" (199). While Gilbert's translation is probably the more technically accurate (in Italian: "perche l'uno guarda l'altro," which taken rather literally means "because the one will watch the other"), the Ricci–Vincent rendering is true to the spirit and makes more obvious Machiavelli's sense that governments need to have internal mechanisms to provide for self-renewal. Clearly, the sense that two distinct and opposing governmental powers will monitor each other's actions, each preventing the other from excesses, is expressed in the original and in both translations.

6. The subject of this similarity to the American Founders is the concern of the next to the last chapter, where a comparison of Machiavelli to certain "factions" in colonial America is drawn. In particular, Madison (the American theorist of democratic freedom, of checks and balances, and of factions) was an articulator of the best of the then-current Machiavellian theories of democracy.

CHAPTER 6. WHY FREEDOM MAY REQUIRE PRINCES

1. All too frequently, theorists *have* been content to "mainly consider *The Prince*," as was Mansfield, "Machiavelli's Political Science," *American Political Science Review 75*, no. 1 (June, 1981): 296. And Garver, for instance, examining *The Prince* in isolation, makes the classic mistake of missing the importance of laws to Machiavelli: "Machiavelli sees two sources of power for the prince, his army and his people; a third possible source of power, laws, is discarded as epiphenomenal . . ." ("Machiavelli's *The Prince:* A Neglected Rhetorical Classic," *Philosophy and Rhetoric* 13, no. 2 [spring 1980]: 108). Of course, as we have now seen, there is massive textual evidence—in *The Prince* and in *The Discourses*—that the laws were anything but "epiphenomenal" to this great thinker, even though this is, perhaps, not so obvious in *The Prince*.

2. In suggesting that Machiavelli aimed to "trick" the Medici into modernizing the Italian nation, I deviate significantly from the most similar rival thesis, that of Mary Dietz. In her "Trapping the Prince: Machiavelli and the Politics of Deception" *American Political Science Review* 18, no. 3 (September 1986), Dietz argued that Machiavelli did not seriously intend to further the monarchical aspirations of the Medici at all. Instead, her Machiavelli was involved in a risky intellectual conspiracy to lure the Medici into a republican trap, where they could be assassinated by the partisans of freedom once they had armed the citizens of the free city of Florence. This implication is developed, and refuted, in more detail in a later subsection of this chapter.

3. Strauss, *Thoughts on Machiavelli*, 16.

4. Ibid.

5. Ibid., 27.

6. Ibid., 28.

7. Ibid., 29.

8. Dietz, "Trapping the Prince," 798.

9. Ibid., 777.

10. Ibid., 788.

11. Ibid., 797.

12. Gilbert places less emphasis on the *fortuna* or chance of having a great legislator in his translation: "Hence, happy is that republic whose lot it is to get a man prudent enough to give her laws so planned that without any need for revision she can live safely under them." (196) Both versions imply that chance has blessed those republics whose founders were wise.

13. John Leonard, "Public versus Private Claims," *Political Theory* 12, no. 4 (November 1984): 500.

14. Ibid., 501.

CHAPTER 7. AMBITION, CORRUPTION, AND NATIONALISM

1. Mansfield, "On the Impersonality of the Modern State: A Comment on Machiavelli's Use of *Stato*," *American Political Science Review* 77, no. 4 (December 1983): 849.

2. Ibid., 855.

3. Price, "Machiavelli's Thought," 385.

4. Ibid., 386.

5. Ibid., 389.

6. Ibid., 391. Of course, private ambitions are only part of what is wrong with mercenaries; their lack of loyalty and fickleness are also cause for caution.

7. Ibid., 395.

8. Ibid., 430.

9. Ibid., 431.

10. Ibid., 433.

11. Here I am following the line of argument of Lionel McKenzie, "Rousseau's Debate with Machiavelli in *The Social Contract*," *Journal of the History of Ideas* 43, no. 2 (April–June 1982): 209–28.

12. Ibid., 221.

13. Ibid., 228.

14. Pitkin, *Fortune Is a Woman*, 15.

15. Francis William Kent, *Household and Lineage in Renaissance Florence* (Princeton: Princeton University Press, 1977), 173; as cited in ibid., 15.

16. Ibid.

17. Skinner, *Machiavelli*, 66.

18. Ibid., 66.

CHAPTER 8. ECONOMICS, EQUALITY, AND JUSTICE

1. A theoretical defense of a liberal notion of equality can be found in Amy Gutmann's *Liberal Equality* (Cambridge: Cambridge University Press, 1980), as well as in L. T. Hobhouse's *Liberalism* (Oxford: Oxford University Press, 1964) and T. H. Green's *Lectures on the Principles of Political Obligation,* London: Longman's Green & Co. 1987). Perhaps, as Gutmann argues, Bentham and J. S. Mill should be included in this egalitarian group. More recently, portions of Rawl's *A Theory of Justice* should be seen as egalitarian. Some who march under the banner of equality are more radical than these liberals and Machiavelli; they would call for the leveling that is anathema to so many defenders of the liberal tradition. These more radical egalitarians deserve more attention, and more criticism, than can be fairly given here. But the mainstream liberals are too responsible to throw out incentives for efficiency in the economy in order to achieve a moral ideal of equality.

2. Karl Marx, "Critique of the Gotha Program," in Tucker, *The Marx-Engels Reader,* 530–31.

3. By manipulating—or breaking—certain of the rules, some Americans in the late twentieth century have had—but not earned—incomes approaching 500 million per year. Convicted inside-trader Michael Milliken is a prime example. Someone once quipped that his half-billion dollar income was more than the Gross National Product of most of the nations of the world. To an egalitarian, such income could never be earned because no single person can create that much value in a year; and from this point of view, rules that permit this to occur are seen as defective, corrupt, and inimical to liberty.

4. McKenzie, "Rousseau's Debate with Machiavelli," 213.

5. Ibid., 212.

6. Ibid., apparently, McKenzie is referring to the passage in *The Discourses* (1:55) already quoted in the text.

7. Ibid., 213; apparently referring again to *Discourses,* 1:55.

8. Ibid.

9. Ibid.

10. Vilari, *The Life and Times of Niccolò Machiavelli,* 29.

11. Ibid.

12. Ibid., 30. However, other sources, including Scheville's *History,* indicate that the correct name was Piero.

13. Ibid., 30–31.

14. Scheville, *History of Florence,* 350.

15. Pitkin, *Fortune Is a Woman,* 84.

16. Ibid., 85.

17. Ibid.

18. Ibid.

19. Whatever Rousseau's feelings might have been about the values and wealth holding patterns of modern capitalist societies, there are modern analysts of today's democratic republics who share this concern about the patterns of wealth holding. Domhoff's empirical research into such holdings in America, for example, is a contemporary effort to make exactly the same empirical argument: that the distributions in America are so inegalitarian as to pose a threat to democracy (G. William Domhoff, *Who Rules America Now?* [Englewood Cliffs, N.J.: Prentice-Hall, 1983]: throughout).

20. The campaign slogan from the 1988 presidential campaign about relying on a "thousand points of light" in private charity, employed by successful candidate Bush from the Republican party, was an instance of this danger to a free people. The goal was to reduce dependence upon government and its resources by reinvigorating private donations from a variety of sources that were available. Machiavelli would see this as standard propaganda from elitist wealth, aimed at enslaving the poor by making them partisans and dependents of the wealthy. It is better, he would urge us, to keep the rich citizens poor by taxing them more heavily and keeping the state rich, so that the poor would depend upon the state instead of the sects of the wealthy.

21. John Rawls, *A Theory of Justice* (Cambridge, Mass.: Harvard University Press, 1971). His discussion of the original position is to be found in section 4 of chapter 1, starting at p. 17.

22. Ibid., 18 and 136.

23. Ibid., 152.

24. Karl Marx, "Contribution to the Critique of Hegel's Philosophy of Right," in Tucker, *The Marx-Engels Reader*, 64.

25. Hayek, Friedrich, *Law, Legislation, and Liberty* (Chicago: University of Chicago Press, 1973); Friedman, Milton, *Capitalism and Freedom* (Chicago: University of Chicago Press, 1962, 1982).

26. Although Williamson purports to be advancing a particular theoretical perspective in economics (that of "transaction cost"), his insights are in fact more general. Imagine, if you will, a standard collegiate textbook with his different assumptions about human knowledge and benevolence. The model employed by most textbooks assumes that economic agents are fully informed, rational, and self-seeking. This model would be more realistic if it were amended to follow Williamson and assume that economic agents were only partially informed and self-seeking with guile.

27. Oliver Williamson, *The Economic Institutions of Capitalism* (New York: Free Press, 1985): 30.

28. Ibid., 43.

29. Although humans are prudential calculators of self-interest, they do not know all that they would sometimes need to know to calculate their interests with certainty; their rationality is limited or "bounded"; ibid., 44.

30. Ibid.

31. Ibid., 45.

32. The principal exceptions will be cases of "asset specificity," where the supplier is asked to supply a product that is of value only to one buyer. For example, if an outside supplier were asked to provide grilles for one car line—grilles that would be of no value to other carmakers—and had to create the machinery for making this intermediate product, then it would be necessary to create presses and molds (assets) that were specific to that production. In these cases, the transaction costs

are much different, and Williamson devotes the earlier parts of the book exploring such cases.

33. Unfortunately, the argument is not equally applicable to all variants of socialism. Market socialism, as applied in the Yugoslav model, for instance, could, in principle, escape between the horns of Williamson's dilemma. Here, even though the means of production are owned by the state in the name of its workers, still there would be a market and competition between firms, so that there could actually be more efficiency. The principal advantage of this variant of socialism is that it can, in principle, provide efficiency of allocation while still avoiding the "alienation" and exploitation of workers. In such a case, a dedicated capitalist would be forced to rely upon Peter Wiles's arguments about the inefficiencies of this form of ownership, namely that there are inadequate incentives for long-term investment (*Economic Institutions Compared* [New York: John Wiley & Sons, 1973]; chapter 5).

34. Hartz and Rossiter, for instance, offer two rather different perspectives on the American tradition—Hartz is quite proud of our Lockean tradition while Rossiter is wary of that liberalism, preferring a position more akin to those of Burke or Hobbes. But one thing they agree on is that at some point in our development, American political culture became Lockean (Louis Hartz, *The Liberal Tradition in America* [New York: Harcourt, Brace, Jovanovich, 1955]; and Clinton Rossiter, *Conservatism in America* (Cambridge, Mass.: Harvard University Press, 1982]).

35. This discussion of "negative" and "positive" liberty should reveal a profound debt to Sir Isaiah Berlin's discussion of them in his "Two Concepts of Liberty," as found in *Four Essays on Liberty*.

36. Grant Mindle, "Machiavelli's Realism," *Review of Politics* 47, no. 2 (April 1985): 214.

37. Ibid.

CHAPTER 9. MACHIAVELLI'S PLACE IN THE HISTORY OF WESTERN POLITICAL THOUGHT

1. Curiously, the intellectual origins for the theory of human nature underlying this realism can probably best be traced to Augustine. In *The City of God,* he had argued that our nature, originally "illumined" by the light of God, had been radically transformed by the Original Sin of Adam and Eve. This transformation had made a heavenly existence impossible in this earthly city, the City of Man. Henceforth, human nature would be more inclined to sin than to nobility.

2. This is one respect in which both differ, for instance, from Hobbes; yet there is also a sense in which Rousseau is more optimistic that the evil can be avoided than Machiavelli is.

3. Despite his lip service to natural law (he lists nineteen such "laws" in chapters 14 and 15 of the first book of *Leviathan*), this oversimplification remains true. For, after listing these many laws, he imposes few obligations with them. (The first and most fundamental law is that "every man has a right to everything.") Further, these "natural" laws are not always binding, unlike the natural law of (say) Aquinas. He concludes his discussion of these nineteen laws by contending that "The laws of nature oblige in conscience always, but in effect then only when there is security" (book one, chapter 15, near the end). The remainder of the paragraph is so thor-

oughly Machiavellian in its voluntarist rejection of moral rationalism that it remains true that he is a voluntarist.

4. Hobbes, *Leviathan,* book 1, chapter 10, 73.

5. Since Jefferson's theory was so akin to Locke's, we may then infer that Machiavelli's notion of liberty was different from both Jefferson's and Locke's.

6. Louis Hartz, *The Liberal Tradition in America* (New York: Harcourt, Brace, Jovanovich, 1955), is the classic work of this genre.

7. Jefferson's views have been accurately associated by Hartz and others with the Lockean tradition in political theory.

8. These views usually are associated with Hobbes' *Leviathan* by political theorists.

9. In describing Madison as a Machiavellian, I mean this, of course, as praise and not condemnation of Madison. Unfortunately, as I will argue, Madison was inadequately committed to the Machiavellian solution to the problem of faction.

10. Of course, there is reason to believe that Madison's ideas changed. Although he was staunchly a Federalist during the ratification debates, he was unable to remain committed to the Federalist party that emerged from it. Instead, by the election of 1800 when Jefferson became president, Madison had become an integral figure in the opposition party, the Democratic-Republicans, and he became a party to *Marbury vs. Madison* as an official of Jefferson's administration, opposing the Federalist Party. From this opposition party was later to spring that "Party of the Common Man" that was the Democratic Party of Andrew Jackson.

One might speculate about what Machiavelli's perspective might have been on the emergence of parties after the ratification of the American Constitution. Perhaps he would have seen the two factions, the rich and the poor, as being represented by the two parties, with the rich represented by the Federalists and the poor ironically by the party of Jefferson, the wealthy slaveholder. Two cautionary notes are in order from the Machiavellian perspective. First, if the parties were crucial to the constitutional balance of power between the two factions, then it is not good that the parties are not provided for by the Constitution. Second, the Federalist Party did not long survive success; after controlling the presidency, the Congress, and the courts during the remainder of the eighteenth century, it did not survive the nineteenth century.

11. Madison, *The Federalist Papers* (New York: Bantam Books, 1982), no. 10, "The Size and Variety of the Union as a Check on Faction," 42.

12. Ibid., 43.

13. Ibid.

14. Ibid. Even though Madison's perceptions were Machiavellian, his perspective was not. While Machiavelli would have worried about the elites prevailing over the people (*il popolo*), Madison's worries were the opposite: that the masses might prevail over the economic elites.

15. Ibid.

16. Ibid., 44.

17. Ibid., 43.

18. Ibid., 44.

19. Ibid., 45.

20. Ibid., 46.

21. Ibid., 46.

22. In an important sense, what is here called the "Madisonian solution" to the problem of faction is not solely his and is probably best viewed as a collective solution, the product of compromise. It is "Madison's" only in the metaphorical sense. Nevertheless, it is accurate to portray it as his because the task of providing a theoretical justification for this collective solution fell to him in *The Federalist Papers,* and the justification of the solution is thus his.

23. *Federalist,* no. 10, 48.

24. Ibid.

25. Here Madison's concern is also quite unlike that of Machiavelli, who had more faith in the masses, even when it came to the defense of the republic. Where Machiavelli would have preferred *pedites* (foot soldiers) to the elites, the preferences of Madison were clearly with the elites.

26. Ibid., 46–47.

27. Ibid., 47.

28. This is an irreverent paraphrasing of Lincoln's Gettysburg Address.

29. As a matter of fact, this is probably not the case. If the evidence of *The Federalist Papers* is accurate, then Madison was probably committed to some type of "positive liberty as autonomy." This hypothesis at least provides a working explanation of why Madison was more closely allied—in the Federalist era—with Washington than with Jefferson, the advocate of negative liberty and negative government. But this conclusion cannot be reached without first considering its alternative and weighing the evidence.

30. Pitkin, *Fortune Is a Woman,* 19–20.

31. Berlin, for instance, is not breaking new ground when he reports that "the doctrine [of liberty] is comparatively modern. There seems to be scarcely any discussion of individual liberty as a conscious political ideal (as opposed to its actual existence) in the ancient world" (129). When the "classical English political philosphers" used the word liberty, they meant the negative idea of the area of non-interference (123). But the notion of positive liberty becomes associated with "the Hegelians" (Green and Hobhouse) who came later than these first liberal thinkers.

32. Berlin's pointed criticism of positive liberty and his defense of negative liberty are not without defects. Elsewhere I have argued for a synthesis of negative and positive liberty in a notion of liberty as purposive. Here the point is simply that either without the other is inadequate.

33. For a more detailed argument about negative and positive liberty, along with an examination of Berlin's philosophy, see my *A Critical Appraisal of the Political Thought of Sir Isaiah Berlin* (Lewiston, N.Y.: Edwin Mellen Press, 1989).

34. Of course, this criticism of Machiavelli for having omitted a theory of negative liberty is meant from the philosophical and not the historical perspective. The point is not that Machiavelli could or should, given the limits of his historical situation, have developed a different theory. Rather, from a critical perspective, we must recognize the theoretical weaknesses of a theory for what they are. Whether or not he could have foreseen the dangers of the "tyranny of the majority" is moot. On the one hand, he could not have benefitted from the historical experiences that, say, John Stuart Mill and de Tocqueville drew upon. To expect him to foresee that people would need to be protected from democratic governments because democratic majorities might strip people of their freedoms would almost

be like expecting Orville Wright to design the original aircraft so as to prevent hijacking.

On the other hand, the criticism of democracies as pandering to appetitive desires at the expense of truth and right is as old as Plato. It would not have required centuries of experience to determine that democratic regimes could and would err in certain ways. If we truly want to protect individuals from errors of governments, even democratic governments, we must afford them the protection of rights. With his keen insight, Machiavelli should have seen that his own premises lead inexorably to this conclusion.

35. In other, more technical words, Machiavelli's moral reasoning seeks a fusion of all that is good in consequentialism with what is right in deontology.

36. Plato's demonstrations in *The Republic* also point in the same direction.

37. Something very similar is also true of J. S. Mill's defense as well as Isaiah Berlin's.

38. The non-whimsical criterion of right that I seek here is similar in inspiration, but not mechanics, to Rousseau's General Will in that both seek a nonarbitrary but artificial criterion of right or wrong (Jean-Jacques Rousseau, *The Social Contract* [London: Dent, 1973]).

39. This issue is not to be resolved quickly; I mean only to cast doubt on the traditional wisdom. The doubt that I am able to cast owes much to previous efforts, including Thomas Nagle's *The Possibility of Altruism* (Oxford: Clarendon, 1970), John Searle's "How to Derive an Ought from an Is" (the eighth and final chapter of *Speech Acts* [Cambridge: Cambridge University Press, 1969]), and especially Kurt Baier's *The Moral Point of View* (New York: Random House, 1965).

40. The Youngbloods captured this musically and poetically in their assertion that "people everywhere just gotta be free."

41. Marx, "Contribution to the Critique of Hegel's *Philosophy of Right*," in Tucker, *The Marx-Engels Reader*, 60. Actually, Marx attributes credit for this insight to Feuerbach, writing that "the criticism of religion" ends in the claim that "man is the supreme being for man" and that this in turn implies the obligation to "end all conditions. . . ."

42. Alan Ryan, *Bertrand Russell: A Political Life* (New York: Hill and Wang, 1988), 206.

43. Carl Cohen notes this similarity, assimilating Machiavelli to the Fascists and using Machiavelli's writings as part of the intellectual ancestry of Fascism in *Fascism, Marxism, and Democracy* (New York: Random House, 1972), a sourcebook on modern ideologies.

44. Robert Nozick, *Anarchy, State, and Utopia* (New York: Basic Books, 1974), chapter 2 and throughout. Nozick uses the idea of "moral side-constraints" on action for a slightly different purpose (to oppose social welfare programs) and does not tie this idea to paternalism, but the point of his argument is aimed equally well at this notion of paternalism.

45. Berlin, "Two Concepts of Liberty," in *Four Essays on Liberty*, 137. Berlin attributes the description of paternalism as "the greatest evil imaginable" to Kant.

46. Bernard Crick, "Freedom as Politics," in Peter Laslett and W. C. Runciman, eds., *Philosophy, Politics, and Society*, 3d ser. (New York: Barnes and Noble, 1967), 194–214.

47. Hobhouse, *Liberalism* (Oxford: Oxford University Press, 1964) and T. H. Green, *Lectures on the Principles of Political Obligation* (London: Longman's Green & Co., 1987).

48. Dietz, "Trapping the Prince," 796.

Bibliography

Almond, Gabriel and Powell, G. Bingham. *Comparative Politics: A Developmental Approach.* Boston: Little Brown, 1966.

Aristotle. *The Basic Works of Aristotle.* Richard McKeown, ed. New York: Random House, 1941.

Augustine. *The Confessions of Saint Augustine.* Translated by Edward D. Pusey. New York: Modern Library, 1949.

Baier, Kurt. *The Moral Point of View.* New York: Random House, 1965.

Ball, Terence. "The Picaresque Prince," *Political Theory* 12, no. 4 (November 1984): 521–36.

Batkin, Leonid. "Machiavelli: Experience and Speculation," *Diogenes* 107 (fall 1979): 24–48.

Beame, Edmond. "The Use and Abuse of Machiavelli: The Sixteenth Century Adaptation," *Journal of the History of Ideas* 43, no. 1 (January/March 1983): 33–54.

Berlin, Sir Isaiah. *Four Essays on Liberty.* Oxford: Oxford University Press, 1969.

Berlin, Sir Isaiah. "The Originality of Machiavelli," originally in *The New York Review of Books,* 4 November 1971, 20–31; reprinted in *Against the Current.* New York: Penguin Books, 1982.

Bien, Joseph. "Politics of the Present: Machiavellian Humanism,"*Philosophy and Phenomenological Research* 42, no. 2 (December 1981): 197–204.

Boak and Sinnigen. *A History of Rome to A.D. 565,* Fifth Edition. New York: Macmillan, 1965.

Brudney, Kent. "Machiavelli on Social Class and Class Conflict," *Political Theory* 12, no. 4 (November, 1984): 507–19.

Chapman, John W. ed. *Nomos XVII: Human Nature and Politics.* New York: New York University Press, 1976.

Chapman, John W. "Political Theory: Logical Structure and Enduring Types," *Annales de Philosophie Politique* (Paris, 1966): 57–96.

Cohen, Carl. *Communism, Fascism, and Democracy: The Theoretical Foundations,* Second Edition. New York: Random House, 1972.

D'Amico, Jack. "Love and Fear in Machiavelli's 'Discorsi'," *Il Politico* XLV, no. 3 (1980, University of Pavia, Italy): 429–41.

de Grazia, Sebastian. *Machiavelli in Hell.* Princeton, N.J.: Princeton University Press, 1989.

Dietz, Mary. "Trapping the Prince: Machiavelli and the Politics of Deception," *American Political Science Review* 18, no. 3 (September 1986): 777–99.

Domhoff, G. William. *Who Rules America Now?* Englewood Cliffs, N.J.: Prentice Hall, 1983.

Dostoevsky, Feodor. *The Brothers Karamazov.* New York: Knopf, Everyman's Library, 1992.

Drury, S. B. "The Hidden Meaning of Strauss's *Thoughts on Machiavelli,*" *History of Political Thought* VI, no. 3 (winter 1985): 575–90.

Ebenstein, William and Alan O. Ebenstein. *Great Political Thinkers: Plato to the Present.* Fort Worth: Holt, Rinehart, Winston, 1990.

Frederick of Prussia. *Anti-Machiavelli: The Refutation of Machiavelli's Prince.* Athens, Ohio: Ohio University Press, 1981.

Garver, Eugene. "Machiavelli and the Politics of Rhetorical Invention," *Clio* 14, no. 2 (winter 1985): 157–78.

Garver, Eugene. "Machiavelli's *The Prince:* A Neglected Rhetorical Classic," *Philosophy and Rhetoric* 13, no. 2 (spring 1980): 99–120.

Geerken, John H. "Pocock and Machiavelli: Structuralist Explanation in History," *Journal of the History of Philosophy* 17, no. 3 (July 1979): 309–18.

Gilbert, Allan, trans. *The Chief Works and Others.* Durham, North Carolina: Duke University Press, 1965.

Gilbert, Allan, trans. *The Letters of Machiavelli.* Toronto: Capricorn Classics, 1969.

Gombrich, Ernst H. J. *Art and Illusion: A Study in the Psychology of Pictorial Representation.* Princeton, N.J.: Princeton University Press, 1969.

Gould, Stephen J. *Ever Since Darwin.* New York: Norton, 1977.

———. *The Mismeasure of Man.* New York: Norton, 1981.

Gray, John. *Liberalism.* Oxford: Open University Press, 1986.

Green, Thomas Hill. *Prolegomena to Ethics.* New York: Thomas Y. Crowell, 1969.

———. *Lectures on the Principles of Political Obligation.* London: Longman's Green & Co. 1987.

Guttmann, Amy. *Liberal Equality.* Cambridge: Cambridge University Press, 1980.

Hart, H. L. A. *The Concept of Law.* Oxford: Oxford University Press, 1961.

Hartz, Louis. *The Liberal Tradition in America.* New York: Harcourt, Brace, Jovanovich, 1955.

Hobbes, Thomas. *Leviathan.* New York: Collier Books, 1962.

Hobhouse, L. T. *Liberalism.* Oxford: Oxford University Press, 1964.

Hulliung, Mark. *Citizen Machiavelli.* Princeton: N.J.: Princeton University Press, 1985.

Kocis, Robert. "Authoritarian or Liberal? Republican Nobility in Machiavelli's Voluntarist Ethics," in *Essays in the History of Political Thought,* Manuel Peláez and Miguel López, eds. Barcelona: Promociones Publicaciones Universitarias, 1988.

Leonard, John. "Public versus Private Claims," *Political Theory* 12, no. 4 (November 1984): 491–506.

Madison, James, Alexander Hamilton, and John Jay. *The Federalist Papers.* New York: Bantam Books, 1982.

Mansfield, Harvey. "Machiavelli's Political Science," *American Political Science Review* 75, no. 2 (June 1981): 292–305.

Mansfield, Harvey. "On the Impersonality of the Modern State: A Comment on Machiavelli's Use of *Stato,*" *American Political Science Review* 77, no. 4 (December 1983): 849–57.

Mansfield, Harvey. *Machiavelli's New Modes and Orders*. Ithaca: Cornell University Press, 1979.

Mao Zedong, *Five Essays on Philosophy*. Peking: Foreign Languages Press, 1959.

Marx, Karl. *The Marx-Engels Reader*. Robert Tucker, ed. New York: Norton, 1972.

McIntosh, Donald. "The Modernity of Machiavelli," *Political Theory* 12, no. 2 (May 1984): 184–203.

McKenzie, Lionel. "Rousseau's Debate with Machiavelli in the *Social Contract*," *Journal of the History of Ideas* 43, no. 2 (April–June, 1982): 209–28.

Mill, John Stuart. *Utilitiarianism, On Liberty, and Considerations on Representative Government*. London: Dent, 1972.

Mindle, Grant. "Machiavelli's Realism," *Review of Politics* 47, no. 2 (April 1985): 212–30.

Nagel, Thomas. *The Possibility of Altruism*. Oxford: Clarendon, 1970.

Norton, Paul E. "Machiavelli's Road to Paradise: 'The Exhortation to Penitence'," *History of Political Thought* IV, no. 4 (spring, February 1983): 31–42.

Nozick, Robert. *Anarchy, State, and Utopia*. New York: Basic Books, 1974.

Peterman, Larry. "Dante and the Setting for Machiavellianism," *American Political Science Review* 76 no. 3 (September 1982): 630–44.

Pitkin, Hanna Fenichel. *Fortune Is a Woman: Gender and Politics in the Thought of Niccolò Machiavelli*. Berkeley and Los Angeles: University of California Press, 1984.

Pocock, J. G. A. *The Machiavellian Moment*. Princeton, N.J.: Princeton University Press, 1975.

Pocock, J. G. A. "Machiavelli in the Liberal Cosmos," *Political Theory* 13, no. 4 (November 1985): 559–74.

Price, Russell. "Ambizione in Machiavelli's Thought," *History of Political Thought* III, no. 3 (winter 1982): 383–445.

Rawls, John. *A Theory of Justice*. Cambridge, Mass.: Harvard University Press, 1971.

Ricci, Luigi and Vincent, E. R. P., trans. *The Prince and the Discourses*. New York: Random House, 1950.

Ross, W. D. *The Right and the Good*. Oxford: Clarendon, 1930.

Rossiter, Clinton. *Conservatism in America*. Cambridge, Mass.: Harvard University Press, 1982.

Rousseau, Jean-Jacques. *The Social Contract and Discourses*. London: Dent, 1973.

Ryan, Alan. *Bertrand Russell: A Political Life*. New York: Hill and Wang, 1988.

Schevill, Ferdinand. *History of Florence*. New York: Frederick Ungar, 1961.

Skinner, Quentin. *Machiavelli*. New York: Hill and Wang, 1981.

Skinner, Quentin. "Machiavelli and the Maintenance of Liberty," *Politics* 18, no. 2 (November 1983): 3–15.

Strauss, Leo. *Thoughts on Machiavelli*. Seattle: University of Washington Press, 1958.

Strauss, Leo. *Natural Right and History*. Chicago: University of Chicago Press, 1951.

Tocqueville, Alexis de. *Democracy in America*. New York: Alfred A. Knopf, 1945.

Tocqueville, Alexis de. *Selected Letters on Politics and Society.* Roger Boesche, ed. and James Toupin and Roger Boesche, trans. Berkeley and Los Angeles: University of California Press, 1985.

Tucker, Robert C., ed. *The Marx-Engels Reader.* New York: Norton, 1972.

Vilari, Pasquale. *Life and Times of Niccolò Machiavelli.* London: Ernst Benn, 1891.

Wiethoff, William E., "A Machiavellian Paradigm for Diplomatic Communication," *Journal of Politics* 43, no. 4 (November 1981): 1090–1104.

Wiles, Peter. *Economic Institutions Compared.* New York: John Wiley & Sons, 1973.

Williamson, Oliver. *The Economic Institutions of Capitalism.* New York: The Free Press, 1985.

Wolin, Sheldon. *Politics as Vision: Continuity and Vision in Western Political Thought.* Boston: Little Brown, 1960.

BOOKS OF RELATED INTEREST

Asche, Solomon. *Social Psychology.* Englewood Cliffs, N. J.: Prentice Hall, 1952.

Austin, John. *Philosophical Papers.* New York: Oxford University Press, 1970.

———. *Sense and Sensibilia.* New York: Oxford University Press, 1964.

Axelrod, Robert. *The Evolution of Cooperation.* New York: Basic Books, 1984.

Ayer, A. J. *Language, Truth, and Logic.* New York: Dover, 1946.

Barrett, William. *Irrational Man: A Study in Existential Philosophy.* Garden City, N.J.: Doubleday, 1958.

Barry, Brian. *The Liberal Theory of Justice.* Oxford: Clarendon Press, 1975.

Bakunin, Michael. *On Anarchy.* Sam Dolgoff, ed. New York: Random House, 1971.

Berlin, Sir Isaiah. *Against the Current.* Henry Hardy, ed. New York: Viking, 1980.

———. *Russian Thinkers.* New York: Viking, 1978.

———. *Personal Impressions.* New York: Viking, 1981.

Berofsky, Bernard, ed. *Free Will and Determinism.* New York: Harper & Row, 1966.

Brandt, Richard. *Ethical Theory: The Problems of Normative and Critical Ethics.* Englewood Cliffs, New Jersey: Prentice Hall, 1959.

Broad, C. D. *Five Types of Ethical Theory.* Paterson, N.J.: Littlefield, Adams, 1959.

Burnham, James. *The Machiavellians.* Chicago: Henry Regnery Co., 1943.

Carter, April. *Direct Action and Liberal Democracy.* New York: Harper & Row, 1973.

———. *The Political Theory of Anarchism.* New York: Harper & Row, 1971.

Chapman, John W. "Rawls's Theory of Justice." *American Political Science Review* 69 (June 1975): 588–93.

———, ed. *NOMOS XIX: Anarchism.* New York: New York University Press, 1978.

———. *NOMOS XX: Constitutionalism.* New York: New York University Press, 1979.

————. *NOMOS XXIII: Human Rights.* New York: New York University Press, 1981.

————. *NOMOS XXIV: Ethics, Economics, and the Law.* New York: New York University Press, 1982.

————. *NOMOS XXV: Liberal Democracy.* New York: New York University Press, 1983.

————. *NOMOS XXIX: Authority Revisited.* New York: New York University Press, 1987.

Dawkins, Richard. *The Selfish Gene.* New York: Oxford University Press, 1976.

Degler, Charles. *In Search of Human Nature: The Decline and Revival of Darwinism in American Social Thought.* New York: Oxford University Press, 1991.

Feigl, Herbert, Wilfrid Sellars, and Keith Lehrer. *New Readings in Philosophical Analysis.* New York: Appleton-Century-Crofts, 1972.

Feinberg, Joel. *Doing and Deserving: Essays in the Theory of Responsibility.* (Princeton, N.J.: Princeton University Press, 1970.

————. *Rights, Justice, and the Bounds of Liberty.* Princeton, N.J.: Princeton University Press, 1980.

Fried, Charles. *The Anatomy of Values: Personal and Social Choice.* Cambridge, Mass.: Harvard University Press, 1970.

Friedman, Milton. *Capitalism and Freedom.* Chicago: University of Chicago Press, 1962, 1982.

Fromm, Erich. *The Sane Society.* New York: Rinehart & Co., 1955.

Gaus, Gerald. *The Modern Liberal Theory of Man.* New York: St. Martin's Press, 1983.

————. *Value and Justification.* Cambridge: Cambridge University Press, 1990.

Gaus, G. F. and S. I. Benn, eds. *Public and Private in Social Life.* London and Canberra: Croom Helm and New York: St. Martin's Press, 1983.

Germino, Dante. *Modern Western Political Theory: Machiavelli to Marx.* Chicago: Rand McNally, 1972.

Gray, Alexander. *The Socialist Tradition: Moses to Lenin.* New York: Harper, 1968.

Gray, John. *Liberalism.* Minneapolis: University of Minnesota Press, 1986.

Greenawalt, Kent. "Policy, Rights, and Judicial Decision." *Georgia Law Review* II, no. 5 (September 1977).

Gutmann, Amy. *Liberal Equality.* Cambridge: Cambridge University Press, 1980.

Hampshire, Stuart. *Thought and Action.* London: Chatto and Windus, 1959.

————. *Two Theories of Morality.* Oxford: Oxford University Press, 1977.

Hancock, Roger. *Twentieth Century Ethics.* New York: Columbia University Press, 1974.

Hare, R. M. *The Language of Morals.* Oxford: Clarendon Press, 1952.

Harrington, Michael. *The Twilight of Capitalism.* New York: Simon and Shuster, 1976.

Hartmann, Nicolai. *Ethics.* Translated by Stanton Coit. New York: Macmillan, 1932.

Hartz, Louis. *The Liberal Tradition in America.* New York: Harcourt Brace, 1991.

Hayek, Friedrich. *Law, Legislation, and Liberty.* Chicago: University of Chicago Press, 1973.

Hegel, G. W. F. *G. W. F. Hegel on Art, Religion, and Philosophy.* Edited by J. Glenn Gray. New York: Harper and Row Torchbooks, 1970.

———. *The Phenomenology of Mind.* New York: Harper Torchbooks, 1967.

———. *The Philosophy of Right.* Translated with notes by T. M. Knox. Oxford: Oxford University Press, 1967.

Hobsbawm, E. J. *Primitive Rebels.* New York: Norton, 1959.

Hudson, W. D., ed. *The Is/Ought Question.* New York: St. Martin's Press, 1969.

Hume, David. *A Treatise on Human Nature.* Oxford: Oxford University Press, 1973.

Kaufmann, Walter, ed. *Existentialism from Dostoevsky to Sartre.* New York: World Publishing, 1956.

Kropotkin, Peter. *Anarchism: Its Philosophy and Ideal.* London: Freedom Pamphlets, No. 10, London, 1897.

Kuhn, Thomas. *The Structure of Scientific Revolutions.* Chicago: The University of Chicago Press, 1962.

Lakatos, Imre and Alan Musgrave, eds. *Criticism and the Growth of Knowledge.* Cambridge: Cambridge University Press, Cambridge, 1970.

Laslett, Peter and James Fishkin, eds. *Philosophy, Politics, and Society,* Fifth Series. New Haven: Yale University Press, 1981.

Lewontin, R. C., Steven Rose, and Leon J. Kamin. *Not in Our Genes: Biology, Ideology, and Human Nature.* New York: Pantheon, 1984.

Locke, John. *An Essay Concerning Human Understanding.* London: Dent, 1961.

———. *Second Treatise on Government.* Edited by C. B. Macpherson. Indianapolis: Hackett, 1980.

Lowi, Theodore. *The End of Liberalism.* New York: Norton, 1969.

Lukes, Stephen. *Individualism.* Oxford: Basil Blackwell, 1973.

Macpherson, C. B. *Democratic Theory: Essays in Retrieval.* New York: Oxford University Press, 1973.

Mandelbaum, Maurice. *History, Man, and Reason.* Baltimore: Johns Hopkins Press, 1971.

Marcuse, Herbert. *Counter-Revolution and Revolt.* Boston: Beacon, 1972.

———. *An Essay on Liberation.* Boston: Beacon, 1969.

———. *Eros and Civilization: A Philosophical Inquiry into Freud.* Boston: Beacon, 1955.

———. *One-Dimensional Man.* Boston: Beacon, 1964.

Maslow, Abraham H. *Motivation and Personality.* New York: Harper & Row, 1954.

Mill, John Stuart. *Utilitarianism, On Liberty, and Considerations on Representative Government.* London: Dent, 1922.

Miller, David. *Social Justice.* Oxford: Clarendon Press, 1973.

Molina, Fernando, ed. *The Sources of Existentialism as Philosophy.* Englewood Cliffs, N.J.: Prentice Hall, 1969.

Montesquieu. *The Spirit of the Laws.* New York: Hafner Publishing Co., 1966.

Morgan, Michael L. *Classics of Moral and Political Theory.* Indianapolis: Hackett, 1992.

Mortimer, G. W., ed. *Weakness of Will.* New York: St. Martin's Press, 1971.

Mosse, George L. *The Crisis of German Ideology.* New York: Grosset & Dunlap, 1964.

Nagel, Thomas. *The Possibility of Altruism.* Oxford: Clarendon Press, 1970.

Oakeshott, Michael. *On Human Conduct.* Oxford: Clarendon Press, 1975.

————. *Rationalism in Politics and Other Essays.* New York: Basic Books, 1962.

Passmore, John. *The Perfectibility of Man.* London: Gerald Duckworth, 1970.

Pennock, J. Roland. *Democratic Political Theory.* Princeton, N.J.: Princeton University Press, 1979.

Pitkin, Hanna Fenichel. *Wittgenstein and Justice.* Berkeley and Los Angeles: University of California Press, 1970.

————. *The Concept of Representation.* Berkeley and Los Angeles: University of California Press, 1967.

Plamenatz, John. *Democracy and Illusion.* London: Longman, 1973.

————. *Readings from Liberal Writers.* New York: Barnes & Noble, 1965.

————. *Man and Society: Political and Social Theories from Machiavelli to Marx.* New York: Longman, 1963, 1992.

Popper, Karl. *The Open Society and Its Enemies.* London: Routledge & Kegan Paul, 1945.

————. *The Logic of Scientific Discovery.* New York: Science Editions, 1961.

Porter, Jene M. *Classics in Political Philosophy.* Scarborough, Ontario: Prentice Hall Canada, 1989.

Raphael, D. D. *Problems of Political Philosophy.* New York and London: Praeger, 1970.

Raz, Joseph. *The Concept of a Legal System.* Oxford: Clarendon, 1970.

Read, Herbert. *Anarchy and Order.* Boston: Beacon, 1971.

Rogers, Carl. *On Becoming a Person.* Boston: Houghton Mifflin, 1961.

Ross, W. D. *The Right and the Good.* Oxford: Clarendon Press, 1930.

Rossiter, Clinton. *Conservatism in America.* Cambridge, Mass.: Harvard University Press, 1962, 1982.

Sargent, Lyman T. *New Left Thought: An Introduction.* Homewood, Ill.: Dorsey, 1972.

Searle, John. *Speech Acts.* Cambridge: Cambridge University Press, 1969.

Sellars, Wilfrid. *Philosophical Perspectives.* Springfield, Illinois: Charles C. Thomas, 1967.

Sellars, Wilfred, H. Feigl, and K. Lehrer, eds. *New Readings in Philosophical Analysis.* New York: Appleton-Century-Crofts, 1972.

Stevenson, Leslie. *Seven Theories of Human Nature.* Oxford: Oxford University Press, 1974.

Strawson, P. F. "Social Morality and the Individual Ideal." *Philosophy* 36, no. 136 (January 1961): 1–17.

Tawney, R. H. *Equality.* London: Allen & Unwin, 1938.

Taylor, Charles. *Hegel.* Cambridge: Cambridge University Press, 1975.

Thayer, Frederick. *An End to Hierarchy! An End to Competition!* New York: New Viewpoints, 1973.

Tocqueville, Alexis de. *Selected Letters on Politics and Society.* Roger Boesche, ed. and James Toupin and Roger Boesche, trans. Berkeley and Los Angeles: University of California Press, 1985.

Von Wright, G. H. *The Varieties of Goodness*. New York: Humanities Press, 1963.

Watts, Alan. *The Way of Zen*. New York: Vintage, 1957.

Wilhelm, Richard and Cary F. Baynes, trans. *The I Ching or Book of Changes*. Princeton, N.J.: Princeton University Press, 1950.

Wiles, P. J. D. *Economic Institutions Compared*. New York: John Wiley & Sons, 1973.

Wittgenstein, Ludwig. *Philosophical Investigations*. New York: Macmillan Co., 1971.

————. *Tractatus Logico-Philosophicus*. New York: Humanities Press, 1961.

————. *On Certainty*. New York: Harper, 1969.

————. *Zettel*. Berkeley and Los Angeles: University of California Press, 1970.

Wolf, Eric. *Peasant Wars of the Twentieth Century*. New York: Harper & Row, 1968.

Wolff, Robert Paul. *The Autonomy of Reason*. New York: Harper Torchbook, 1973.

————. *In Defense of Anarchism*. New York: Harper & Row, 1970.

————. *The Poverty of Liberalism*. Boston: Beacon, 1968.

————. *Understanding Rawls*. Princeton, N.J.: Princeton University Press, 1977.

Wolff, Robert Paul, Barrington Moore, and Herbert Marcuse. *A Critique of Pure Tolerance*. Boston: Beacon, 1970.

Index

Agathocles, 5, 63, 65, 70, 88, 99, 115–19, 122–24, 151

Ambitio, 75, 165, 184

Ambition/ambizione, 31, 74, 75, 126; and class, 24, 31, 73–76, 119, 120, 126, 133, 136, 143, 151, 156, 169, 171, 172, 182–85; and corruption, 21, 76, 77, 110, 120, 135, 136, 139, 144, 148, 156, 165, 166, 175, 180, 192, 193; and property, 11, 120, 165, 172, 184; as a vice, 75, 76, 88, 115, 117, 120–24, 140, 150, 155, 164, 165, 184, 19; external, 166, 168; in Machiavelli's plays and poetry, 12, 31, 120, 121, 164, 226; neutralizing, 28, 76, 77, 121, 143, 165, 195, 209; reversing, 144, 145, 151, 155, 160–62, 218

Aquinas, 28, 29, 36, 41–43, 85, 108, 223

Aristocracy, 17, 35, 36, 137, 190, 191; and corruption, 35, 136, 137, 179, 192, 208, 220; Aristotelian, 25, 134, 136, 194; difficulties presented by, 148, 179; feudal, 22, 110, 144, 171, 178, 182

Aristotle, 25, 42, 50–53, 105, 134, 135, 164, 196, 223

Augustine, 28, 36, 39, 41, 43, 85, 95, 222

Berlin, Sir Isaiah, 9, 12, 18, 27, 54, 107, 108, 207, 210, 216, 217

Borgia, Cesare, 99, 115, 126, 152, 184, 226

Brutus, 24, 63, 71, 74, 95, 115, 116, 124, 126, 155, 156, 159, 160, 219, 221

Capital/capitalism, 27, 45, 163, 176–78, 185, 186, 188, 189, 191, 206

Chance. See Fortuna

Checks and balances, 134, 137, 140, 168, 170, 194, 199, 204, 205

Cicero, 29, 97, 108, 157, 221

Collectivism, 10, 165, 166, 172, 173, 176, 198, 208, 209, 213, 214, 217

Commerce/commercial: and class, 35, 161, 170, 180–82, 184, 192, 193, 223; and economic development, 9, 21, 24, 45, 181; as a modernizing force, 45, 110, 147, 177, 178, 182; capitalism, 24, 26, 31, 45, 151, 159, 178–82, 193, 218, 223; fostering, 21, 35, 216, 217

Consequentialism: and corruption, 95, 115, 116, 118, 130; and glory, 117, 118; and liberty, 95, 133; and moral voluntarism, 114, 116; as a doctrine, 66, 95; defined, 98, 99, 114

Constitution, 135, 138, 149, 171, 194, 205; and class, 133, 140, 170, 172, 183, 190, 194, 206; and corruption, 78, 179, 183; and liberty, 24, 25, 30, 66, 83, 124, 129, 132–34, 138, 140, 145, 177, 211; and property, 22, 179, 180; and stability, 25, 30, 132; Aristotelian, 25, 134; as law, 115, 121, 128, 129, 131, 132, 134, 136, 140, 195, 204, 207; creators of, 61, 63, 66, 139, 171, 194; general, 25, 69, 133–35, 137, 186; mixed, 25, 30, 75, 133, 135, 137–40, 194, 199, 200; of Florence, 21, 121, 155, 162; of Rome, 140, 204; of USA 84, 104, 128, 198–201; process of, 22, 25, 59, 61, 63, 66, 86, 90, 92, 98, 116, 130, 133, 139, 146, 149, 185, 227; renewing, 25, 30, 116, 126, 133, 134, 139, 140, 149, 155, 188

Constitutionalism, 27, 30, 66, 127–29, 131, 132, 139, 143, 198

Corrupt/corruption, 191; and class, 77, 138, 139, 169, 170, 176, 178, 180,

191, 200, 215, 218; and liberty, 138, 143, 171, 191, 207, 218; and moral consequentialism, 114–19, 130, 160, 164; and moral voluntarism, 102, 103, 105, 113, 114, 116–18, 125, 127, 130, 154, 160, 191, 195, 196; and morality, 84, 90–101, 106, 109, 194; and princes, 24, 25, 30, 69–71, 73, 93, 117, 125, 126, 136, 148, 152, 154, 156, 159–61, 179, 191; and property, 71, 76, 83, 131, 144, 152, 171, 177–79, 181, 184–86, 191; as a human potential, 28, 29, 55, 59, 63, 68–70, 78, 88, 91, 109, 117, 129, 135, 191, 211; as a vice, 75, 125, 149, 151, 166, 203, 207, 212; causes of, 28, 75, 76, 83, 87, 88, 110, 116, 136, 144, 148, 151, 165, 166, 171, 172, 175, 184, 185, 193, 204, 211, 218, 221; condition of, 30, 38, 65, 67, 78, 101; difficulties presented by, 25, 70, 74, 78, 83, 88–90, 99, 115, 134, 154, 155, 160, 179; neutralizing, 63, 66, 69, 72, 133, 134, 140, 149, 187; of family, 64; of Florence, 65, 126, 152, 170, 182; of Italy, 71, 88, 126, 151, 154; of religion, 36–39, 49; of Rome, 70, 116; process of, 30, 31, 68, 70, 76, 77, 108, 149, 178; reversing, 28, 30, 31, 75, 88, 90, 101, 123, 131, 134, 144, 149, 154–56, 159, 161, 179, 191, 192, 209; using cruelty to end, 65, 73, 101, 118, 126, 149, 155, 156, 159, 160, 214

Democracy/democratic, 204, 207, 211, 212, 214; and equality, 17, 20, 22, 26, 27, 31, 131, 147, 171, 175, 176, 179, 186, 189, 190, 194, 201, 206, 210, 218; and liberty, 17, 21, 23, 24, 27, 31, 32, 49, 119, 144, 147, 149, 177, 178, 194, 196, 197, 206, 211; and militarism, 109, 215; and moral voluntarism, 24, 84, 99, 109, 119, 127, 128, 130, 192, 193, 199; and princes, 44, 72, 73, 118, 191; and property, 177, 179, 180, 188, 189; and rationalism, 44, 54; and representation, 22, 37, 137, 139, 202, 203, 205; and stability, 22, 73, 185, 191, 217; Aristotelian, 25, 37, 134, 194, 202; as a doctrine, 134, 199, 202; as

a modernizing force, 22–24, 74, 116, 144, 147, 190; as a vice, 73, 211; as an ideal, 17, 66, 71, 73, 74, 108, 109, 125, 143, 144, 148, 149, 151, 161, 169, 170, 175, 177, 195, 197, 204, 208, 209, 226; necessary conditions, 9, 26, 28, 31, 36, 66, 149, 176, 178, 179, 181, 186, 188, 191, 193, 208, 210; of Florence, 181, 182, 210, 224–26; of U.S.A., 198, 199

Deontology (moral), 98, 99, 114, 118, 130, 196

Development (political and economic), 20, 22, 23, 26, 65, 68, 84, 133, 140, 199, 213, 216. See also Modernization

Developmentalism (psychological), 24, 61, 69, 78, 191, 196

Duty, 19, 23, 64, 83, 95–98, 114–16, 118, 128, 130, 133, 165, 184

Egoism, 208

Empire/imperial, 1, 89, 90, 153, 156, 173, 184, 222–27

Empirical: conditions, 99–101, 103, 116, 216; data, 19, 44–46, 50, 59, 60, 67, 68, 121, 205; knowledge, 37, 44, 67, 68, 73, 74, 85, 89, 91, 99, 124, 181, 185; observations, 19, 99, 126; science, 18, 35, 45, 60, 106, 108, 197

Empiricism: and humanism, 35, 43, 45, 52, 86, 93, 98, 148; and moral voluntarism, 85, 86, 110; as a modernizing force, 42, 45, 52, 53, 60, 85, 103, 112, 135, 147, 159, 194, 196, 204

Equality, 76, 180, 205; and class, 177–80; and corruption, 71, 76–78, 83, 171, 175–77, 179, 184; and liberty, 26, 27, 76, 131, 149, 169, 175, 176, 179, 180, 182–84, 186, 189, 190, 194, 201, 206; and property, 71, 76, 78, 84, 131, 171, 175–77, 184, 185, 189, 194, 201, 203, 204, 208; as a doctrine, 9, 11, 12, 17, 175; as a modernizing force, 20, 22, 26, 190, 191, 193, 218; as an ideal, 10, 17, 31, 83, 174–76, 191, 194, 210; of Florence, 182, 183; of Rome, 183; using cruelty to create, 171, 179, 191, 194

Executions, 95, 122, 140, 219, 221

Executive, 20, 30, 35, 36, 104, 115, 156, 195, 198, 199, 223, 226

Faction: and class, 25, 170, 183, 194, 219; and liberty, 25, 30, 31, 148, 168, 170, 171, 176, 182, 194, 195, 199, 200; and sectarian violence, 27, 120, 151, 200, 204, 216, 220, 223; as a vice, 76, 101, 151, 168, 169, 200, 201, 203, 211; as an ideal, 120, 169–71, 176, 183, 194, 199, 201, 216, 218; causes of, 200, 201; neutralizing, 137, 138, 140, 171, 183, 194, 201–6; of U.S.A., 198–200, 205, 208
Feudal/feudalism: and class, 22, 35, 36, 110, 159, 162, 164, 169–71, 176, 178, 179, 183, 188, 193, 223, 224; and corruption, 24, 169, 186, 188, 218; and liberty, 22, 164, 169, 180, 181, 184; and property, 26, 176–82, 184, 186, 188, 192; and sectarian violence, 151, 159, 162, 218; difficulties presented by, 30, 36, 45, 86, 89, 144, 162, 163
Fortuna: as a cosmic force, 37, 45–48, 50–54, 62, 69, 70, 86, 102, 136, 139, 151, 154, 159, 167, 196, 197, 205, 218; as a doctrine, 12, 46, 48–52; as a Roman goddess, 47; as a woman, 46–48, 54, 86; in commentaries, 53, 100; in Machiavelli's plays and poetry, 12, 20; in The Prince, 42, 46, 47, 51, 54, 167
Fortune. See Fortuna
Freedom. See Liberty

Glory/gloria: and corruption, 67, 68, 75, 83, 99, 100, 116, 118, 120, 124–26, 132, 149, 150, 152, 154, 182, 184; and liberty, 25, 66, 68, 70, 127, 144, 146, 197, 211; and moral voluntarism, 97, 98, 119, 125, 192, 211; and morality, 90, 96, 99, 114–16, 118, 124, 130; and princes, 71, 74, 155, 156, 209; as a human potential, 28, 39, 53, 55, 60, 62, 63, 66, 68, 88, 117, 121, 133, 191, 211; as a modernizing force, 71, 84, 89, 98, 117, 121, 163, 172; as a moral value, 23, 24, 61, 66, 70, 75, 99, 105, 106, 112, 117–19, 121, 122, 124–27, 138, 144, 150, 152, 156–59, 162, 163, 192,

194, 211, 218; as an ideal, 12; modernizing, 18, 22, 24, 218; of Italy, 163; of Rome, 126, 145; using cruelty to create, 156; versus power, 5, 66, 70, 75, 88, 102, 116, 117, 119–27, 144, 145, 151, 156, 160, 161
Guicciardini, 121, 225, 227
Guilds, 31, 35, 148, 170, 181, 190, 224, 225

Hamilton, Alexander, 198, 199
Hobbes, 29, 62, 66, 84, 92, 98, 102, 130, 195–98

Individual/individualism, 27, 49, 146, 172, 180, 190, 198, 202, 203, 206, 208–10, 213, 217
Instinct/instinctivism, 61, 62, 75
Italy/Italian, 37–39, 48, 65, 71, 88, 105, 121, 126, 144, 147, 148, 150–54, 156, 159–64, 167, 168, 181, 182, 184, 186, 191, 193, 211, 215, 216, 218, 222–24

Jefferson, Thomas, 9, 139, 198, 199, 206, 207

Laissez-faire. See Capitalism; Liberty: negative
Law/laws: and constitutions, 25, 30, 59, 61, 69, 70, 73, 78, 131–34; and corruption, 68–71, 73, 75–77, 84, 88, 95, 99, 111, 116, 117, 125–27, 131, 132, 140, 149, 152, 154, 156, 172, 177, 179, 193, 195, 200; and glory, 98, 100, 119, 124, 144, 155, 192, 211; and liberty, 115, 118, 130, 145, 149, 170, 200; and moral deontology, 30, 67, 68, 73, 78, 83, 86, 90, 91, 94, 95, 97–99, 101, 114, 118, 127–30, 133, 134, 207, 210, 212; and moral voluntarism, 23, 24, 29, 44, 45, 62, 67, 72, 74, 78, 83–86, 94, 98, 99, 102, 103, 105, 114, 129, 130, 157, 159, 160, 187, 191, 193, 199, 211, 212; and princes, 70–72, 74, 136, 152, 154, 156, 158, 160, 179, 196; and rationalism, 103, 107, 115, 128, 129, 196, 198, 211; as a modernizing force, 136, 151; authority, 72; civilizing power of, 18, 24, 25, 30, 55, 59,

62, 63, 65, 66, 68–70, 72, 73, 78, 88,
91, 111, 115, 117, 119, 129, 130,
134–37, 139, 152, 154, 184, 201; of
Rome, 132, 183; positive, 103–5; scientific, 24, 28, 60, 61, 68, 133, 194,
197; using cruelty to create, 94, 99,
100, 152, 155
Legislative, 20, 25, 69, 74, 94, 97, 98,
102, 104, 113, 114, 116, 117, 124,
125, 171, 212, 219, 220
Legislator(s), 59, 69, 71, 74, 86, 125,
137, 145, 154, 180, 195, 196
Liberty: and class, 25, 145, 171, 172,
179–82, 189, 194, 200, 201, 205,
211; and corruption, 28, 130, 137,
207; and equality, 76, 175–77, 179,
180, 184, 186; and glory, 66, 68, 130,
145, 195; and property, 133, 162,
186; as a modernizing force, 32, 112,
218; as an ideal, 9, 10, 26, 39, 74,
129, 137, 158, 196–98, 201, 205,
206, 210, 211, 215–17; defined, 26,
190; in commentaries, 168; necessary
conditions, 24, 25, 130, 133, 134,
137, 138, 145, 149, 170, 186, 194–
96, 217, 218; negative, 26, 27, 129,
190, 195, 199, 206, 207, 209–11,
216, 217; of Italy, 71, 121; of Rome,
132, 145, 177; of U.S.A., 27, 198,
199, 202; positive, 11, 26–28, 31, 78,
190, 194, 198, 199, 205–11, 216–18;
purposive, 190, 195, 198, 213, 216;
using cruelty to create, 10, 138, 139,
145, 150
Livy, Titus, 73, 148
Locke, 9, 23, 26, 27, 29–31, 92, 98,
102, 113, 129, 130, 132, 189, 195,
198, 206–8, 210, 216, 218
lo stato, 66, 70, 164, 167, 169
Lucretia(s), 63–65, 116, 160, 219

Madison, James, 31, 84, 104, 195, 198–
206, 208, 218
Mansfield, Harvey, 52, 87, 88, 108,
116, 164
Margrave, 35, 223, 224
Medieval, 29, 36, 55; morality, 85, 94,
95, 108; religion, 18, 29, 37, 38, 42,
97, 107, 170; worldviews, 21, 28, 29,
36, 42, 43, 45, 46, 48, 49, 83, 86,
196, 223
Militarism, 10, 18, 31, 144, 161, 214

Military, 10, 21, 75, 77, 100, 101, 132,
140, 145, 151, 153, 161, 162, 177,
183, 204, 210, 214, 215, 220–22, 226
Mixed constitution, 135
Modern/modernity (condition), 17, 20;
and class, 22, 35, 147, 177, 191, 192,
206; and corruption, 64, 65, 74, 149,
185; and empiricism, 42, 43, 45, 52,
53, 60, 85, 103, 196; and glory, 22,
89, 150; and humanism, 17, 20, 22,
32, 47; and liberty, 9, 23, 26, 45, 78,
138, 144, 151, 185, 193–96, 206,
208; and moral voluntarism, 9, 11,
18, 23, 28, 29, 85, 86, 89, 92–94, 97,
98, 101, 106–8, 110, 196, 208; and
morality, 30, 106, 107, 110, 115, 215,
216; and nations, 150, 151, 162–64,
199, 213; and religion, 42, 49, 107;
and worldviews, 36–38, 42, 43, 86,
196, 197; as a human need, 9, 21,
147; authority, 30, 151; defined, 20;
economic, 20, 21, 35; in commentaries, 164, 167; necessary conditions,
24, 116, 159; versus teleology, 35, 42,
43, 106
Modernize/modernization (process), 20,
163; and corruption, 65, 159; and glory, 24, 121, 124, 144, 150, 163, 218;
and liberty, 22, 28, 147, 161, 216,
218; and nations, 18, 151, 159, 163,
215; and princes, 21, 159, 163, 191;
and property, 9, 10, 20, 31, 151, 162;
and   religion,   38,   40,   49;   and
worldviews, 36, 40; as a human need,
9; as teleology, 20, 32; authority, 20–
22, 26, 29, 55, 152, 163; economic,
20, 22, 26, 35; in Machiavelli's plays
and poetry, 65; theory of, 20, 22; using cruelty to foster, 23, 30
Monarchy/principality: and corruption,
22, 24, 25, 30, 67, 71–74, 89, 93,
101, 116, 122, 125, 134, 136, 145,
149, 154, 155, 157, 158, 179, 191;
and equality, 148, 190, 191; and glory, 70, 88, 90, 101, 102, 129, 136,
146, 152, 153, 155–59, 162, 209; and
humanism, 45, 46, 53, 54, 148, 164;
and liberty, 74, 139, 140, 143, 145,
146, 155, 194; and moral voluntarism, 87–93, 96, 97, 102, 103, 105,
109, 117, 118, 157; and property, 76,

162, 164, 180; Aristotelian, 25, 43, 134, 137, 154, 160; as a modernizing force, 22–24, 30, 66, 67, 71, 74, 97, 99, 147, 151, 152, 159, 163; as a vice, 54, 63, 87, 136, 137, 143, 146, 199; as an ideal, 62, 138; in commentaries, 36, 146–50, 206; of Florence, 148, 156, 159, 161; of Italy, 148; of Rome, 63, 116, 124, 156; Montesquieu, 30, 140, 177, 180, 184, 199

Morality. See Corruption; Duty; Obligation; Rationalism; Voluntarism

Multinational states, 173, 174

Nation/nation-state (political unit), 149, 198, 199, 214; and collectivism, 208, 209, 211, 213, 214; and corruption, 74, 76, 89, 151, 159, 161, 165, 193, 211, 214, 217; and divided loyalties, 89, 151, 159, 161, 163, 195; and liberty, 121, 128, 159, 161, 203, 211, 215; as a modernizing force, 18, 164, 166–68, 172, 173, 186, 193, 213; as a vice, 173, 214; defined, 167, 168; harmony, 168, 215; modernizing, 18, 23, 40, 151, 159, 206; of France, 164; of Germany, 167; of Italy, 121, 127, 150–52, 215, 218; of Switzerland, 152; of USA 199, 203; unification, 17, 21, 121, 126, 127, 149–52, 159, 161, 164, 166–68, 186, 190, 193, 214, 217, 218

Nationalism (ideology), 10, 30, 31, 108, 110, 146–48, 151, 161, 162, 164, 167, 168, 172, 173, 195, 210, 213–15, 217, 226

Nationality, 167, 168, 213

Natural Law, 9, 27, 29, 85, 93–95, 97, 103–5, 107–9, 113, 129, 216

Natural rights, 26, 27, 105, 113, 129, 198, 199, 211

Nihilism, 102, 110–13

Numa, 38, 89, 115, 116, 126

Obligation: and corruption, 102, 109, 115, 116, 127; and moral deontology, 94, 99, 130; and moral voluntarism, 29, 45, 67, 72, 74, 78, 79, 83, 84, 86, 87, 92–94, 98, 99, 102, 104, 111–18, 185, 191, 192, 194, 196, 198, 208, 211, 212; and princes, 89–91, 117,

122, 125; as a human need, 212, 213; natural, 40, 86, 93–95, 97, 105–7

Open (cosmos), 28, 35, 40, 41, 43, 46–53, 55, 193, 196, 209

Original Sin, 29, 60

"people, the," 39, 73, 74, 76, 78, 90, 100, 129, 136, 137, 139, 140, 145, 151, 153, 157, 158, 161, 165, 170, 171, 182, 183, 203

Pitkin, Hanna Fenichel, 45, 51, 55, 64, 86, 100, 170, 182, 183, 206

Pocock, J. G. A. 49, 52, 70, 198

Political economy, 31, 177, 187

Populism, 31, 188–90, 194

Prerogative, Lockean, 30, 195

Principality. See Monarchy

Property, 9, 11, 71, 112, 134, 157, 169, 177–80, 182, 184, 186, 188, 189, 191, 201, 203, 204, 206, 208, 218, 220

Rationalism: metaphysical, 43, 52, 194, 223; moral, 83–86, 93, 97, 103, 107, 113

Rebirth/regeneration of constitutions, 44, 45, 69, 133, 139

Relativism, 18, 106, 108, 110–14

Religion: Christianity, 18, 28, 29, 37–43, 47–49, 94–98, 108, 113, 222; general, 5, 18, 36–39, 43, 49, 89, 97, 102, 117, 122, 126, 128, 168

Republic, 147; and class, 22, 25, 27, 76, 78, 131, 138, 145, 148, 165, 169–72, 178–82, 185, 186, 189, 191, 204; d constitutions, 30, 61, 68, 69, 88, 98, 130, 132, 139, 140, 145, 147, 149, 154; and corruption, 28, 71, 77, 87, 89, 154, 160, 165, 191, 200; and equality, 77, 78, 176; and glory, 24, 39, 98, 100, 116, 117, 126, 144, 146, 154, 160; and liberty, 21, 72, 119, 149, 192; and princes, 71, 74, 76, 144–46, 149, 155, 156, 159, 196; and representation, 21, 37, 54, 137, 201–3; Aristotelian, 37, 130, 134; as an ideal, 17, 24, 25, 30, 31, 44, 108, 140, 143, 146, 147, 196, 206, 209, 218; creating, 18, 97, 117, 133, 146, 149; necessary conditions, 124, 159; of Florence, 11, 12, 38, 96, 115, 121, 131, 132, 134, 147, 150, 151, 154,

160, 162, 182, 189, 210; of Italy, 154, 159, 186; of Rome, 25, 29, 61, 63, 64, 95, 116, 119, 124, 132, 140, 145, 147, 183, 208; Plato's, 37, 43, 44, 67; using cruelty to create, 101, 102, 140
Romulus, 25, 63, 65, 71, 74, 84, 88, 95, 99, 102, 115, 117, 119, 122–24, 126, 152, 154–56, 159, 160, 162, 163, 209, 219, 222

Savonarola, 11, 37, 38, 181
Science. See Empirical
Sect/sectarian: and class, 179, 190, 200, 223, 224; and corruption, 183, 200, 201, 203; and divided loyalties, 77, 78, 159, 162, 163, 190, 200, 224; and religion, 203; neutralizing, 203–5, 223; violence, 27, 89, 151, 169, 179, 183, 199–201, 204, 210, 216, 220, 221, 223
Skinner, Quentin, 69, 70, 72, 75, 83, 117
Social contract, 19, 29, 72, 83, 135, 185, 196, 197
Social welfare. See Liberty: positive

Soderini, Piero, 35, 54, 115, 120, 131, 132, 151, 181, 189, 215
Stato. See lo stato
Stoic, 29, 95
Strauss, Leo, 28, 93, 106, 108, 127, 146–49, 208
Straussians, 18, 28, 108–10, 149

Teleology: Christian, 40–43; metaphysical, 40, 42, 43, 46, 48, 52, 85, 106, 197, 223; moral, 32, 53, 99
Titus. See Livy, Titus
Tocqueville, Alexis de, 20, 22, 147, 209

Virtù, 53, 63–65, 69–71, 100–2, 110, 159, 191, 196
Virtue, 53, 63–66, 68–70, 72, 75, 77, 89, 94, 95, 105, 106, 108, 110, 113, 114, 117, 121, 122, 139, 151, 156, 159, 161, 169, 171, 180, 187
Voluntarism/voluntarist, 11, 23, 29, 83–86, 93–95, 98, 99, 103, 106, 107, 110, 113, 116, 117, 125, 193, 194, 196, 197, 218

Weber, Max, 20, 21